HARD
KNOX

by
CHUCK KNOX
and
BILL PLASCHKE

HARD KNOX

The Life
of an
NFL
Coach

HARCOURT BRACE JOVANOVICH, PUBLISHERS

San Diego   New York   London

Requests for permission to make copies of any
part of the work should be mailed to:
Permissions, Harcourt Brace Jovanovich, Publishers,
Orlando, Florida 32887.

Library of Congress Cataloging-in-Publication Data
Knox, Chuck.
Hard Knox : the life of an NFL coach / by Chuck Knox
and Bill Plaschke.—1st ed.
p.   cm.
Includes index.
ISBN 0-15-133450-1
1. Knox, Chuck.   2. Football—United States—Coaches—Biography.
3. National Football League.   I. Plaschke, Bill.   II. Title.
GV939.K5A3   1988
796.322'092'2—dc19
[B]   88-15695

Designed by Janet S. Taggert
Printed in the United States of America
First edition

A B C D E

To Shirley, my life.
Without her, nothing would be possible.

— C. K.

To my brains, my strength, and my love:
Grover, Mary Margaret, and Lisa Ann

— B. P.

Contents

vii

Contents

— **Acknowledgments** —

We wish to thank the following: our wives, Shirley Knox and Lisa Ann Jacobs, for perseverance beyond the duty of the ring; the Knox family, from brother Bill to son Chuck to daughters Chris, Kathy, and Colleen, for their time and honesty; Gary Piepenbrink, the most patient of editors; Gary Wright of the Seahawks, the best public-relations man in the English-speaking world, but you knew that; the Seahawks' assistant coaches, and the assistants from all of Chuck's staffs—they've truly survived the hard knocks; the entire Seahawks office, from Ruthie to Mary Phillips to Joe Vitt, who tells a great story; the boys at the Glass Tower and Sessions, from Jimmy to Johnny to Mook; Bill Knight, who backed the *Seattle Post-Intelligencer* feature story that led to the book; Dave Distel and the *Los Angeles Times,* who backed the coauthor; and to wise man Blaine Johnson, who said writing this book would be like running a marathon. Right about now, we could use a cup of water over the head.

HARD
KNOX

Introduction

Kirkland, Washington
Winter, 1987

There. I think I understand how this thing works.

You stick in that little tape with the open end down. Man, I've never seen a tape that small. I've licked bigger Easter Seals.

Let's see, you close the compartment and push that little silver button at the same time you push that other little silver button. OK, now a little red light is supposed to come on and . . . there. I've got it. It's operating now.

Testing, one two three. It works. Easy. Eighth-grade Sewickley.

They call this a *micro*-something tape recorder. I've never owned one. I never trusted them. I still keep all my notes on those six-by-nine spiral notebooks, and I use big felt pens. That way, I can get up in the middle of the night and throw on the light and there it is, there I am. I can't erase myself.

I would just as soon have written this book like that and then mimeographed the notebooks and passed them out down at the local beer halls. The word would have gotten out.

But some people say the best way to write a book about yourself is to talk into a tape recorder. That way, it all sounds like you. OK. So I borrowed this little thing.

Anyway, greetings.

It's one of those winter days when you turn on your windshield wipers even though it's not raining, hoping maybe they can clear away the gloom. But I'm in a pretty good mood because I'm sitting here in my office. Nice office. I've had my three hots and a cot in places smaller than this office. Big desk, big chair, my own television set, my own VCR. Even have my own bathroom, a door on it and everything. No wasting time walking down halls and standing in line.

Damn nice office. You can see the mountains from this office. What mountains, I'm not quite sure. Hell, I didn't even know where Mount Rainier was until earlier this summer, when my wife, Shirley, and I drove up there and got lost and finally stopped and ate a lunch on some hill with wine and cheese, like out of one of those magazines.

You want to know a funny thing about driving to Mount Rainier, or any big mountain? The closer you get, the harder it is to see. Finally, when you reach where you're going, you have no idea where you are unless you step back and take a look, remembering what you saw before you got there.

Sometimes my life feels like that. Maybe that's why I'm writing this book. To step back and take a look, remembering where I've been.

After fifteen years as a head coach in the NFL, I have the seventh-best record of all the coaches in history. I've won something like 63 percent of my games. I've been Coach of the Year four times. I've coached six divisional championships and had a wild-card team four times. That's ten out of fifteen years in the play-offs, which is OK, I guess, except my children's Christmas memories don't involve a Santa Claus, and that hurts me worse than you'd think.

What I'm best known for, I suppose, is that all three teams I have coached have gone from hopeless to hell-raisers. The Los Angeles Rams, Buffalo Bills, Seattle Seahawks. All three had losing traditions when I got there. I helped all three get to the play-offs. They say I'm the only coach in history to do that, to make the play-offs with three different teams. I guess I'm the most proud of that. It lets the world know I'm a *professional* football coach.

Yeah, *Chuck Knox, pro football coach*. It used to sound good. But I've stopped introducing myself like that. Recently I've decided to go back to just Chuck Knox. I'm not a super-star. I'm not a hero. I don't glitter. I survive.

Do you know how long it took me to get an NFL head coaching job? How does nineteen years sound? I spent two years as a high-school assistant coach, three years as a high-school head coach, then four years as a college assistant, then ten years as a pro assistant before finally getting my shot.

Even when I've won, I've just survived. I've coached in four conference championship games, but you know how many of those games I've won, how many Super Bowls I've coached in? None.

A big-game loser, that's what the critics called me. A guy who loses when it counts.

I used to think they were right. For much of my early life, if there existed a definition of *winning*, I sure as hell didn't know where to look it up.

I was a poor kid. I grew up in the little western Pennsylvania town of Sewickley, in a four-room apartment on Walnut Street with no central heat and sometimes no glass in the windows, which meant on some winter days the wind would come through and darn near blow the covers right off you.

We also had no telephone or television, which meant there was nothing between me and my father when my father got mad. That happened a lot.

Charlie Knox was a Irish immigrant with a lousy mill job and a drinking problem. His pride put him in constant need of a fight to prove himself. But he didn't know who or how. So he fought me. When that kind of thing happens today, the child is taken away from the parents and placed in a home. Back then, the fights *were* home.

My friends were black and Italian and the kind of people who existed on the downside of the rich folk's noses.

My best friends? Probably the streets. That's were I learned the most. All these little sayings I'm full of, they come from the streets. Sportswriters call the sayings "Knoxisms." I don't call them anything, probably because I consider them just plain old "eighth-grade Sewickley." I better explain that expression. If something represents common street smarts, I refer to it as being "eighth-grade Sewickley." I use it all the time. Maybe I use it too much. It seems the older I get, the less people understand it.

Funny thing was, shortly after eighth grade, I couldn't wait to get out of Sewickley. At age fifteen I tried to join the Navy, figuring a beating in boot camp couldn't be any worse than a beating at home. They discovered my age and sent me back.

Then as soon as I graduated from high school, I betrayed my father and my neighborhood by leaving a perfectly good job at the steel mill and sneaking off to Juniata College. Then I rubbed it in by getting married and having a baby by the time I was a junior in college.

But all of this was going to be OK because I was going to be a football star, right? Well, I never was. I haven't played a down of football since my senior year in college, when I was just a mediocre five-foot-eleven offensive lineman for a Division III school—not exactly a breeding ground for NFL coaches.

I didn't have much money and didn't have much power. But it was shortly after walking proudly away from Juniata that I realized, if you have dreams, you might not need either.

I could dream, all right. Beginning with my first head coaching job, at Ellwood City High in western Pennsylvania—a couple of years and odd jobs after college graduation—I was consumed with one thing: I would be a football coach, and it would be for professionals, and I would not even look at the huge odds against me.

I wanted so bad to advance that I would attend every coaching seminar and convention I could get to—even ones where I wasn't invited—just to pick other coaches' brains. I would sleep in cars in college parking lots, sleep on other coaches' floors. In hundreds of greasy spoon restaurants, I'd draw hundreds of plays on paper tablecloths. When I came up with something really good, I used to go out to the restaurant's front yard and demonstrate on the grass.

Whenever I start feeling my Seahawks job is hard today, I just have to think back to then. Nobody has it tougher than a high-school coach.

Then when I reached the college coaching level, as an assistant at Wake Forest and Kentucky, I realized the struggles were the same. With tiny budgets and no name recognition, I learned about driving all night to stick your foot in a recruit's door. I learned how sometimes the way you smile, the way you sell, is as important as the way you coach. I learned I didn't like that.

I didn't like it so much, I left the security of the colleges to join the pros as an assistant with the New York Jets, back when the American Football League was new and the Jets were terrible, and everybody thought I was throwing away my life. After helping build the Jets to Super Bowl caliber, I left to become an assistant for the sorry Detroit Lions. Another mistake, they said. Coach from the AFL can't coach in the NFL.

Then, after spending six years in Detroit thinking I was paying my dues, I wasn't even considered when the Lions head coaching job came up. I was thrown out the front door.

It was only by a miracle that I squeezed into my first head coaching job, with the Los Angeles Rams. As it turned out, I was barely able to squeeze out of there and make it to the Buffalo Bills, my second head coaching job. In both Los Angeles and Buffalo, I won but I couldn't win. I was a loser in the big games and in earning the big money from the owner, and finally in Buffalo I wound up losing almost all faith in a system that had failed me twice. So I left—but only to take over yet another neglected child, the Seattle Seahawks.

So, you can see, I am not just Chuck Knox, pro football

coach. I am . . . damn, sometimes, I wonder just who I am.

It's like today I'm farther up that mountain than I ever dreamed, but I look around and I can't tell where I am. Everybody says I should enjoy the view. But to do that, first you have to understand what you're looking at. Explain this view:

I've got two cars. I've got more than two people who will drive them for me. I've got a house where you can walk out the front door and look at a lake. I've got a condo with a view of a golf course. I get paid not just to coach, but to make speeches to businessmen with twice my upbringing, twice my schooling. I play golf with politicians. I go to dinner with civic leaders. In Buffalo, I even represented the city in a drive to attract new corporations.

But damn it, a part of me is still eighth-grade Sewickley.

I don't use credit cards. I don't even carry a wallet. Some of our best furniture was bought used, then refinished. Extravagant things still embarrass me a little. I once bought my daughter Chris a car, but made up a little loan book so she could pay me back. It was only four months before I said, the hell with it, and gave her the car, but she got the point. My three girls used to beg for a stereo, but I always told them to listen to the radio. Looking back, I find it hard to believe that I would never even buy them books. Instead I would take them to the library and sign them up for a card.

I just can't rid myself of Sewickley. The best explanation I can give for that is, I don't want to. Take the football field sidelines: every game I'm surrounded by old Walnut Street friends. I won't tell you which ones they are. You can easily pick them out. I even have one particular Sewickley friend who spends every season at my house.

Understand that the story I'm about to tell is very hard for me. I've never told it. I've never talked about it. To anyone. Some of this stuff even Shirley didn't know, and I've been married to her thirty-five years. I don't talk much about myself. According to the NFL media, I am considered possibly the worst coach for quotes. Every Wednesday during the season, I have a conference call with the writers of the opposing team. From what I hear, they dread this call. They fall asleep during this call.

But see, I've come too far to let my guard down during those situations. I've worked too hard. I know what it's like to have nothing, so now I desperately protect whatever my football teams and I have. In silence, there is that protection. If somebody wants to get an edge on me, they will have to search for the cracks themselves. They will have to find that advantage themselves. I'm not going to give it to them. It's eighth-grade Sewickley.

It was not my idea that I break this silence. The book people came to me. And at first I rejected them. Even when they talked money, I didn't listen. You can buy and sell whatever a man wears, but there is no price on what he has inside. So I turned them down. Then I realized, maybe somebody will read this and have hope. Maybe there are people out there just surviving like I was, people who think they don't stand a chance. Maybe they'll read this and think, If that fella Knox can do it, so can I. I thought about that. That made sense.

So I said, "What the hell."

1

Sewickley

Twenty-three steps. I will remember that number, and those steps, for as long as I can remember how to count. From Walnut Street up to the front door of the three-room apartment where I grew up, it was twenty-three steps. When things in our little home became crowded and tight, it was twenty-three steps down to freedom. When Pop took one drink and one swing too many, it was twenty-three steps to safety. When Mom couldn't keep peace, or I couldn't sleep because of the noise in my head, the rest of the world was always just twenty-three steps away.

The town was Sewickley, a burg of six thousand, thirty minutes west of Pittsburgh, as the Ohio runs. It was no different from any other place in western Pennsylvania's steel valley. One waterway and, directly across that waterway, one mill. We had the Ohio River's beauty, and we had the new soot and garbage it delivered us each morning. We had the steel mill's life support, and the pain it caused those who spent their lives inside. So, like all those other little places, Sewickley was a city confused. There were the rich people who lived in the hills overlooking the town. Then there were the rest of us, the ones they overlooked.

The Italians, the Irish, the blacks. The just plain poor people—like me. We lived together in the center of town, among the alleys and pockmarks that developers had yet missed, in a building known as the Dixon Flats. Football people today compliment me on how well I relate to black players and I laugh.

My section of Walnut Street, a one-block area between Beaver and Thorn Streets, was the center of black business activity. There were two predominantly black saloons, a black pool room, a black barber shop, and the office of my first dentist, a black man. Name of Doctor Randolph.

It's funny, not until I just mentioned that did I realize it was really like that. I noticed color then about as much as I do now. When you and your neighbor are equally despised by people of a different class, then your neighbor becomes your brother. Even if he could never be your brother unless he dyed his skin or changed his accent. Spend a few years in 1940s Sewickley, where in each grade at school they used to stick the minority and poor kids in one class, and the rich and favored kids in another. If you had an English or WASP-sounding name, you were placed in class 1A or 2A, or whatever, depending on your grade. If your name ended with an *i* or *o*, or some other vowel, or you were from the Dixon Flats, you were stuck in 1B or 2B, or whatever. You were stuck with all the problem kids, and you were treated differently. If put in a special class, you could spend six or seven years with the same kids, and even the same teacher.

I remember once after a fight I was thrown out of school for the day, and before the principal sent me home he said, "Getting into fights is just like you and your kind from Walnut Street." My mother heard this and was furious. She ran down to the school and screamed at him in that Scottish brogue of hers: "Mr. Principal, I can accept that my son was wrong to fight, but I cannot accept your remark. The measure of a man has nothing to do with where he is from. The measure of a man is in what comes from his mouth and what is in his heart."

So, yeah, spend a few years in my class, and you'd be the same way I am today. Nothing special about it.

Sewickley friend Dominic "Big D" Roppa: I remember when Chuck was coaching the Rams, we were on a bus going to a game, and one of the players was in the back complaining about something. All of a sudden, Chuck stood up and said, "Shut your damn mouth. I know where you're coming from. I've been down that road. I've been down worse roads. You ain't seen none of the stuff I've seen. We'll do it my way and we'll get it done my way." The player shut up. Chuck always had a way with players.

Our tenement was no different from any other tenement in the under bellies of those small towns. Only thing unusual was that it sat on top of a bar called Chick's Place, where people came to drink and sometimes collapse outside the front door. You could see it every night from one of our windows.

Four twenty-three Walnut Street. Second floor. Four rooms, four people. Me and Pop and brother Billy, two years younger, slept in the bedroom. Mom slept in the kitchen. The arrangement actually worked better for Mom than us. She had the heat from the kitchen stove, which was always turned on. We had nothing. In the morning we would have to walk across a cold linoleum floor to get to the bathroom. I still remember that floor. Like too many things, I have carried it with me. To this day, people who see me dress in locker rooms always find it odd—the first articles of clothing I put on are my socks.

None of this would have mattered, except we had windows that always seemed to be broken. You can accept sleeping without central heat. The bitch is, waking up with damp covers.

People sometimes make a big deal out of this, and I wish they wouldn't. I got along fine. I survived. You just shook that chill off, jumped into your clothes, and ran down those twenty-three steps. When you got around your friends, you were warm. That's the only kind of warm a person needs.

We called ourselves the Walnut Street Gangsters. We didn't

carry guns or knives, or anything like that, but we weren't afraid to use our fists. If you came through and challenged us, we would go after you. Some of our gang—not me, of course—would get in fights every other day. Almost like clockwork, it was. Those friends I made then, they are still my friends today.

I don't care how many times you invite me to play golf in your backyard or take a private plane to your cabin in British Columbia. I prefer a back room somewhere, with folding chairs around a card table with a red checked tablecloth and, in those chairs, guys like Big D and Mook and Bummy and the Munizza brothers. One of them will remember to bring the scotch. One of them always does. The rest of them will bring the memories. At the end of the night I might be laughing and crying and embarrassing myself. That's OK, that's me, and sometimes I think they are the only ones who really understand that. They're my guys, and although I have picked up some new guys along the way, those friends from Walnut Street will always be my guys. It's eighth-grade Sewickley.

We didn't have a phone in our apartment either, but that's a joke. Who the hell were we going to call? We also didn't have television or radio; but again, so what? What was there to listen to? You want adventure, you want crime, you want suspense—hang around outside Chick's Place. Do it on payday.

> *Sewickley friend Bobby "Mook" Marruca: We could never call Chuck, so we always had to come over. It was pretty rough. I never wanted to go inside. I was always embarrassed for Chuck. We would wait out on the step for him to run down. We all lived in bad places, but sometimes we wondered how he made it.*

Oh, it wasn't as bad as it might seem. Shoot, it was a place to sleep and we had food. That's all you need, three hots and a cot. When things are going bad, that's what I tell my players: how can they complain, with three hots and a cot?

There is, of course, the one big physical reminder of those years. Watch me on the sidelines. I walk funny, I admit it. It looks like I've got this built-in swagger. It looks like one leg is shorter than the other. That's because it is. The right leg is shorter than the left leg. Sometime in my early years, I contracted a form of polio. Because we couldn't afford a doctor or anything, it went undetected. My leg got screwed up.

When I played in college, at Juniata in Huntingdon, they nicknamed me "Daddy-O" because of the swagger. Since then I would never have thought about it, except that on every team I've coached I've always caught one of my players making fun of me. They mock the way I walk. It's OK. There are a lot worse things they could make fun of.

There could be a lot worse childhoods, too. That's why I rarely talk about mine. No reason for anyone to feel sorry for me. I don't want anybody thinking I deserve a break from anyone. A man must make himself from whatever he is given. *Play the hand you're dealt*—it was my first and foremost Knoxism. It's easy to figure out why. It means look adversity in the eye, then kick the hell out of it.

> *Billy Knox: That apartment. I used to be so embarrassed about it. I would always have friends drop me off a block away, then I would walk home. There was that Chick's Place bar and all those fights and no windows in our joint. It was terrible.*
>
> *You know what Chuck used to do, of course. Used to have his fancy girlfriends drive up and pick him up in their big cars, drive right to the front door. Imagine, right there on 423 Walnut. He would strut outside and wouldn't give a damn if everybody knew where he lived. Used to act proud of the place. I could never figure that out.*

Today a lot of successful people who grew up in our situation protest, "It's OK, we never knew we were poor . . ." Billy and I knew damn well we were poor. The good town of Sewickley was more than happy to inform us. Every year they took us to this summer camp called the Pittsburgh Home for the Improvement of the Poor. These do-gooders would put us on a bus and cart us twelve miles away to some park or something, give us baths and dress us in these pretty brown shorts and throw us in barracks. We would spend a week out there, getting a taste of the outdoors. Like we didn't spend all of our time outdoors on the streets anyway.

I wouldn't have minded any of it, except it turned out we set an all-time attendance record for the Pittsburgh Home for the Improvement of the Poor. Four straight years. With apologies to those social workers, I learned more from the streets. By the time I was five years old, I knew about getting conned. I learned that the world is full of phony baloneys who like you only because of what you have.

I had been given a new baseball bat by some charity. The older guys down the alley had an old bat that had been cracked, nailed together. They came down and started palling around with me and made me their friend. Then all of a sudden they wanted to trade bats. Even at five, I wasn't that stupid. I told them no. They went away, and then came back later when they heard somebody had given me a dime. They said they wanted to be friends again, and as a gesture of their friendship, they would give me a nickel for my new dime. Said a nickel was worth more because it was bigger. I believed them. They took my money and ran.

I may not be the smartest guy in the world, but you can bet I haven't been conned much since then. I began watching the players down at the Silver Grill pool hall, and I learned. Now I can smell a con. I can *feel* a con. It helps when you are dealing with players who fake injuries and team owners who fake money problems. I warn my team now: You can get away with a lot of things, but don't dare try to give me a nickel and say it's a dime.

I was a pretty good-looking kid then. I was always one of the more athletic kids, and I even had a nickname: Nick. They all called me Nick because I had this nick on my head from where I had fallen in my house and cut myself. With my hair so short, the thing stood out. I didn't mind the name. I told the boys, fine, but call me *Big* Nick, so they did. By the way, I still have that scar. Age being the thief that it is, pretty soon they will be calling me Nick again.

Billy Knox: I wonder how Chuck really got that nick on his head. Really. Maybe he fell or maybe he . . . well, ask him about our father. Ask him about all the lickings we took.

He says all this stuff in his past didn't affect him, no windows or heat and all that, but he can't say that the old man didn't affect him. He can't say he didn't fear our old man. We all feared our old man.

A bit about my parents, Charlie and Helen: My father was a short, big-armed, big-necked fellow from Ireland. The part of my build that looks like an ice box, that comes from him. I think he used to play soccer in Ireland. I'm sure some soccer players there got hurt. I'll say this, he was tougher than I'll ever be.

My mother was tall and big and just as hard, from Scotland. She came over on a different boat. They both migrated west until their paths crossed in Sewickley, where they were married.

Neither one ever really understood much about America. From the minute they got off at Ellis Island, they were made to feel like their backs were to the wall. They were fighters made to feel like fighting was the only thing that worked. First, they couldn't find decent jobs. My father finally caught on at the mill, but not working inside. He cut the grass, painted the walls, cleaned up, that kind of stuff. My friends would see him working outside the executive offices, and for a while I got away with telling them those were *his* offices. My mother worked as a maid for the people who lived on top of the hill—the Alexanders, the Byers, the kind of people whose names you never forgot because they sounded so much richer than yours.

Because of my parents' low wages, they couldn't get a decent place to live. And they never had enough clothes or food for two growing boys. Life wasn't quite dealing with them square. So they battled it.

Mother did it quietly. She quietly just got stronger and stronger. She never caused any trouble, never yelled at us or anything. She lived until she was seventy-four and, right to the end, wouldn't take anything off anybody, good or bad. Wouldn't take aspirin for a headache. Would never even tell us she felt sick. She would never buy a car, even though after my father died she worked the graveyard shift as a practical nurse. She didn't trust cars. She would walk or take a cab. She never trusted much of anything but herself. When I was at Wake Forest University as an assistant coach, she once came down on a bus for one of my daughter's birthdays. On her lap the entire way was a cardboard box that held a homemade birthday cake. She wouldn't believe anybody else could make one properly.

After my father died and I was finally able to afford to move her out of our tenement, she wouldn't go. Didn't see any reason why.

> *Shirley Knox: When Chuck became a high-school coach in the area, Mrs. Knox would rarely miss a game. She insisted on walking the sidelines, and the whole time she would shout in her thick Scotch accent, "Get'em, get'em!"*

My father didn't handle things in quite the same way. He physically attacked life. If that sometimes meant he felt a need to attack Billy and me, well, I guess that's what he did.

His world was one of grinding workdays and vacations when you spent one week on the couch. His world was coming home at six o'clock, washing his face, and then running back downstairs to ride the night away in a beer truck with our neighbors, the Munizzas. After their deliveries were finished, my father might jump off the truck and into a pool hall or tavern to spend the rest of his night.

His day was eight hours of demeaning work at the Duquesne Foundry, being asked to do things like make the boss's new shrubbery look good, or wash the boss's car. His night was six hours of escape into a bottle. My father worked hard, then drank hard. But there needed to be a release there somewhere, a way to let loose the energies and frustrations trapped in the bottom of that rut.

That release was his temper. Often, the target was his children.

> *Bobby "Mook" Marruca: No two ways about it, old Charlie Knox was a hot-tempered son of a bitch. He was a big drinker, a tough drinker. He would get mean. I would come over to get Nick and I could hear the old man upstairs whaling on him. All those years growing up with Chuck, I never once set foot in his house. Never would.*

There is pretty much only one way to put this: my father would beat me, and he would beat Billy. Today you might have all kinds of psychologists running around our house. Back then it wasn't anything. A man had a right to peace and quiet in his own home, and if his kids didn't give it to him, he could do whatever.

My father, I guess, did whatever.

He would hit us for coming home fifteen minutes late. He would hit us for coming home, period. He would chase us underneath the bed and pull us out by the legs and hit us. Then sometimes we would have to climb out of bed and go down to some bar and carry him home in the middle of the night, right about when he was stone drunk and preparing to fight somebody. We would get him inside our apartment and lay him down. Then he would get up and hit us because we hadn't let him hit the other guy.

On mornings after, he would wake up and go downstairs

and tell the people out on Walnut Street, "Damn it, I gave
the boys a licking last night and never should have." At least
that's what people would tell us he said. He would never say
that to us. I can honestly say some of my best weekends
were spent when my father was locked up by the cops on
Friday for being drunk, and my mother wouldn't go down to
get him until it was time for work on Monday.

Most of the time, I suppose, my father truly felt I deserved
it. I was always getting into trouble, which is fine for most
kids, if you can afford trouble. We could barely afford shoes.
Trouble was not in our budget. Once I broke my arm three
times in nine months. How? Who remembers? Kids in western Pennsylvania break limbs like kids in other places break
shoelaces. For me it was worse than for others, because for
me, a broken arm meant two visits to the doctor. One to get
the cast, the other for Pop to cut the doctor's grass to pay for
the cast.

So I break my arm for the third time. I'm about ten. I come
walking toward home with this arm dangling down and I'm
thinking, Why even keep going? Pop will kill me. Why not
go right to a hospital, where at least he can't get to me? Why
not go to a friend's house, where maybe I'll be able to sleep
the night?

Like most kids, by the time I finished plotting my escape,
I was at my doorstep. Up the twenty-three steps I jogged, like
they weren't even my feet. I sat down to dinner. Billy is sitting next to me. Pop is on the other side of the table. I'm
eating with one arm, leaving the other arm hanging at my
side. No big deal, no way anybody would notice. Except Pop
does.

"Whattya do to ya arm?" he asks in his Irish brogue.

I say nothing.

"Ya broke it again, didn't ya?"

I say nothing.

Anybody who has ever read any of this kind of story is no
doubt expecting a heartwarming punchline. Something about
how the father comes around the table and comforts the son

and says that he understands what it's like to be a boy, and hey, let's go to the doctor before that arm starts growing back funny.

Wrong book. If there's a punchline in my life, I've missed it. My father looked at me and cursed.

"If ya broke that arm, I might as well break the other one!"

And he comes after me, right across the table, lunging for my neck. Dishes clatter to the floor. My mother begins crying.

We had a fire escape at the back of the house, and I guess I could have run for that, but I didn't. I never ran; I don't know why. I don't think anybody ever knows why he runs or doesn't run. This time, like every time, I sat there and let him hit me until his anger disappeared. Then he could feel like a man again and take me to the doctor.

I guess he hit me because part of him loved me, and the other part hated himself for not being able to give me everything such love would require. He wanted me to be a man, but felt he couldn't give me enough to become one. And I never even hit back. Not even when I got big. Even when I couldn't take it, I didn't hit back. Say what you will, the man was my father. I wouldn't fight him physically, but I fought in my own little, sometimes foolish ways. Like the time I tried to join the Navy.

Billy Knox: I remember when Chuck came home bragging one time that he wasn't going to have to take any shit anymore. He said he was going to join the Navy. He quit the football team and went down and signed up and got ready to get on the train. But then the officers discovered one teeny problem: Chuck had forged his birth certificate to say he was eighteen. In reality, he was just fifteen years old. Nice try. He was back in our one bed that night.

I didn't see anything wrong with joining the Navy. I had just hurt my knee playing basketball. I had been in a cast for three weeks, and they were draining the damn knee every other week. If I couldn't play sports, then I couldn't escape every day; and if I couldn't escape, then I had to *really* escape—and get the hell out of there for good.

Only way the Navy found out I wasn't old enough, after they inspected us for hernias and everything, was that they took a second look at my birth certificate and spotted the forgery. Hell, if I had gotten through, I probably would have been an admiral today. Why not? I think your abilities will enable you to rise in whatever you do, whatever profession you try. That's why I coach and teach football not like it was football, but like it was life. It's all interchangeable.

As I got older, I became less rebellious. I finally just felt sorry for my father. None of it was his fault. He came to this country too late in life, he never really had a chance. He stopped making me mad. He just made me feel sorry.

> *Bobby "Mook" Marruca: I remember walking downtown with Chuck. You could always tell when his old man was raising hell in one of the pool halls; Chuck would see him out of the corner of his eye and steer us the other way. He didn't want us to see his dad like that. He was embarrassed for him.*

The situation at home being what it was, to prove my worth within I had to make my mark outside. If I wanted any self-confidence, I realized I would have to get on my hands and knees and scrub for it. So I did. That's the way it should be. Sounds corny, but even back then, I learned to win.

> *Sewickley friend Tony Cicco: Yep, Chuck knew what it took to win. At the Sewickley Theatre I was an usher, then the manager. I used to fight with Chuck every Saturday night. He had figured out a way to pay for one ticket, then sneak into the bathroom and pass his ticket stub out the window to somebody else. Soon all the kids were doing it. After a while we finally put grates on that window. I wanted to charge the kid for the grates, but hell, he barely had shoes.*

I started my working career by hitchhiking up the Sewickley hill to caddy for the rich people at the Allegheny Country Club. I would chase their golf balls, I wasn't proud. I wanted to be like them. I liked it in the clubhouse. I saw guys ordering scotch and soda, and dipping these gold-braceleted hands into what seemed like barrels of free pretzels and nuts and stuff. There were all kinds of people waiting on these guys, people coming up and shining their shoes. I wanted to have all that. Today I wear a gold bracelet that some might think out of style. I think it reminds me of what I didn't have. Whatever, I'm not taking it off.

Most of my time at the country club was spent in the crowded basement of this caddy shack. We would go down there and wait for our tips, which could never be given to us personally. Golfers gave the tips to the head man in the locker room, who was supposed to bring them down. He was an old German fellow named August. But he never brought them. So we would huddle together down there and chant, "August keeps the tips, August keeps the tips." I'm sure they heard us, but they never did anything about it.

I haven't forgotten that. Today I tip too much. If I say to a bellman or shoeshine guy, "Are you a businessman?" there's a message in that. It means, if you want a little money, come take care of me, and I will more than take care of you. Shirley gets mad at my tips. But that's a part of me will never change.

After not making the Navy, at age fifteen I lied about my age again. This time to the railroad, and it worked. I got a job breaking down boxcars. Shoot, I didn't consider myself fifteen. Even today, I never look at age in anybody. I look only at productivity. There is age, and then there is experience, which has nothing to do with age. Experience is not what happens to a man, it is what a man does with what happens to him. Even though a man has been working at a job twenty years, if he's making the same mistakes the twentieth year as he did the first year, I wouldn't call him experienced. It's eighth-grade Sewickley.

In addition to the railroad and some little jobs, I spent most of my childhood shining shoes down on Beaver Street for Mr. Maculuso. This is where I learned things like, Catholic priests have big feet and don't tip much. And, you can distinguish the different kinds of shoe polish by their smell. I would clean the polish out from under my fingernails and we would go to the Saturday night dances, and there would be people whose shoes I just shined that day. I could always tell who was polished with what. I will never forget those smells.

> *Dominic "Big D" Roppa: He says he never forgets the smell of polish. Shoot, the man never forgets the shoes. I remember once he walked up to a guy in Sewickley, a guy he hadn't seen in twenty years, guy's name was Frank. Chuck said, "I remember you, you used to wear loafers." The guy was stunned.*

People wonder why I succeed with what they consider less-gifted players, and win championships with less-gifted teams; well, this is why. I wasn't gifted with anything. I earned everything. I learned what it took to win because if I didn't, I would be living twenty-three steps up from Walnut Street this day.

Ability is not enough. A player must have the burning desire in his gut to make something out of that ability. This world is full of unrewarded geniuses. That's what I call people with talent who never achieve anything. Those people are not my people.

I have a soft spot for players and teams who physically don't have what it takes. That's because they are forced to *learn* what it takes. Spare me the football player who has everything and thinks he needs nothing, because, chances are, he's never had to learn anything. Coach-killers, I call those guys. Can't teach them anything. Cost coaches their job because they never play up to their potential.

Give me the guy who's been on his knees enough that he can tell a shoe by its smell.

Shining shoes also taught me the importance of fashion. I began to collect clothes, although not like you would collect clothes. I would collect one good pair of shoes in March, add a good pair of pants in September, buy a good shirt to go with the outfit in January. That would be my collection. And it was important to me. Out on the streets with people, I not only wanted to look nice, I *needed* to look nice.

People from the old neighborhood remember me as looking a lot nicer than I should have looked coming from a family so poor. It's eighth-grade Sewickley. When you only have one suit, you make damn sure it always looks perfect.

Look at me today. Even when I'm overweight, I'll be wearing clothes where all you see is the crease and the shine. I even make sure we coaches look good on the sidelines. I'm for wearing fancy sweaters or colorful parkas—whatever looks sharp. I can't help it. When I keel over from a heart attack, chances are slim I'll go to the hospital embarrassed.

> *Bobby "Mook" Marruca: We would go to these dances and Chuck would be dressed to the nines, with the pegged pants and shined shoes. He'd walk out the front door and his father would say, "Ay, there goes the King of Swing."*
>
> *We each only had one suit coat, so we would swap coats every week for a different look. One problem. It would get hot in the gyms and we would have to take off our coats, but we wouldn't trust anybody else to hold them. So we would lay them down and make a pact. I watched Chuck's coat and he watched my coat. While we were dancing, making out with a girl, any time—we always had to have one eye on the coats.*

Sometimes taking care of my clothes still didn't do much good. My first good coat was torn on the window crank of Mook's car. I got real mad, and then I got scared. I was sure my pop would whip me when I came home on this cold night with a big hole in my coat. I snuck in the back, up the fire escape, and he never knew. I bought another coat a couple of months later, and it got stolen. Oh well.

If you're around me when I'm talking about the past, you'll hear a lot about Mook's car. Mook always drove because I never had a car. Mook would actually drive me on all my dates, drop me off and wait and everything.

Even today I don't drive much. Shirley taught me how when I was nineteen but I've never gotten used to it. I have the cars, but other people drive them for me. That way I can sit in the passenger seat and listen to my marching band music on the cassette player and tell the driver, every ten minutes or so, to slow down. Now, that's traveling.

Daughter Kathy: What does he mean, "doesn't drive"? My father drives all the time—from the passenger side. He is the most intense backseat driver in automotive history. Every few miles it's "Honey, if you don't slow down, you're going to get a ticket" or "Honey, look out for that truck seventeen miles down the road." He drives, all right. Drives us right through the roof. Finally we have to say, "OK, you care so much about this trip, we'll stop the car and you drive." That pretty much quiets him. I think he doesn't drive for the same reason he doesn't smile on the sidelines. Too much to think about. Too many things to go wrong.

This will make critics of my so-called job-hopping laugh, but growing up, I always had a travel streak in me. Mook and I could never date girls in Sewickley; we would always have to go down the road to Avalon. Isn't it always like that? The prettier girls always seem to live in the next town over? Something about that sense of mystery, I think. Something about the adventure. I think the grass is always greener on the other side not because it looks greener, but because it's so exciting just jumping the fence to get there. From Sewickley to Avalon, from Los Angeles to Buffalo to Seattle, that sense of adventure in me has always stayed the same.

None of it is any different from the time in high school when me and some buddies hitchhiked to South Bend to watch Notre Dame play football. To this day, I have no idea how far that was from Sewickley. We didn't tell anybody; just, one Friday night, I borrowed something warm to wear from a friend named Jumbo Rupert and we took off, getting there in time for the game the next day. After we cried in front of an usher, he let us in to where we could stand and watch from the back row. We hitchhiked back that night. It's a miracle some maniac didn't pick us up and put us six feet under. It's a substantially larger miracle that Jumbo Rupert never asked for his sweater back. It's not a miracle that I never offered it.

I was always finding somewhere to go, anywhere other than 423 Walnut Street. And I would always find some way of getting in trouble on my way there.

> *Sewickley friend George Ammon: Chuck and I were driving through Avalon once, just cruising real slow, when all of a sudden he told me to stop the car. I said, "What for?" He shouts, "Just stop the car, willya?" So I stop the car and he jumps out and runs to the car behind us and pulls some guy out of the front seat. They go at it right in the street, beating the hell out of each other. They finish, and Chuck walks back to the car, gets in the passenger side, and calmly says, "OK, we can go now." I still don't know what the hell that was all about. With Chuck, sometimes you didn't ask.*

You have to understand me and fights. My father always said, don't come home crying after getting a beating, or you'll get another beating. He told me, if you're bigger or equal to him, you should win fairly. If the other guy is bigger, you should grab whatever is near and hit him with it.

So you should always win. That's how I always fought—

to win. The only exception to my dad's rule came the time I was sitting on a sidewalk bench, I was about thirteen, and some guy comes up and belts me. He was twenty-six. Why did he hit me? No idea. I come home with a black eye and my father asks where I got it and I'm afraid to tell him. Much later when I finally explain—I wanted to eat dinner first— my father surprises me. Because the guy is twenty-six, my father doesn't want to beat me, he wants to beat the guy. He goes all over town looking for him. When he found him, he was going to kill him, so thank goodness he never found him. I think part of the reason was, no store or bar owner would help him. They were worried that my dad would find the guy in their place and wreck the joint.

In between all these dramatics, I made time for a little high-school football. Actually, I liked basketball just as well, maybe because I was the only one out there not afraid to throw an elbow and foul out of a game. I was a five-eleven forward and fouled out of my share of games. On the football team I was a linebacker and offensive lineman. But more than anything else, I was known for playing dirty. I was never great, but I worked hard and did anything to win. I think I got my reputation from the one-on-one drills we used to run. I'm talking, one-on-one with helmets that had no face masks. I loved it, the man against man, just you and the other guy, may the strongest survive. Even today I use those drills, I guess I am one of the last coaches who still do. But it helped me.

Some players say I coach like a frustrated player. I think it's more accurate to say that I coach like a player, period.

> *Sewickley friend Tom Sanders: All the kids at school tried to stay away from him during one-on-one football drills. He was flat-out dirty.*

Here's what my high-school yearbook said under my senior picture. You figure it out.

> CHARLES KNOX—*Behold the athlete. Big husky Nick, hustling forward, hard-hitting tackle, a splendid mimic,*

> *jitterbug expert, smooth talker. Find him with George or*
> *Mook, but you will have to go to Avalon. Steady worker.*
> *"Dust yourself" he says. Democrats' staunchest defender.*

The thing I did best in high school, I think, was learn the game of football. Even back then I was studying play diagrams and theory books, and things like that. I like to think that I was one of the first people in western Pennsylvania to seriously scout other teams. I would go to other games on nights we didn't play and sneak over the fence. Maybe it figures that I became the first person in western Pennsylvania ever injured while scouting. One night it was dark, and some official was running to catch us, so I just leaped over the top of the fence. Most of me went over fine. My arm didn't. It got stuck in barbed wire that I swear appeared out of nowhere. It gave me a big gash, but by then I was smarter than to go home. I went right to the hospital, got it stitched up— the old man never knew a thing.

> *Bobby "Mook" Marruca: What a fool kid he was.*
> *Damned barbed wire tore his shirt and put a huge hole in*
> *his arm. As I remember, he still watched the game. I could*
> *never figure out if we were there really to scout the team,*
> *or scout the other girls. Turns out, I guess it was the team.*
> *For all that blood, I hope so.*

By the time I was a senior I had a reputation. I guess you could tell that from the yearbook.

But for some reason, I could never be big enough. I was the leader of the gang, but I wanted to be more. Maybe I wanted to get so big, I could strut away from Walnut Street after high-school graduation and never come back. Maybe that's what I wanted.

One night me and the boys were cruising downtown Pittsburgh when we pass one of these tattoo parlors. A couple of us decide to go in and see what it's all about. We get inside and one of the fellas says, "Hey, Nick, I bet you're not man enough to get one of those."

"The hell you say," I told him.

So I did it. I got CHUCK tattooed right across the meat of my arm.

> *Billy Knox: That dumb sucker. He came home with that thing on his arm, I liked to die. Ugliest tattoo I've ever seen. Once again, Chuck just had to be the biggest man in the neighborhood. Why don't you ask him what ever happened to that tattoo?*

It took me about twenty-four hours to regret the tattoo. I worried about it, thought I was ruined for life, and then realized, wasn't anything I could do about it. I had to play the hand I was dealt, even if it was I who had done the dealing.

Man, but I always had to be the tough guy. The principal used to get so mad, he would bring me down to the boiler room in high school to whip me. Before bending over, I would always take my little wallet out so it wouldn't cut into my butt. Maybe for that reason, today I don't carry a wallet. Don't like anything rubbing against me.

By the time I was a senior in high school, something else finally hit me: You needed more than tough. You needed control of that tough. You needed the smarts to learn how to best use that tough. I didn't think anybody thought I had any of those things. Take that back. I *knew* nobody thought that.

Here I was, a senior prep linebacker in football-hot country, and no college was interested. No college ever stopped by to watch me play. No college even called. Looked like I would end up right where I didn't want to be.

I hated the mills, I hated what they did to my father, but by the middle of my senior year it was predestined. I was going to the mills. Either that or I was running away from home. Considering I had already tried the latter option a couple of times, I had no choice.

Until Midget. His name is really Tommy Perricelli. He lived down the road a bit, in a little town called Ambridge no different from our town—at least, didn't smell any different.

He is a little, bald, round-shouldered man, five foot three, who just kind of hung around the high school football players and called the local colleges when he saw a good one. You have them in your town. Call them bird dogs, scouts, whatever.

After one game my senior season, this little man shows up in our locker room. I hear that he's looking for guys for Juniata, a little college up in the Pennsylvania hills somewhere. I had never heard of it, but that didn't matter. It wasn't in Sewickley and that was enough. Anyway, I see this little man, and for whatever reason, I see my escape hatch. I run over to him—I'm still in my uniform—and I try quietly to convince him that I would be a good recruit.

Tommy "Midget" Perricelli: I walk in this locker room and this real tough kid, the toughest kid on the field, walks up to me. He says his name is Chuck Knox. Then he grabs me and starts shouting, "If you come back here for me, you'll be coming back for a helluva football player. If you just come back for me, you'll be getting a great one." He's almost screaming now. I think he's going to kill me. While this guy is shaking me, I can only think of one thing: I'm coming back. And it will be for him.

2

Juniata and Ellwood City

It was August 15, 1950, the kind of Sewickley day when, you get out of the shower, you dry off twice. Climate control being what it was up in 423 Walnut Street, I was actually glad to be standing on a sidewalk a couple of blocks away.

I was waiting for Midget—Tommy Perricelli—to drive by and pick up me with my one good suit and my dreams. I had been granted a two-week tryout by Juniata College, which I told my friends was a beautiful liberal arts college nestled in the central Pennsylvania hills and—aw, hell, they knew I didn't know anything about the place. I had never seen it. Never applied there. Didn't know anybody there. Couldn't even spell it.

In fact, I had not even decided to take the college up on their tryout offer until a few days before Midget picked me up.

I had worked all summer in a construction yard—Mook was my yard boss—and I had sweated and stunk and decided, What the hell, I could use the change of scenery. I had saved all my money—about six bucks—and decided I would go to college and see how far that would take me. I couldn't tell my father, because he had planned on me entering the mill as soon as I was old enough. I just quietly told my mother

and she rummaged around and found the old bag that my
father had used to bring his stuff over from Ireland. He came
over in 1928 and this was 1951, so you can guess what the
bag looked like. Seeing as we never took any vacations—a
vacation for my father was not having to go to work—it was
all the luggage we had. When I crammed all my stuff in the
bag, we realized that the strap was broken. So we had to wrap
a couple of big ropes around it.

On August 15 my mother escorted me and this awful bit
of my father's past down the twenty-three steps to the sidewalk to wait for Midget. I couldn't wait in front of the house,
in case my father somehow got out of work early and walked
past, so I dragged everything down to Prince's Candy Shop
and waited there. Along Midget comes, and I see two other
kids in the car, Reds Orler and Dino Patricelli, two kids from
Ambridge. I don't know them, but since we are all in the
same boat I decide not to start anything. I throw that old bag
in the back and hope nobody sees it. I get in the car in my
nice peg pants and shined shoes and hope nobody can tell
that these are the only decent clothes I've got.

It was an ordinary car ride, about three hours long through
some mountain roads, but for some reason it has stuck in
my mind. Maybe it's because today only two guys in that car
are still alive, me and Midget. Dino dropped out of school,
married a cheerleader, and then died of a heart attack. Reds
got cancer and died. Sometimes when I feel funny getting
old, I look back to that car ride and realize how lucky I am.
I'm not a real sentimental guy or anything, but looking back
on that car ride . . . I don't know.

So we get to Juniata and I've never seen anything like it.
There are trees and grass and open spaces. No mills. No
stench. I think, I'm going to like it here. I can even breathe
here.

The football coaches gathered us together and told us,
breakfast at seven-fifteen, first workout at nine. I thought,
Hell, I'm better than that. I don't have to get up at seven-
fifteen for a nine o'clock workout. I could get up late and

grab a doughnut at this shop down the road. That's eighth-grade Sewickley.

The first day, that's what I did. I went down and bought a couple of those big sinkers, had a cup of coffee, and went to practice. Well, they start working us, and the sun starts getting us, and about halfway through I have to run over to the sideline. And I do it. I throw up. I actually throw up with everybody looking. Everybody is thinking, What a big pussy. Including me.

Somehow I survive the camp and make the team and am granted a four-hundred-dollar tuition waiver. I can't believe it. Here I am, nothing much but a kid with an opinion that he's tough, and they're going to *pay* me to go to school. So I call some friends at home and get them to run down the street and get my parents, to drag them to the phone so I can tell them that I really will be going to college.

Judging from our conversation, my mother was knocked out. My dad, well, they said he didn't exactly respond the way I thought he might.

Billy Knox: You should have seen the old man when Chuck called back with the news that he was going to college. The old man flipped. Told him, "I've got friends in the mill with college educations. What good is a college education? You trying to be better than me?" I've never seen the old man so hurt.

It was simple. My father didn't trust an institution like college. He didn't trust the outside world. He didn't trust anybody who was giving something away for what looked like nothing. He trusted only what he knew, and that was the mill.

Sewickley friend Jimmy Munizza: The old man flat disowned him. I would call him down to the beer truck and say, "Mr. Knox, the boy is just trying to better himself."
The old man was hard. The old man wouldn't listen.

| *Said his son wasn't going to better himself with some stupid education.*

From several hundred miles away, my father hollered and hollered. I tried not to listen. But I couldn't put it out of my head.

By the time school was a couple of days old, I realized that from where I came, you never got away. You lived in a mill town in the 40s, you became like that mill town. You became a contradiction. You became hardworking and tough, and childish and scared. You wanted to end up better than anybody, but who in the hell were you to think you were better than anybody? Many left town back then to find out who they were. Many came back because in the end they felt ashamed for looking.

Five weeks after I left for college, I had reached that stage. My father, my upbringing, everything—it all came crashing down on me. In going to Juniata I thought was opening the door to the world outside, but instead that door led to some closet jammed full of my past, and soon I was buried in it.

I was having these dreams of going back to the Dixon Flats and nobody knowing me and nobody wanting to loaf with me (western Pennsylvania definition of *loaf:* "hang out"). I couldn't sleep and couldn't think straight. Really, why was I trying to outdo my father? Sewickley was good enough for him, wasn't it? Why was I still trying to be such a big man? Why couldn't I just do the expected for once and go home.

And let's face it, at college then, I *was* different. I was the sorest of thumbs. When it came time to go with friends to a movie or something, I had no money. I had one pair of shoes. I had only one set of good clothes, and no class. I just didn't belong.

Five weeks after starting college, I decided I had to go home. I called the Juniata coach, Bill Smaltz, and told him I was quitting. I jumped on a bus and got off in Sewickley. It was going to be the end of my football and otherwise worldly career.

Until Midget. Thank goodness for Midget.

That damn Tommy Perricelli, he had found out I was coming back, and when I got off at the Sewickley bus station in a driving snowstorm, he was waiting for me.

> *Tommy "Midget" Perricelli: The coach had called me at home and told me about Chuck. I thought, This boy doesn't want to quit. This boy is just confused.*
>
> *I got in my car and drove to the bus station and waited for him. Confused was right. He got off the bus all red-eyed and babbling about his father and his duty to his family and all sorts of things.*
>
> *Now it was my turn to grab him. I asked him if this was what he really wanted. I asked if he was doing this for himself, or for some stupid ideal that life shouldn't change, that life was all written up somewhere, and he had to follow.*
>
> *I screamed at him all the way home. I told him his life may be without money and warmth, but it was not without choice. And he was blowing his biggest one.*
>
> *We pull up in front of 423 Walnut Street. His father is working night shift, but his mother is upstairs. As he leaves the car to go up there for good, he changes his mind. Suddenly, he's not going up there. He's staying with me. He's not quitting after all.*

What can I say? I was just a confused kid. I saw how the rest of the world lived and I thought I could never be a part of it. Midget convinced me I *could* become a part of it, I *could* own the rest of the world. It *was* my choice.

My problem was, I thought when I left Sewickley I would be done fighting. Midget told me, no, I'd just started fighting. He said nobody owns the world without getting a couple of bruises from it. That's all I needed to hear. I liked a good fight. So I decided, what the hell, and took that challenge.

Everybody has his own theory about destiny—like, how in the hell two people heading in the same direction can end

up so totally different. I have my theory, and it's based upon
that night in the snowstorm. In every man's life, he encoun-
ters several forks in the road. For some reason, some men
will always know which is the right path, and others will
always choose the wrong one, and there isn't much we can
do about it. I believe that. From that night on, I have somehow always managed to stay on the right path.

*Tommy "Midget" Perricelli: So he changes his mind and
decides he's going back to college. But by then, Mrs. Knox
has seen us through the blanket in the window. She comes
running down the stairs, wondering why her Chuck has
come home so unexpectedly. I think quick. I say, "We
were just in the area recruiting some other boys, and
thought we'd stop by." She doesn't know any better, so
she brings us in for some crackers and tea and tells Chuck
she'll make his little bed for him and he can go back to
Juniata in the morning. Chuck says fine.*

*Uh, not so fast. I know if Chuck stays the night, Mr.
Knox will come home and convince him the other way,
and Chuck won't go back to school. So I pull him in the
corner and, well, I lie to him. I tell him, if he doesn't come
back to school that same night, he'll be ineligible for the
season. He says, "Really?" I say, "Really, son." He doesn't
quite understand, but agrees that he doesn't want to be
ineligible, so we thank Mrs. Knox for the crackers and tea
and get in the car and take off to start the rest of Chuck's
life.*

*Sound like a cozy ending? Bull. It was snowing like all
hell, and we could barely see in front of us. The three-
hour drive took six hours through those mountain roads,
and we get to Juniata at 4:30 A.M. Only thing good about
that drive is, about halfway there, Chuck lifts his head
from a crook in the passenger door, turns to me, and tells
me, "You know, I'm going to be a football coach one day.
I'm telling ya, Mr. Perricelli, I'm going to be a big-time
coach." I say, "Right, Chuck. Now go back to sleep."*

That Midget. I don't know if anybody has ever done more for me my whole life than he did that night. What happened to him? You probably know and don't even know it. Watch me on the sidelines sometime. There will be this little bald-headed man behind me or next to me, wearing a Seahawks sweater and pants. That's Midget. He is still a bachelor, and he still lives by himself above this abandoned bar in Ambridge. But I decided he would never be alone during the football season. So during the fall he lives with me, wherever I'm at. He stays in one of our spare bedrooms during the week, and sometimes at home games he takes over my hotel suite on Saturday night so I can be home with Shirley. On game days he stays close to me, carries my briefcase in from my car, walks the sidelines, and sits in my locker-room office afterward. He flies to all the out-of-town games on these senior citizen flight passes. Stays with me in my room on the road.

Some people think my continued association with Midget is strange. I don't.

> Tommy "Midget" Perricelli: I'm getting to be an old man and don't have much anymore. I still live above that damn bar, right down the road from where I first met Chuck. Most everybody else has either died or moved away. But Chuck, although he's all the way across the country, will always be there for me. He don't forget nothing or nobody. Not even an old midget.

Once I decided to stay, that first year at Juniata wasn't so bad. I found my niche with a couple of other outcast western Pennsylvania kids.

> Former Juniata teammate Pat Tarquinio: Chuck was one of those real tough nuts from a western Pennsylvania river town. He looked tough and talked tough, like he had to prove something. He had that swagger, it made us call him "Daddy-O."

I was lucky I was from the same area as him, because he took all of us western Pennsylvania kids under his wing. It was like he was comfortable only with his own kind. If you were his own kind, that was good, because if not, well, this was the guy who was involved in most of the fights on the field, all kind of scuffles. You didn't want him against you.

That first year I latched onto the only two kids at Juniata who seemed tougher and at least as poor as I was. They were the Krucelock brothers, from some mill town somewhere. Jack and Paul Krucelock.

The thing with them was that they would go into the dorm, into everybody's room, and try on sport coats. If one fit them, that's what they would wear that night. I remember one rich kid who had just gotten there and he had brought with him a new sport coat. A couple of nights after his arrival he saw Paul "Cruiser" Krucelock wearing that coat at a dance. He said, "Hey, man, you got my jacket." Cruiser said, "Don't worry, man, I'll have it back to you by morning." Maybe he did.

Jack was famous for bringing a set of drumsticks with him to every dance and playing the drums during the band's break. At which point the manager would throw him and Paul and me out the door, ass over drumsticks.

But the Krucelock boys were pretty good ball players, which taught me a philosophy I still use today: Never ask if guys drink or smoke or wear other people's coats. Ask if they get the job done. Never care how they look, or how they pronounce their name, or who their friends are. Care only that they get the job done.

Knox's Juniata coach, Bill Smaltz: Knox was darn lucky he got to hang out with anybody, because everybody was afraid of him. He came to Juniata with a quick temper about twice the size of his 180 pounds. The other freshmen said they didn't want anything to do with him. From what I understand, in that raggedy suitcase of his, he managed to squeeze boxing gloves. Now I ask you, what kind of kid, when he goes off to college, brings along boxing gloves?

That first year at Juniata I essentially fought and raised hell. My goal in life was still centered on being the big man. Then school ended and it was summer, and I had no choice but to come home. Come home to my father. And come home to maybe the most important realization of my life.

Jimmy Munizza: The boy gets home and the old man is madder'n hell. Remember, the boy ain't been home since he left the previous fall. The old man scolds him—I think the boy was too big to be beaten on anymore—and then the old man does him one worse. He sends him into the mills. He sets him up with the dirtiest, awfulest job there is, right in the belly of the mill. The boy would come out everyday soot-black from head to toe. And you know how much Chuck liked to look nice.

It was the longest summer of my life. Those damned dirty mills. I'd be working and sweating and the old workers would come up to me and say, "See what happens if you don't get an education?" They would point to some other young filthy guy, maybe a former local football star, and say, "See him, he decided to chase women instead of books. Now he's chasing the clock."

I saw, I saw. It took me thirty minutes every night to get my body clean, a task which I seemed to finish just in time to go back to work the next morning. I realized what this life was really like. I realized, You don't do football, what the hell are you going to do? This? It was either the mill or run numbers or tend bar. I realized there was nothing in Sewickley for me, absolutely nothing. I told myself, Go back to Juniata in the fall and get this damn show on road. Do something with your life. Don't ever come back to old guys and filth and wasted dreams. I returned to school in the fall a little older and a lot smarter. I returned ready to change my life and stop the partying and fighting and become a real man.

One month after the start of my sophomore year, on a Friday night at a high-school football field in Huntingdon, I met my first real woman.

Shirley Knox: You have to understand, in Pennsylvania small towns back then, before every home football game, everybody would parade through the town before going down to the field. The marching band, the cheerleaders, everybody. I was a junior cheerleader at Huntingdon High, so before every home game I would do the same thing. On this one Friday night I remember marching around the school and down the dirt road to the stadium. There, right at the front gates, I saw Chuck for the first time. To this day I remember how he looked. He was wearing a Sewickley letter jacket with a big Indian head on the back. His collar was up, and he was wearing peg pants, white socks, black shoes. He looked like he was trying to be a real tough guy. He was obviously one of those Juniata players who still liked to hang around high-school girls. I saw him and was attracted to him and thought, I wonder if this guy is tough enough to ask me to dance later tonight?

My buddies and I always went to the local high-school games to scout the talent. That is, the football talent. On this one particular Friday night we were hanging around outside the gate, waiting for all those marching band people to get their butts inside the stadium so we could go in ourselves.

Then I see Shirley, this cute little cheerleader. Definitely the best-looking one there. She was checking me out too, I knew she was. I must have felt it.

Shirley Knox: That night after the game, we had a dance like always. He was there. He asked me to get out there and jitterbug with him. He could really jitterbug. He seemed so self-assured. I said yes. We danced. And I haven't danced, so to speak, with anyone since.

Before we danced, I introduced myself, but I guess I didn't need to. She knew my first name from my tattoo. She told me her name was Shirley Rhine.

I really fell for this girl. I knew right away I was ready to settle down. I know it sounds awful young to be thinking like that, but in case you hadn't noticed, I had grown up fast. I was just nineteen, but I had been around a lot of blocks. I felt I had the life experience, I guess, of about a thirty-year-old. I knew she was only a high-school kid, but I decided right in those first couple of months of our dating, she was going to be Mrs. Knox.

It all fit in with the plans I had made after leaving the mill the previous summer. I was going to make it on the outside as a coach. I was going to make it on the outside as a man. This Shirley Rhine was to be my wife. And once I had her, I would never have to go back.

Shirley Knox: We had a most unusual relationship. We would go to the movies and to a soda fountain called The Palace, where we'd drink a coke—all very common. But then, since he had no idea how to drive a car, we would walk home. Home was two miles away, across a bridge. When we got home he would insist on walking back to his dorm, two more miles the other way across the bridge. My father would offer to lend us his car so I could drive Chuck, but he would refuse. Only if it looked like he might die of cold would he let anybody drive him back.

This is where I learned the meaning of an expression that I often pass on to my teams before big games today: The faint heart never won the fair lady. I would have walked two hundred miles to go on a date with Shirley. Also, I was always a little embarrassed about not being able to drive a car. Nobody in my family ever even owned one, so I shouldn't have been embarrassed, but I was.

Shirley can laugh about those days all she wants, but I also wasn't afraid to ask her to teach me how to drive, and she did. When I was nineteen, thanks to her, I got my driver's license. I had no car to go anywhere, but by gosh, I now had the paper power to get there.

I stayed at school to work after that sophomore year, and by the following fall, things were really cooking for this guy. As a junior I was offered a job as proctor in a dorm, which I accepted because it meant a free room. I loved it and turned it into even more. I somehow acquired the dorm's laundry concessions, getting Buck's Laundry to pay me to pick up the students' wash and bring it in.

So now I've got the four hundred dollars in tuition and a free room and enough money for free laundry. Things are happening. For one of the first times in my life, I think I was having fun. The dorms were these temporary barracks built in World War II. You could easily put your foot through the thin walls. Any excessive noise, as a proctor I got to jump all over people. This was where I found my voice, my "Shadddd-up back there!" that still works today.

I also found out that, strange as it may seem, that voice did wonders in the classroom. It helped me with speeches and readings, and eventually got me through my senior oral exam, which I needed to pass to graduate.

Pat Tarquinio: You should have heard him in literature class. He once took a Shakespeare reading and turned it into a halftime speech. It was that "To be or not to be" thing. He wasn't just reading Hamlet, *he was coaching* Hamlet.

Yet while in control, I was still a little out of control, which you could see on the field the opening day of my junior season. It was then I got thrown out of my first and only football game as a player. We were playing Moravian College, and this linebacker had been subtly punching me the whole game. Finally, after one play, in the open, I swung back. I thought I had the right. My coach, Bill Smaltz, did not.

> *Bill Smaltz: He had been getting fifteen-yard penalties called on us for three years. He just couldn't stop fighting when he heard the whistle. Now he's swinging at this kid, and I don't know if he told you, but it cost us a punt inside their ten-yard line. The penalty moved the ball in good territory and they drove to score. I was so mad after the ref threw Chuck out, I threw him out again—as in, Get the hell off the bench and out of the stadium! I banished him to the team bus, where he sat the rest of the game.*
>
> *Then the next day in practice, I singled him out in front of the whole team and told him, if he had another late hit called on him all year, I was going to ship his butt back to Sewickley. One more fight, and he'd be spending the next thirty-five years of his life in that mill!*
>
> *Probably the only thing that saved him from getting expelled right then was, when he swung at that guy, he missed.*

As I remember it, I coldcocked the guy. I thought I knocked him out. No, really, I was sure I did. Regardless, Smaltz hit me with the scariest sideline speech I've ever heard, so scary that I've used it on occasion since. I find out where a slumping player is from and threaten to send him back there. We believe in positive reinforcement, but sometimes it works better the other way. Not until you've experienced the fear of returning in shame to a town and a father that doesn't want or need you can you realize what a great motivating tool that fear can be.

By then I had decided I could not go back to Sewickley.

Just after my junior season, I cemented that. I married Shirley. She had just graduated from high school, and I was ready to finish college. And I was tired of being alone. If I had grown up in a different area, under different circumstances, I probably wouldn't have felt that way.

Look at today, with my own children. By the time they reached their junior year in college, they were just starting to feel independent. But back then I had felt that way since about age six, and was ready for it to end.

Her ring was a simple gold band bought at Bernie Schwarz's in downtown Huntingdon. We couldn't afford a honeymoon. We had to live that first year with her parents. Shirley had to make all our children's clothes, and later, when we moved out on our own, she had to make the lampshades and drapes so that we could save money. All of those things have become our good, sweet memories. In fact, there's probably only one part of the wedding I would do differently. I would have forced my parents and friends to show up.

> *Bobby "Mook" Marruca: It was the damnedest wedding I ever heard of. Nobody from Sewickley came. Not me, not his parents, nobody. It was like it was a secret wedding. None of his friends were there. He came back the next summer, all married and everything, and nobody could believe it. Looking back on it now, it's so strange. They have been married thirty-five years, one of the most successful marriages I know, yet when it all started, nobody was there.*

Yeah, I wanted my whole world at the wedding, but we couldn't afford anything but a quick little ceremony, and nobody could afford to drive over for it. It wasn't worth the two or three days' pay it would cost my people. I didn't want to embarrass them by asking.

Besides, my father probably wouldn't have shown up anyway. The wedding just made him madder than ever. He was saying things to people at home like, "Anybody can get married. It doesn't take a college education to get married. Why in the hell did the boy get married?"

I finally got the nerve to take my wife home the following summer, after I had graduated.

Might I add here, I graduated with distinction, which is the Juniata equivalent of graduation with honors. Just don't ask how.

Anyway, I finally felt man enough to introduce my wife to my father. This was just after we had our first child, Chris. I didn't know what to expect. If my dad didn't like my going to college, and didn't like my getting married, what on earth would he say about a baby? But I had to go home one last time before entering the work world, to show him that I *had* made it, that no matter how weak he had made me feel, I found enough strength to grab onto a dream, and that dream had already carried me out of there. Also, I needed to drop in to see how life *used* to be, and to show him what he'd missed. In other words, I went home after my senior summer preparing for a fight.

> *Shirley Knox: I had heard so much about Mr. Knox, and about how tough he was, that I was kind of scared going home that first time.*
>
> *We get to Sewickley, and we walk up the steps into that tiny apartment. It's so hot and cramped, and there's this small but huge man—big arms, big neck—just looking at me. I'm holding the baby and he's staring at me and I'm thinking, We're both going through the window. But he smiles. He takes the baby out of my hands. He stares at her and talks this rough Irish baby talk, like he doesn't know what to say but has to say it anyway. I turn around and Chuck is nearly in tears.*

It was something. My father saw the baby, he saw how the piece of him that became me had become someone else, a new Knox. It was as if my father recognized in that one little child, all that I had accomplished and all that I was searching for.

After twenty-one years, it was only through a little baby that my father finally saw *me*. I can't explain it any better. He couldn't either, and didn't. It was just that, finally, he was dad and I was son and everything fit right and worked right and felt right. He was proud. It was something.

> *Shirley Knox: The rest of the weekend Mr. Knox would carry little Chris on his shoulders, carry her all through Sewickley, stopping by the Silver Grill and the candy shop and everywhere, showing her off like she was a pretty flower.*

By the time I had left Juniata after that senior year, I knew I wasn't good enough to play football anymore, but I felt I could be good enough to coach. The operative phrase here is *could be*. I knew I wasn't good enough yet, but I knew I was willing to study and work. I'm not sure anybody else knew it, but I did.

> *Pat Tarquinio: He was the senior tackle and I was the quarterback, and one day he walks over to me and says, "You'd be a good coach, and as soon as I get my first head coaching job, I'm calling you." I thought, Sure, he will. I couldn't believe his confidence in himself.*

Immediately upon graduation, the only coaching opening I could find was right there in Huntingdon, as a sort of unpaid graduate assistant coach at Juniata. To make ends meet, I found a job teaching ninth-graders over at Huntingdon High; I taught them, among other things, a class called Problems of Democracy. Personally, I don't believe there are many problems with democracy—I guess if it wasn't for democracy I wouldn't be here today—but that's for another book.

We moved into a tiny apartment above the *Huntingdon Daily News*. We made no money, so the following year I moved down the road to be a full-fledged underpaid assistant coach at Tyrone High. I left the safety of college and took the job, but only because I had a wife and little Chris and another baby on the way, Kathy.

This meant another move, and by now Shirley was starting to get the idea.

Shirley Knox: Here I was, an only child who had lived in the same house all her life, and suddenly we were moving to our third place in three years. And this place in Tyrone was the clincher. It was a mansion that had been converted into three apartments. The Tyrone head coach lived on the spacious second floor. We lived up in the attic, or the third floor, in what was essentially the maid's quarters. We had only two rooms, and soon, when Kathy was born, we had two babies.

We could just take one year there. Things got so tight, Chuck finally decided to accept an offer to go back to Juniata as a teacher and assistant football coach. This would put his dreams on hold, but food and baby clothes couldn't wait, so he had no choice. There was just one catch. Juniata would only take him that fall if he began work on his master's degree that summer. So he did, at Penn State. To make money he moonlighted at night. It was some summer.

Did Shirley tell you what I did at night? Probably not. I'm not embarrassed—I sold used cars. Classes in the morning, educating the prospective car buyer at night. No, I didn't rip anybody off. I've done a lot of things in my life, but all were honest labor, and that's often as much as a man can ask for, honest labor.

By the way, I even sold a car to the mayor of Tyrone, although it was a flood car, meaning it had been in a flood and just dried out. It ran, he took it, I made my nut.

If nothing else, I think selling used cars helped me appreciate offensive linemen. Nobody wants their job, but everybody needs them to get around. And if I've never been much of a big-shot kind of guy, it's maybe because I could never envision a big shot writing prices on car windshields in soap.

One day later that summer, just as I was finishing my nine hours toward my master's, and just as we were preparing to move back to Huntingdon, I see an ad in a newspaper. It's for a high-school football coach in a little town called Ellwood City. I didn't know why they would want a used-car salesman, but I sent in my application and got called and went for an interview.

I knew Ellwood City from my days at Sewickley, it was another tiny fifteen-thousand-person mill town just down the river. I also knew Ellwood was the smallest school in its division, so it was always playing bigger teams, always the underdog. My kind of town, Ellwood City was. And it needed a football coach. I drove over and gave the interview my best shot. The interviewers seemed surprisingly impressed. They said they had heard about my work at Tyrone, and my work at all these clinics that I had started attending. To this day, I don't know how they found any of that out. But they told me nothing about my chances, and I drove back to Tyrone knowing nothing.

When I returned I got a phone call from Juniata, saying, by the way, when I showed up in a few weeks, we would have to live in a campus house with five coeds upstairs. Great. I dropped to my knees and prayed that the next call would be from Ellwood City.

Shirley Knox: I thought it was going to be so cute, Chuck as a proctor for all these girls. I was looking forward to it.

But then just before the school year started, we got another call. Chuck could not believe it. You'd have thought it was the Pittsburgh Steelers.

Just as we were preparing to pack to move the family back to Huntingdon, the phone rang in our cramped little maid's quarters. I picked it up, and all I remember is somebody on the other end saying the words "Ellwood City." I could hardly keep from shouting.

They asked me over the phone whether I wanted the job or not—just like that. I still don't know why I impressed them. Maybe it was because I was from western Pennsylvania. Maybe it was my accent.

But I asked nothing except "When do I start?"

Only, I wasn't there yet. I first had to inform the president of Juniata that I had decided to give up a career as a college professor to coach high-school football. I talked to him, and he put it pretty straight. He told me I was blowing my chance at higher learning merely to instruct kids playing a sport of brutes. I didn't think much of his attempted persuasion until I stopped at Kelly's Bar that night on the way home to Tyrone. All my pallies there, they said the same thing. They couldn't understand why I would give up something with class for something that smelled like grass. Remember, I wasn't going off to coach the Rams, I was going off to coach sixteen-year-old Wolverines. I could see their point.

I got home that night, fell asleep, and was awakened at four o'clock in the morning by a phone call. It was those same guys from Kelly's. "The mistake of your life!" they shouted into the phone. "You're making the mistake of your life!"

The next morning I woke up and decided, I've made mistakes before. This is as good a time as any to make another one. It came down to not caring about anything but football. And now I was finally going to be a man in charge of a football team.

I immediately moved the family to Ellwood City, where we eventually lived in one of our greatest houses ever, in the best location possible.

Shirley Knox: You aren't going to believe this: We lived right across from the football field. I mean, right across the street. I didn't think it was possible. But Chuck found a way.

It was a tiny gray frame house with white shutters. It was old and creaky, but Chuck made just one home improvement. He turned the basement into a projection room, where he would sit all evening watching films after spending all day at school.

I threw myself into that first job. I couldn't get enough of it. I was consumed by it. A lot of what I do now, I instinctively learned to do then.

Former Ellwood City player Karl Florie: He walks in on a not-very-good team—by far the smallest team in the division—and he's not much older than we are. He's twenty-four, which to this day is the youngest coach ever for a school that size in our conference.

I was a senior, the center, and I snapped the ball one-handed. He saw this the first day of practice and said, "Let's try a two-handed snap." I told him I already felt comfortable doing it one-handed. He said, "Two-handed is the way you're going to do it now." And that was that. It was the last time I talked back. So sure of himself for being so young.

Ellwood City was where I first realized the importance of studying the game. It was also where I first realized that, provided they were qualified, I wanted only old friends to be on my coaching staff. That's the Sewickley Gangster in me— You know the devil you've got, you don't know the devil you're going to get.

Pat Tarquinio: Sure enough, by the time I get out of college, Chuck has a head coaching job at this little hick town called Ellwood City. He calls me, just like he promised; and I come on down to be his assistant.

What I found there was a guy who lived for X's and O's. Sometimes it was embarrassing. Once he cleared off a table at a restaurant and started diagramming a play on the

> *table cloth. Another time, he ordered us all out of a res-*
> *taurant, then dropped to his knees on the front lawn and*
> *demonstrated a new blocking stance. It was one o'clock*
> *in the morning, and the few people still on the streets were*
> *looking at us like we were crazy.*
>
> *Other times being with him was just plain unbearable.*
> *Like when he dragged all of us down to watch the spring*
> *game at North Carolina State. We left after the school day,*
> *and he drove all night, fourteen hours, and got us there*
> *just in time for the afternoon game. After the game there*
> *was a party with the college coaches, and we had to at-*
> *tend that. By this time we were all nodding off, lying down*
> *on the host's couches and floor. But Chuck was still going*
> *strong, asking questions, diagramming plays. He finally*
> *turns to us and shouts, "We didn't come here to sleep.*
> *Get up and learn something!" What a maniac.*

I guess I was a little intense, but you have to understand the situation. Western Pennsylvania football was big, and this school was small. Nobody believed in us. It was kind of like every situation I've been put in, before and since. We didn't have a chance, so it was my job to find one. As it turns out, we went 2–8 the first year, but the mighty Wolverines did beat rival New Castle, a school about three times our size for the first time in twenty-nine years. I may not have departed there with a bunch of wins, but I left with that little football program thinking big. Sometimes that's just as important.

> *Karl Florie: We didn't win many games, but by god, by*
> *the time he left, we certainly thought we were going to*
> *win.*

This is where my coaching philosophy was generated. I realized that everything I had learned while trying to survive on the Sewickley streets was applicable to my survival here. I'm not going to get into a big thing about how football mirrors life and all that stuff, but when you think about it, the struggle is the same. And through those Knoxisms, I made myself comfortable with that struggle.

> *Pat Tarquinio: We noticed that when things got tough, Knox started talking in clichés. He was saying things like, "Nothing succeeds like success; The proof of the pudding is in the eating; Be careful about the press, don't be a quick quote, or they will burn you." Imagine that, talking to sixteen-year-olds about the press.*

Sure, I deal in clichés, and everybody mostly makes fun of them. But they remember them. Ask Pat Tarquinio why it is that he managed to remember something that was said thirty years ago. I'm never so proud as when an old player remembers an old saying of mine.

I stayed at Ellwood City three years with a team that was small and not very good. So I had a lot of practice with Knoxisms. In odd ways, I also developed my style of motivation.

> *Karl Florie: I'll tell you about Knox's motivation. There was the time we had lost at Aliquippa, a bigger school that Knox hated like he hated all big schools. We lost because we couldn't score from the one-foot line. As the school bus was leaving the parking lot, chugging to get up this hill, it started smoking. There was smoke everywhere.*
>
> *The kids in the back panicked and shouted, "The bus is on fire! The bus is on fire!" Sitting in the front, Knox never moved. He just turned around and through the smoke shouted, "Get some belly, get some belly."*

Shoot, I knew the bus was not on fire. But if those boys had some belly, they never would have lost that game. That is still one of my biggest problems, not thinking players are tough enough. Call it a chip on my shoulder, call it whatever. I never have related well to guys who have had it easy, whether it's the naturally talented player who doesn't work, or the rich owner who gives orders without having to know the game. At one time or another in his life, everyone should be forced to get a little belly. Otherwise, how does he know it's there when he needs it?

My 1984 Seahawk team, the one that went 12–4 without Curt Warner, now those were guys who weren't scared of a little smoke on the back of the bus. Their bus had been on fire since Warner went down in the first game of the season. They were used to it. I was named Coach of the Year, but they were the ones with the belly.

My biggest complaint about high-school coaching had nothing to do with buses and players, though. It had to do with there not being enough time to coach. You had to take roll in classes, monitor study hall, and fill out truancy reports. To this day, I do my best to help high-school football coaches, mainly because there is not a more difficult job. You aren't just a coach, you're a mother and father and baby-sitter—not to mention doctor and lawyer and everything else shy of wet nurse. Whatever nickel they make, it isn't enough.

Probably the most important thing a high-school coach can do—and all of western Pennsylvania is going to scream if they hear this—does not involve winning. It is sending kids to college. It is moving them down the line. The job of a high-school football coach is not to make his own future, but to build others' futures. The rest will take care of itself. If his kids are good enough for college, he'll be recognized as good enough for college coaching. Everybody will share in that success.

This wasn't so easy for me. At times, getting my team into college was like getting twenty-two Chuck Knoxes into college.

Karl Florie: When it came to college, Chuck was really funny. He first had to convince some of us kids that college was even worth it. A lot of the laborers' kids were going through the same problems he apparently went through when he left Sewickley. Nobody was sure college was worth it. Then once he convinced us to go to college, he had to convince a college to take us.

Me, I didn't want anything to do with college. But one day Chuck grabbed my arm and forced me into his car with a guy named Joe Cochran and said he had something to show us. About one hundred miles later, we pull up at this small Pennsylvania school called Clarion State Teacher's College. He had been talking about this school for weeks. I thought, Oh no, here comes another pitch. But we don't go to the school. We go to the middle of the town, where Chuck takes us into the soda fountain and buys us a milk shake. As we're drinking, several pretty girls walk by. He suddenly says, "Yeah, you're going to like drinking milk shakes for four years in this town."

I look around and think to myself, Well, yeah. Four years later I graduated from there. If it wasn't for Chuck Knox, I never would have gone anywhere.

The best part about my experience at Ellwood City, though, wasn't the kids or colleges. It was my father. Having finally accepted me, he was now following all of my games. My mother would actually attend some, walking the sidelines and shouting in her Scottish brogue, "Git'em! Git'em!" But my father had his own way.

Jimmy Munizza: The old man would spend most of fall Friday nights holed up in his apartment. Every once in a while he would stroll down to the beer truck, and everybody would say, "Hey, Mr. Knox, how is your boy's team doing?" He would always shrug and say, "How the hell should I know?" But then in the next breath he would say, "It's twenty-one to twenty at the half." Then he would quietly walk back upstairs. He was listening to the game on the radio, listening to every play. Just too proud to admit it.

It happened in the winter of 1958, after what was to be my last season at Ellwood City. My father died. In the winter, in a snowstorm. I'd have been a fool to think it would happen any other way.

It was just three months before I would get the call to big-time college coaching. It was one day after he had slid his first retirement check into his pocket.

> *Jimmy Munizza: Mr. Knox's emphysema started acting up. Mrs. Knox got scared and asked if she could run to find a phone to call a doctor. He told her no, because the doctor wouldn't work on the weekend. She ran to my house and I called the doctor. But Mr. Knox was right, he wouldn't come. Mr. Knox was getting sicker and sicker, so I had no choice. I ran up to their apartment, hauled Charlie Knox over my shoulder, and carried him down to my beer truck.*
>
> *I laid him down in the front seat and drove through the snow to the hospital. We got to the emergency room, but even the staff there couldn't find a doctor for him. I don't know if they thought he couldn't pay, or what. There was all kinds of confusion.*
>
> *All of a sudden Mr. Knox started shouting, "Call for the big boy. He'll know what to do!" He was talking about Chuck. Imagine that. Attendants just wheeled him up to a room and told him to wait. In that room, while waiting, he died.*

A couple of months later, Jimmy Munizza's wife, Frances, is working at the beer distributorship when she swears she had a vision of my father. He is emblazoned on the wall, surrounded by a number, 625. She tells Jimmy and his brother John and they say, "Well, ain't that something. Charlie has come back from the dead to give us a lucky number."

So they start betting 625 in the local numbers game. Betting and betting it, but it never comes up. So now they think Charlie was trying to tell them something completely different, something about the evils of betting. So they stop betting completely.

A couple of days later, the number hits.

And maybe that's what my father was trying to tell them: Hang with your lucky number; don't quit on your lucky star, and by god, it may not always be your friend, but it will never quit on you. Tell *them?* Maybe that's what he tried for twenty years to tell me.

Sometimes I think I'd give it all back if he could see me now. I would sure show him. Or I would give anything just to see *him* now. I can picture it, my dad joining me on one of my road trips, stalking the sidelines, ripping the referee.

Now when I go back to Sewickley and sit around with the boys, when the scotch is fresh and the smoke is thick, I inevitably ask them to tell me stories about my father. Any stories. Doesn't matter if I've heard them before.

3

Wake Forest
and Kentucky

It is early one Thursday afternoon at Ellwood City High, in March of 1959. It is my general science period. I am in the middle of pulling the insides out of a frog. I am not making this up.

This schoolgirl knocks on my classroom door. "Phone call for you in the office, Mr. Knox," she says.

Why would anyone call me at school in the middle of class? I think, Shirley isn't pregnant, at least not last I looked, so we can't be having another baby. Then I wonder if somebody is sick. I know I can't handle another death so soon after my father. I get some boy in the front row to tend the classroom, and I hustle down to the office and take the call. I listen for a few minutes. I nearly drop the phone. On the other end is Paul Amen, the head football coach at Wake Forest. He says he is looking for somebody to fill a vacancy as assistant coach, somebody with experience in western Pennsylvania, because they want to begin recruiting there.

"Would, uh, this person happen to be me?" I ask, trying to block out the dull roar from a sudden change of classes that has filled the halls behind me.

"Uh, maybe," says Amen, very cool and businesslike. "Why don't you fly down here Sunday and we'll find out."

"See you there," I say, hanging up the phone, grabbing for both my handkerchief and my breath.

I finish my teaching duties and race home to tell Shirley. I get right to the edge of the football field, a couple of hundred yards from the house, and then suddenly stop as if struck by cardiovascular trauma.

Did he say *fly?*

> *Shirley Knox: Chuck had never flown before. He came home excited about the job possibilities but unnerved about flying. Mr. Amen had told Chuck that because of the hastiness of this trip, he would probably have to fly standby. Chuck had said fine. Then he comes home to me and says, "Honey, how do I find a plane and what in the hell is standby?"*

The way I figured it, what I didn't know about standby and flying and all that, I could find out in the next couple of days. And I did.

Turns out I enjoyed the flight, which is odd because I've always been afraid of heights. Perhaps it's because tall buildings were so foreign to me as a child—twenty-three steps up was about my limit.

Even today, in Seattle, I don't like going up the Space Needle. If forced, usually by business reasons, I'll go. But once at the top I'll never look out or down. Shirley and I traveled through Yellowstone Park the other summer, and I had a heckuva time with those mountain roads, so she drove. When we stopped at those scenic lookouts, only she got out of the car.

I occasionally like to take my assistant coaches down to Fort Lewis, an army base near Seattle, to watch the troops in their confidence-building exercises. One of these is called the "Swing for Life"—you go up on this narrow eighty-foot tower and then swing on a rope down into some water. One of my coaches got up there to try it and was so scared he had to be helped back down. Nobody asked me to try it. Smart thing for all of them.

The problem with the Wake Forest trip was not the flight, but what happened once I got there. I discovered I was competing for the job with two guys who had been recommended by Army coach Red Blaik, who had been Amen's boss at West Point for thirteen years. As far as Amen was concerned, what the colonel said was gold.

Two hours into my visit I figured I had about as much chance of getting this job as the Ellwood City Wolverines had against the Army. I only had two things going for me, and one of them depended on Shirley's cooking.

> *Longtime Knox assistant coach Ken Meyer: I guess I was the one who discovered Knox for Wake Forest, although it was certainly by stumble rather than design, and considering he lived right next to the damn Ellwood City High football field, somebody else would have found him sooner or later. I was there to recruit one of Chuck's kids just after the 1958 season. He insisted that I stop by his house that Saturday morning before I got started.*
>
> *I'll never forget, they had this cheap little bamboo rug on the floor. Right away Chuck drags me into this basement where a projector has been set up, and starts showing me films. It's not quite eight o'clock. This goes on for quite a while. And then Shirley, bless her heart, comes in with this great breakfast. I was hooked on the dedication of the coach and the cooking abilities of his wife.*

I never forgot Kenny Meyer for picking up on that. Who do you think was my offensive coordinator during four straight championship years in Los Angeles? And who do you think is my quarterback coach now? Same guy. In my mind, the most important feature of any good executive is his memory.

The other thing I had going for me at Wake Forest happened during the interview. Right in front of me, Amen picked up the phone and called Bill Smaltz, my old Juniata coach, who was now an assistant at North Carolina State. I heard just one side of the conversation; it was more than a bit unsettling.

"Bill, this is Paul Amen over at Wake, I got a question for you."

Silence.

"Doing just fine, Bill. The question is, being from western Pennsylvania, and knowing the hundreds of high-school coaches up there, if you had to hire one from that area for your staff, who would it be?"

Silence. Incredible, drawn-out, sweat-producing silence.

"Thanks, Bill."

Amen put down the phone, and in his most solemn military manner, he turned to me.

"Said he would take this fella named Knox. Chuck Knox."

Bill Smaltz: I didn't know Chuck knew that I had recommended him. All these years, I thought my input was a secret. Oh well. It was an obvious recommendation.

When I heard Amen say my name . . . if I thought my nervous stomach could have handled it, I would have done handsprings. Smaltz gave me the best recommendation you can receive, an unsolicited one.

To this day, when hiring somebody, I never call a candidate's references. I make all my calls *before* I get the guy's references. And I never mention the guy I'm considering. I'll call different authorities in the position I am trying to fill and ask exactly what Paul Amen asked Bill Smaltz: just who they think is the best man for the job. An unsolicited recommendation, that's the only thing I settle for anymore.

In this case, it still didn't ensure me the Wake Forest job, at least not on the spot. Amen sent me home and told me he would call me in three or four days.

After my jubilation, I was suddenly wary again. When you're a young coach, three or four days feels like three or four last-second field goal attempts.

> *Shirley Knox: After he was home about ten minutes, I wanted to buy him another plane ticket and send him back out. Every time the phone rang, he would jump. I couldn't go near it for three days. It would ring; he would jump and grab it, then he would shake his head and hand it to me, saying, "It's for you," as if my phone call had just cost him his job.*
>
> *Oh yeah. He didn't sleep for those three days either. I tell people the hardest part about being his wife has never been all the moving, but the waiting around for some-body to tell us where to go.*

I had arrived back at Ellwood City on a Tuesday morning. On Friday morning, Amen calls. I remember the words like they were spoken this morning.

"Chuck, I'm prepared to offer you a position as line coach at Wake Forest University," he said. "The salary will be fifty-five hundred a year. Since we are currently undergoing spring football practice, I'd like to get you here as soon as possible."

"How about tonight?" I said.

And that was that. I was finally a real coach, a full-time coach, not an attendance-taker or raffle salesman.

In case you're wondering—as my wife certainly was—that salary was less than I was making at Ellwood City.

> *Former Wake Forest head coach Paul Amen: The thing that impressed me about Chuck was that he was so eager to learn, so interested in all the aspects of the game, and he had such an inquisitive mind. I don't want to say he wanted this job bad or anything, but it wasn't until much later that he told me he had taken a pay cut.*

I was, I kept repeating to myself, an assistant coach at Wake Forest University. I would say it slowly, and by the time I got to the university part I was shouting. I said it even while picking up the phone and making arrangements to fly down there.

Flew standby, of course. By now I was convinced your life won't get anywhere if you wait for a confirmed reservation.

> *Ken Meyer: Great story about how he got the job. But now ask Chuck what happened when he arrived at Wake Forest. You see, he never bothered to find out that, at the time, Wake Forest was one this country's leading Baptist universities. He never found out about the strict rules involving everything, from the football budget to the football coaches' social lives. Ask about the first time he said, "Gee, I sure could use a drink."*

Quite a place, this Wake Forest. I first realized what I was getting into when Amen told me, yes, they would move my family and household goods down, as long as I didn't need any more than $250 for it. This was the first time we had moved in anything other than the back of a station wagon, so I didn't know what $250 would do. Amen told us, and it wasn't much, so he showed us how to cut corners, urged us to sell things, to get rid of our junk *before* we came down. We did, enabling us to move for just about $250.

In the process, Amen taught me a relocation lesson that I sometimes follow today: never give your future employee a carte blanche on moving expenses. You do that, nothing is going to get thrown out; your employee is going to toss everything on that van, and the bill is going to be twenty-five thousand dollars. Then after he gets to your town, he has a huge garage sale, which you helped subsidize without receiving any of the profits. Instead of that route, you must ask around, find out what a fair moving price is, say, fifteen thousand, then tell him that is all he is getting, not a penny more. Guaranteed, he will have his garage sale *before* coming down. Then he can make his move in about ten thousand dollars, pocket the rest, and be a very happy employee.

So we manage to survive our first moving-van move, but there's this problem. The mover and a very pregnant Shirley and the kids arrive at Wake Forest right in the middle of a spring practice. I am called from the field. I run up to our second-floor faculty apartment, show it to Shirley, and then holler down to the moving man.

"All the stuff goes up here," I say.

"No, it don't," he says.

"No, it don't *what?*"

"No, it don't go nowhere until I have my two hundred and fifty dollars."

Damn. I've got no money; I haven't been paid my running allowance yet. Shirley has about ten bucks. Our whole life is in this moving truck and the guy won't even shut if off. I can't think of anything to do but run back to the field and find Coach Amen. He makes a big deal of stopping practice. I ask him if I can have my check now. He says it's customary to reimburse the $250. I say, fine, but the definition of reimbursement says that somebody has to have the money in the first place, and I don't have anything. He finally relents and sends somebody over to cut me a check. But by now I've missed too much practice, so I can't stay around to help the movers unpack and assemble things. For the next two years, our dining-room table's legs were on backward.

Quite a place, this Wake Forest. I had no idea it would be so strict, so proper, so "by-the-book." I had no idea what book they were talking about.

Coach Amen called me in shortly after I arrived and made it very clear about his coaches' conduct. We couldn't drink. We had to wear a T-shirt underneath our open-neck coaching shirts so our chest hair wouldn't stick out. There was even a rule on how to answer the phone. It was always "Wake Forest University, Coach Knox speaking."

The Wake Forest rules were bewildering at first, but I could handle them. Even the drinking. We would hide a six-pack in a brown bag out behind the apartment. It was eighth-grade

Sewickley. The enforced decorum was actually good for me. Because of it, I finally got rid of the one most visible, disgusting image of my past.

> *Paul Amen: The only thing that really surprised me about Chuck was the tattoo. I definitely didn't like it for our school. It definitely had the wrong connotation.*

It was almost as if, when I arrived at Wake Forest, the tattoo got bigger and bigger. More blue. Harder to hide. I started buying my shirts with longer sleeves.

One night at a party, a team doctor walks up to me. "Nice tattoo," he says.

"I'm not proud of it," I say.

"So get rid of it," he says.

"How?" I say.

"For free, that's how," he says, speaking the magic words.

Well, he fixed me but good. A couple days later I went in to his office and he put my arm to sleep and actually cut the damn tattoo off, sliced it right off. It hurt like hell for two entire weeks. It wouldn't have been so bad, except that I had to go on one of those long recruiting trips the next day. We had to drive for seven days, and oh man, did that son of a gun hurt!

> *Ken Meyer: Talk about bad timing. Why did Chuck cut that thing off right before a trip? I'll never know. But he couldn't drive the damn car, because he couldn't hold his right arm up. And every time he shook hands with some kid, you could see the color drain from his face. Every high school tried to impress him with a hard handshake, and Chuck couldn't refuse. It damn near broke his stitches. Coming home, right about West Virginia somewhere on some back road, the stitches finally did split. Blood everywhere, a guy with an open wound in the front seat of my car. It was some trip.*

Today, all I have in place of that tattoo is a small trace of a scar. You would never realize what had been there, which is fine with me. The way I figure it, it's one thing to remember your past, it's quite another to advertise it.

Meanwhile, I became so immersed in my football mission that I didn't notice much of anything else. In fact, I was so immersed in my mission that, well, I almost didn't notice the birth of our third daughter, Colleen.

> *Shirley Knox: It was September 22, right in the beginning of the season. Chuck went out to the field just as I was going into labor. Back then, we just didn't bother the husband with things like that. I know it sounds funny today, but that's the way it was. So I have a girl, and the doctor calls Chuck over at the coach's office and tells him, "Coach Knox, I have a substitute here for you." Bad move. Chuck thinks it's a boy. That's all he'd been wanting for the longest time, a boy. But that's not what the doctor meant. When Chuck got here and saw Colleen . . . he was so proud he was almost crying, but you could also sense some disappointment. Three children, and not a football player among them.*

Yeah, I knew Shirley was having the baby as I took the field, but the philosophy back then was a philosophy that unfortunately has changed today. Your job is important to you. Your job is what pays for the first eighteen years of that baby's life. Do your job, your baby will still be there after you punch out.

People came up to me that day and said, "Coach Knox, your wife is having a baby, what are you going to do?" I told them, back in the steel mills, you don't work, you don't get paid. Back in the steel mills, if your wife has a baby in the middle of the day, you work all day, come home, get cleaned up, and *then* go on up to the hospital. It's like the coach of my first pro team, Weeb Ewbank, once said: "You just have to be there when the keel is laid, not when the ship is launched."

When the doctor called me down at the practice field and told me about the baby, I only had one question and that was, are Shirley and the baby healthy? They were, so I went back to work. Call me what you will. Just because I'm wearing some fancy sweat suit and cleats doesn't mean I'm not still a working man.

It was at Wake Forest that, for the first time in my career, my devotion to this game began rubbing off on my players. Although sometimes that would rub Amen the wrong way.

> *Paul Amen: I would enjoy watching his players come running when he blew his whistle, hooting and hollering and ready to fight. But there was a problem. Chuck kept wanting to jump in there and demonstrate blocking techniques on them. I told him to be careful just how far he went. He didn't have pads, he didn't have a helmet, and they did. I told him sometimes players, in what they claim is extra effort, will go out of their way to pop a coach.*

It was the start of the one coaching habit that I have finally broken. Maybe the habit came about because I was never the player I wanted to be. Maybe it's because I just like a good fight. But I didn't feel I was properly coaching unless I was butting their heads, pushing them off the line, blocking them on their rears. Football is a show-me game, not a preach-to-me game.

When it started at Wake Forest, it was cute, but Paul Amen was right. I have all kinds of scars on my forehead from overzealous players who wanted to take a shot when they saw a coach in a three-point stance with his hat turned backward. But then, some of those scars were caused by me, like as recently as the fall of 1986, when I nailed a relaxing Seahawk with a head butt on the first day of camp.

Looking back on it, my Wake Forest on-field devotion was actually quite funny, because the one thing I learned in two years there, and later on during two years at Kentucky, was that, of the three levels of coaching, college is the one where on-field devotion is not always the primary concern. This is because college is the one level where you have direct control of who your players are. And getting those players to your school, *that's* what is important.

In high school, you can only choose from your student body. And in the pros, through the virtues of the reverse-order-of-finish draft, everybody theoretically starts equal. Everybody gets forty-five guys and can do with them what they will. Because of this, I was able to take floundering teams like the Rams, the Bills, and the Seahawks and make them contenders. In high school and the pros, therefore, the question is always, how well can you do with the players you have? Can you motivate them better, direct them better, organize them better, and then get them to play better than the other guys?

Good coaching wins at any level. But in college it's more a question of resources. For reasons of location and prestige, certain colleges have consistently fielded winning teams for the last seventy-five to one hundred years. They have tradition, stability, and winning records because they attract the best talent. The toughest college jobs are not at the Nebraskas or the Michigans, but at the schools that have to play these people, the Wake Forests, the Iowa States, the Kansas States. Because of their recruiting disadvantages, a lot of these schools simply can't compete.

Although I was in big-time college football only four years, I do know a little bit about recruiting. If you had taken one of those two-week East Coast trips with me at Wake Forest, in an old car, staying at old motels and without enough expense money even to phone home, you would know something about it, too. We were never on the kind of budget where we could simply fly to Pittsburgh and rent a car for a couple of weeks. We would borrow a car from some alumnus and drive it up through Royal Oak, up to Staunton Military Academy, on up to Winchester, hop on the Pennsylvania Turnpike, make some calls off there, turn around and do it all in reverse.

It would be a trip of at least three weeks, with fast food and flophouse hotels. And the bosses back home would say, don't worry about your family, don't spend our money calling them; we'll take care of them. Damn, today, some of our traveling coaches and scouts call home twice a day, once to check in and then again a half hour later to go back over what they talked about in that first call.

That was just the traveling part. Once you arrived at your destination, sometimes it got messier. What if another school's coach had gotten to a certain kid first? You promised your head coach you were going to get this kid, and then somebody else is all over him like a cheap suit. Suddenly the kid's locker-room door is closed, and the other coach is in there with him—what are you going to do?

And when we went head-on-head with another school, Wake Forest often didn't stand a chance. We were competing against guys who would sit at the kitchen table and peel off hundred-dollar bills for the old man. We couldn't afford that. We were going against guys who would launder money for the kids like this: put some graduate assistant on a booster's payroll, make the guy show up once a month for a two-hundred-dollar check, then let him keep fifty dollars and give you back the other hundred and fifty to give to your players. We couldn't afford it even then. All we could tell kids was, it's not that much money or that worth it in the long run, and then try to describe our less tangible benefits.

We were even going against guys who would take these kids out to lakes fishing, so nobody could get ahold of them until signing day. This was compounded by the fact that, back then, signing day was not a binding day. Unless you kept tabs on your kids throughout the summer, any school, anywhere, could come in and steal them before the opening game. Today, at least, they have a National Letter of Intent Day, which makes a kid keep his word.

So of course we had a lot of back-stabbing and bad-mouthing going on, a lot of everything happening to convince poor high-school kids to save some coach's job. I've seen coaches publicly call each other liars. I've seen fist-fights between coaches in school auditoriums, right in front of cheerleaders.

I was lucky because in the area I recruited, they couldn't make up lies about me. Everyone knew that any outrageous story was probably true. And more often than not, that endeared me to the mill-town kid and his family, who often reminded me of my own family. It often gave me an edge, and I took that edge and expanded on it to where I sold *myself*, not my school, and that seemed to even things up.

> *University of Kentucky assistant coach Ralph Hawkins: I know Knox doesn't like recruiting, but let me tell you, he was the best I ever saw. The absolute best. Coming from the streets, he knew almost every ethnic group's lingo, their dialect, and enough words to fit any language. He could speak Italian, Polish, and play their little finger games.*
>
> *You recruit differently in different parts of the country. In western Pennsylvania you need to make the parents feel comfortable in their own house, if that makes any sense. That's what Chuck did best. He talked like the street, too, so the kids loved him. Right away they realized there was nothing they could go through that he hadn't gone through. He would take care of them.*
>
> *And he didn't just sell the kids. He made it a point to know the uncles, know the brothers. A lot of coaches on recruiting trips go to bed early so they can get a head start on the next day. Not Chuck. He was recruiting all the time. After he left the parents' house and tucked the kid in bed, he would take the older brother out to a bar and sell him.*

I was huge on selling a kid's relatives and friends. Once though, it almost backfired when I wanted to get this kid named Bluebaugh from Canton Central Catholic. I had worked so hard on his buddy, a kid named Tommy Becker, that in the end Becker also wanted to come to the school. In order to sign Bluebaugh, I had no choice but to sign Becker, who I felt was only mediocre. I was in trouble until—you'll never guess—Bluebaugh quits school after two years and Becker letters for three years. That's recruiting.

It was at Wake Forest that I learned the fundamentals of recruiting. I'm not saying I'm qualified to give lessons in it, but I did get some western Pennsylvania football players to come to a nonfootball, deadly strict, Deep South Baptist institution. Maybe that should be worth something.

First thing you do in recruiting is judge the talent, determine where the players are. Then you just sell those players on your school.

Easily said. Not so easily done.

A few of my rules for recruiting the eighth-grade Sewickley way:

Number one: You can buy a father, but never the mother.

Although I wasn't at a college where we could afford to buy anybody, I saw this happen all the time. It was common practice to get to a kid's house, take the old man in the kitchen, and say, "Hey, your son is going to get the same education with us as anywhere else—oh, excuse me, I see where you have linoleum on this kitchen floor; maybe a rug would look nice . . ." Or, "You've worked all your life to put your son into college, and now that he's made it, even though you're broke, you should be so proud—oh, and I see you could use a refrigerator, hmmm . . ."

Some fathers would rationalize and go for it. The pitch sounded good. But don't dare try it on the mother. Try any of that on her, and you are out the door. Wham. Gone. The difference is, the mother is willing to get on her hands and knees and scrub that linoleum floor so her son can go to a good college. Money to her is nothing.

You have to go to the mother with little facts about the school that you have written on index cards and memorized: "Yes, ma'am, we know your boy is a Catholic; we'll have Father So-and-So there to take care of his spiritual needs.

Yes, ma'am, we have the whatever-it-is school of medicine there; they'll take care of his academic needs . . . blah, blah, blah."

Do all that, and before you know it, the mother will be inviting you to dinner. Once that happens, you've got the kid. He's yours.

Number two: Talk to the kid like he's already at your school.

This is a little phone technique I developed. Say things like, "Next year you will be playing games in five different cities, all of them fun cities, and from what I hear, you guys will be favored to win the championship." Or, "Say, we just had a barbecue here today with all of your future teammates. We missed you."

Number three: When he comes for his one official visit, leave nothing to chance.

This goes along with my philosophy that anybody can coach the big things, but the winner is the guy who doesn't miss the little things. When the kid flies in, do you have a good route planned from the airport to the school? Will you drive him through the nice part of town, no matter how remote it may be from the actual school? Do you know who he's going to meet and in what order he's going to meet them? And for pete's sake, does everybody know his name? You don't need the head coach saying, "Hi, I'm Coach Smith, what's your name?" He has to be saying, "Hi, Frankie, I'm Coach Smith, how's everything back in Pennsylvania?"

You can leave nothing to chance. I learned a lot about coaching big football games from recruiting small-town kids.

Ralph Hawkins: I gotta tell the Frank Antonini story. It happened when I was new to the University of Kentucky, where Chuck went after Wake Forest. I was supposed to follow Knox around on one of his final recruiting trips before he went to the New York Jets. The object was this kid named Frank Antonini of Ambridge High near Sewickley, one of the best kids in the country. We get to his

*house at two o'clock in the afternoon. Chuck walks in the
door, hugs the mother, speaks Italian to the father, and
the old man turns to his boy: "Frankie, go down in the
basement and get the wine." Up comes this huge jug of
homemade wine, out comes this huge hunk of cheese and
some meats and soon the house is full of all these neighborhood people who have heard of Chuck as the local boy
who made good. Later on the daughter brings out a pineapple upside-down cake, says she made it just for Chuck.
We stay until ten o'clock that night. The kid is a lock.
But Chuck isn't done.*

*He goes downtown to the Jacktown Hotel bar, calls all
the local high-school coaches, brings them all in, throws
every bit of money he has on the bar, about eighty-five
bucks, and says, "All right, boys, Big Money is here; the
clinic has started." Till way past closing, Chuck was diagramming plays on napkins, blocking other coaches around
the room, getting right into their hearts for the inside track
on whatever other great prospects they might have in the
future.*

*Big Money—ha! But we got Antonini and others like
him.*

Tell you what, high-school coaches in western Pennsylvania take care of their own. Especially when they found out
that Big Money was making about five thousand less a year
than they were.

I admit I saw recruiting as a challenge, an incredible challenge, and in a way I guess I actually enjoyed it. But in the
end I hated where it led. I hated its phoniness, and that led
to my eventual departure from the college game. My problem was that once I recruited a kid I felt a personal commitment to him. If you were a good recruiter, it meant you later
had to be a good baby-sitter. And that kind of responsibility
took even more time away from my coaching duties.

I felt that the mother had entrusted her boy to me. I had
to make sure he went to class, make sure an outlet for his

spiritual beliefs was available. A lot of schools will say, "Yeah, we'll take care of your boy's spiritual needs," then the coach will consistently call 7:00 A.M. Sunday meetings that last until 1:00 P.M. I couldn't do that with a good conscience.

I tried to take a big interest in each of my kids, and that led to things like kids coming to me when they were home-sick, kids running out of money and needing to borrow some from *me* (what a joke), kids wanting to use my phone to call their girlfriends. It was one thing after another; and while I felt it was my duty, I also knew that I didn't want to do this much longer. Remember, I wanted to be a coach. A teacher. Not a salesman or a baby-sitter.

I took the biggest step toward that end after two years at Wake Forest when Bill Crutchfield, another assistant coach, told me about an opening at the University of Kentucky. Not that their school was any better than our school, but their school had one thing our school didn't—a head coach named Blanton Collier.

Most know him as the Cleveland Browns coach who took the team from Paul Brown and, in eight seasons from 1963 to 1970, won an NFL title, three conference championships, and a division championship. Overall he won 66 percent of the games he coached (79–40–2), which would have put him in the overall top seven of all coaches, if only he had coached the accepted record-book minimum of ten seasons.

It was typical of Collier to retire two years shy of formal greatness, because he was not in it for the glory or the awards. He was in it—as you can tell by the fact that he was a high-school coach for seventeen years before joining Kentucky—for one reason only: to teach. He was in it to make the people who worked and played for him as successful as they could be. When you cut through all the bull, that's coaching. It was through Blanton, in just one season at the University of Kentucky, that I discovered that definition.

Call him my greatest influence, call him my mentor, call him whatever. This soft-spoken, gentle man, almost the opposite of everything you'd expect a coach to be, is a part of everything I've ever accomplished.

You don't hear much about his college days—when I first learned from him—because he wasn't your typical college coach. In his eight years at Kentucky, he wasn't once a salesman. He would spend three hours going over a blocking technique with a junior college coach, and then five minutes with a recruit. That was the reason he was only at one college, University of Kentucky, and then only long enough to get back to the Browns, where he had earlier served as an assistant.

I knew that when he accepted me as a University of Kentucky assistant, in the long run it would be the break of my career. But it wasn't certain at the start that there was even a job I could fill. When Collier interviewed me, he wasn't sure whether he was looking for an offensive- or defensive-line coach. The offensive-line coach there at the time was Bill Arnsparger, and he was willing to take either position. Because my specialty was offensive lines, he went ahead and gave me that job and moved Arnsparger to the defensive line. Guess who later drew up the brilliant defenses of the great Miami Dolphins teams? Bill Arnsparger. In that sense, Collier's decision was a break for both of us.

But apart from Blanton Collier, the job offered few immediate attractions. Kentucky provided a salary increase—from $5,500 to $8,200. But I had to pay $1,000 a year for the rental of a faculty house, so my actual take was $7,200. Financially, I was going nowhere, and not very fast.

> *Shirley Knox: And once again, you should have seen the house. When they said they had a faculty house for us we thought, you know, faculty row. Hah! How about, faculty skid row. Our house was beat up, run down, and just about ready for a long nap. Of course, neither it nor us could ever sleep, what with the cockroaches running around in the kitchen. The first person who introduced himself to us*

| *was our next-door neighbor. He was the guy who cut the university lawn.*

The only thing good about this place was the next-door neighbor, the Kentucky maintenance man. In a lesson neither Shirley nor I will ever forget, he taught us how *not* to barbecue chicken. He would go out in his little backyard and throw that tomato sauce on the chickens while they were cooking. It would burn the chickens right up, and let loose an odor that I can still smell. Almost like burning rubber. We were too afraid ever to say anything to him. But if you're ever over at the house for a barbecue, and we happen to be having chicken, notice how Shirley won't put that sauce on until *after* they are cooked.

| *Shirley Knox: I will say this much for Kentucky. We finally got through a job, start to finish, without having any more babies.*

On my first day at Kentucky I walked into their tiny coaches' offices—we took a backseat to the basketball program—and I was just amazed. I sensed even then that I could have been walking into a coaching Hall of Fame. By that time, assistant coach Don Shula had left for the Detroit Lions, but in one corner was assistant coach Howard Schnellenberger; in another corner, assistants John North, Leeman Bennett, and Bill Arnsparger; in another corner, George Boone and Ermal Allen. Counting me, every man on that staff would go on to NFL success. Five of us would be head coaches (Schnellenberger, Bennett, North, Arnsparger, and I). Another would be a player personnel director (Boone). Yet another would be Tom Landry's top assistant at Dallas (Allen). And down the hall sat the quietest, most unassuming of them all, Blanton Collier. I learned right away that he was the most academic of all coaches, a theorist with a 150 IQ, the only coach in history who needed to keep squelching rumors about his moving to the state capitol to become superintendent of schools.

Blanton told us that a football field is an extension of the classroom, and that real teaching is not teaching at all, but the ability to inspire learning. He used to tell us, "*You* know that two plus two equals four, but if your son thinks it's five, then your teaching won't do any good unless you can find a way to get him to accept it. With that acceptance comes learning." He summed it up this way: "Believe in the teachability of the student. Everyone can learn. You just have to find the right way to teach him." I later simplified that: My players are smart enough if I'm good enough to teach them.

I say it even today. It is the basis for everything I have accomplished with the so-called underachievers, with the Rams and Bills and Seahawks of the world. To me, no football player is too young, no football player is over the hill, no football player is dumb. They are all smart enough, all champions—if I and my coaches are good enough to teach them.

Blanton would constantly challenge his coaches with this, constantly challenge them to get better. He'd walk into one of our position meetings on Friday and quietly say, "I've been thinking all week about this play, let me see what you think." He would draw it up, and most of us would automatically agree with him that it was a great play. After all, the master wouldn't spend a week on anything less.

But often Blanton was just testing us. Sometimes he had only thought of the play five minutes before. He fully knew it was a stupid play; he just wanted to see who was bright enough to realize it and challenge him. It also worked the other way. He would come in and say, "Hey, sorry to bother you, I just thought of this little play here while shaving this morning; see what you think." It could be a play he had been mullling over and designing for days. He wanted to see if you could recognize its value.

Blanton did not want his coaches simply guessing what he was thinking. He wanted honest opinions. This is how I treat my coaches today. I even hit them with the bit about thinking something up while shaving. It's like the great Kentucky basketball coach Adolph Rupp said, if you don't shake those balls up every now and then, they won't bounce like you like. Coaches are no good to you if they're just yes-guys.

Blanton Collier was unique. He was one of these Einstein characters, a genius whose every word was worth listening to. In the off-season the assistants would go to his house with spiral stenographer's pads and sit at his feet and take notes while he talked. It was so refreshing, invigorating. He would turn football into the technical and philosophical. A genius. Yet this same guy would run around all day with his shoes untied. Sometimes he would drive two miles past his house, the same house he'd lived in for years, before realizing he had gone too far.

He taught me so much. From him I learned you must hold your coaches directly accountable for the actions of the people they coach. He taught me that there are no problems in life, only challenges. He taught me that just because something is negative doesn't mean it is bad, only that it's off-target.

An example: He came in once after looking at films of a loss, after our offensive linemen let people get through them. He was all tight-lipped and everything, and said, "I don't understand how we can teach these principles and then look at the films and see that the players aren't getting it done."

Having learned his theories by then, I looked down and said, "Daggone it, I've just got to do a better job."

He said, "Well, you're working pretty hard. Maybe you just need a different approach. When talking about blocking, you always use the phrase 'follow-through,' and it's not sinking in. Maybe it's just semantics. Instead, why not try a more descriptive term. Why don't you call that technique a 'stick'? See if that registers with them."

I went out of there all charged up and told my players, "I want all of you to stop trying to 'follow through.' I want you to start 'sticking.' 'Stick' through the other guy, stick it to him. Forget about all else but stick, stick, stick."

That day in practice, and for the rest of that season, we

were sticking defensive linemen all the way up into the stands.

That was Blanton, a man who could choose one player, at one position, and improve him more than anybody else on the team. Any player, any position. All his players didn't have to look alike, or play alike either. Blanton knew that guy with the fat ass couldn't comfortably get in the same stance as that more solid guy next to him. So he let him do his own thing, as long as it worked. Today, so do I. As much as Blanton loved technique, execution was number one, and technique was number two.

It's a fact, we need more teachers like him in football. I think Bill Walsh of San Francisco is a great teacher. I think Don Shula of Miami, another disciple of Blanton's, is a great teacher. The players know who the bad teachers are. The fans can even watch and tell who they are. They are the guys ranting and raving on the sidelines, worrying about the petty things, like players who leave their paper cups on the field, and what the players are going to wear, and what they are going to eat today. Some coaches are so concerned with how players look, those become the big things. I tell the players before the season that I'd like their helmets under their left arms during the National Anthem. I tell them just once, and I only tell them because some players are always worrying about it. But do you know, some teams practice that? And some guys are fined if they don't do it right?

Yes, everybody knows who the bad teachers are. They are the guys who don't last.

On March 22, 1983, at age seventy-six, Blanton Collier died. A couple of months later I was talking to Paul Warfield, the former Browns receiver who had just made the Hall of Fame. I asked who was introducing him at the induction ceremony, a spot usually taken by a player's team owner or something, a really big name. Warfield said it was going to be his high-school coach, because that was his first teacher. But he also said he wished Blanton Collier, his other favorite teacher, could have been up there as well.

I think if I ever make the Hall of Fame, I would feel the

same way. More importantly, I'd like to see Blanton Collier make it before I do. Every year I talk to writers, and every year I try to promote him. Every year I've failed. But I'll keep trying. It's like Blanton said back then, and like I have said a thousand times since: There are no problems, only challenges.

4

New York

Why do I keep doing this to myself? You tell me—why?

Such went my conversation with the mirror.

The year was 1963. It was a spring morning in Lexington, Kentucky. I had just hung up the phone. The man on the other end had been Weeb Ewbank. He had just asked me to leave the security of the University of Kentucky to become—get this—the youngest assistant coach for a professional team that didn't yet exist, in a professional league that was exactly one year old.

And I had just told him yes.

What, are you crazy? What are you trying to prove? Don't you care about your family? Why put it all on the line for the funky American Football League, for something called the New York Airplanes or Jets, or whatever the hell they are?

That morning, the mirror and I went at it pretty good.

Earlier that month, during spring workouts at Kentucky, Ewbank had called and asked if I would just listen to his proposal. Of course, I told him no. I didn't listen right away. Don't ever call me about another job during the middle of a busy time in my current job. I don't want to think about more than one thing at once, about anything other than the place I'm working, the guy who is giving me my food and a roof over my head.

A lot of people make a big deal out of that kind of thing, calling it loyalty. It's not loyalty, it's eighth-grade Sewickley. You take care of the man who feeds you, and at that time I was being fed by the University of Kentucky.

I told Weeb to call me when I had time to talk, after our spring game, which signified the end of spring practice. He did. He asked me to come in for an interview for their offensive-line coach position. At the time, I thought, This is *pro* football he's talking about. And to tell you the truth, I didn't care if it was pro football on the moon. It was pro football. It was the highest level of my profession.

In other words, I didn't think much. I caught the next plane.

Even before I left for the airport, people had started talking. Everyone told me that going after a Jets job would be too risky, that the league and team and job could fold at any time. They said I would set myself back years.

I listened, but I didn't hear. I couldn't hear. Staying at Kentucky with all its security, *that* would have been risky. It sounds funny, but you know what I mean? Once I knew I was going to make it out of the mills, I knew that whatever I did I had to do at the highest level. I couldn't settle for something less and then end up wondering if I shouldn't have taken my father's advice and just stayed home. I couldn't let other people wonder about me either. Any chance I got, I had to take that chance.

I found out that Weeb had heard about me through the recommendation of Blanton Collier, who had just left Kentucky to go to the Cleveland Browns. Usually the guys who trusted Blanton were the guys who thought like Blanton. That reassured me: even if this all went to hell, maybe from Weeb Ewbank I would learn something.

I thought about all of this while flying to Baltimore on a Friday afternoon to spend the weekend with Weeb. And I mean, *with* Weeb. How many times have you gone on a job interview and slept at the boss's house? For me, this weekend made once. As I later learned, Weeb was the kind always to take advantage of a good spare bedroom somewhere, even if it was his own.

After not much more than small talk on Saturday morning, I was offered the offensive-line job. It was for an $11,000 salary—a $2,800 raise from Kentucky, which wasn't much, especially since we would be moving from Lexington to Manhattan. I arranged for Shirley to meet me at the Louisville airport after my flight home Sunday afternoon. On the ninety-minute drive to our Lexington home, we talked about it. I'll never forget that conversation.

> *Shirley Knox: He was really torn between following everyone's advice and following his heart. He wanted my input. I didn't know enough about it. So my input was this: Do whatever you want to do. I'm with you on whatever you want to do. No, I didn't want to move to New York. Yes, we had three children under the age of ten and it would be a nightmare. But no, I couldn't stop him. Sometimes you can look into my husband's blue eyes and see the dream. This was one of those times.*

That's what she said, all right, "Whatever you want to do." At the time, she was the only one who said that to me. Twenty-five years later, she's still saying it to me. Until recently, I'm not sure I ever fully appreciated that about her. *Whatever I wanted.* With her it was always whatever I wanted.

That settled it. The woman who claimed she didn't know anything about it knew all about it. Shirley convinced me that sometimes in life it has to be whatever you want, and nothing less. So we took the job.

At that point I decide it's time to really look into the job. So I do. And I damn near die. Turns out, the Jets weren't so much the Jets as they were the New York Titans, an original AFL team that died in bankruptcy in March of 1963. In had stepped a deep-pocketed ownership syndicate led by Sonny Werblin, a group that saw a chance to breathe a new name and a new image into the new league's most important marketplace.

The new owners burned the Titans' blue-and-gold for green-and-white. They hired proven winner Ewbank from Baltimore and claimed dibs the following season on a spot in new Shea Stadium. They thought they were creating a wonderful new team with a space-age name. But when I looked around, all I could see was Titanic ghosts.

There remained the crumbling, emptying Polo Grounds, where in 1962 the Titans had averaged just 5,166 fans for seven home games. In their three seasons, the Titans had gone 19–23, having been outscored 1212–961. And by the time I arrived they had been completely drowned out by the rumblings of the NFL's New York Giants, who had played in the title game four of the last five years.

The big-time Giants had Frank Gifford and Y. A. Tittle. The cheapskate Titans? They had this parting quote by inaugural head coach Sammy Baugh, who was fired after two seasons amid criticism for not using a playbook: "Before you can have a playbook," he said, "you first have to have paper."

So here we were, going from the small-town South to the big city where nobody knew us from a piece of bluegrass. If I had known everything then . . . well, no, I still would have gone to New York. But at the time, my dream plainly fell into the category of hopeless.

Actually, the transition wasn't as difficult as I imagined. I went up there early and found this great four-story house in New Milford, New Jersey. Had a great summer kitchen in the basement. A wonderful place for Shirley and the three girls. I knew it would be a hard move, going to such a big city, so I was glad to be able to make it easier on them.

Shirley Knox: That was the funny thing. He really thought that house would make life easier. I get there with three kids at my skirts and realize something: it is the worst house in Western civilization. The top three stories

*were all bedrooms, one on each floor. Everything else was
on the first floor. He never had to climb those stairs with
a vacuum cleaner, so he never imagined that as a problem. Actually, he's never had to go anywhere with a vacuum cleaner. And that summer kitchen he talks about? It
was a bar. That's all.*

*Chuck gets so preoccupied with his job that he doesn't
think about the little things in ordinary life. The house
had a roof, right? Good enough for him. Lucky thing,
though. Three months later, the FHA appraisal didn't come
through with the right amount, so we were let out of the
loan and off the hook and got the heck out of that place.
It was the last time I let him pick a house without me.*

What a house, what a town. And my, what a job. You know
how you sometimes celebrate when you get your first paycheck? With mine it wasn't a celebration but a realization: I
better get a second job. My money wasn't even going to carry
me across the George Washington Bridge. I immediately took
a test as a life insurance and mutual funds salesman. I passed.
I'm still not certain it was possible to flunk.

That first off-season, I spent my spare time selling the
Winfield Growth Fund. Still remember the name. Still even
own some, although the company's been bought out a couple
of times and changed names. I was forced to call people cold,
introduce myself as a New York Jets coach, and hit them
with the pitch. First thing they would say was "New York
what?" Second thing they'd say was "No."

If it wasn't for coworkers and uncles of cousins of friends,
I'd never have had a chance. One night I went over and
pumped the fund to the Jets public-relations director, Frank
Ramos, and his wife, Jackie. We're sitting at this dinner table
and I'm going hard, almost raving about the benefits of this
daggone Winfield Growth Fund, when Jackie offers me another helping of this special pot roast. Mmm, sounds good,
thank you very much, ma'am. Thank *you*, she says, and
promptly pours the gravy right down onto my lap.

She starts crying, Frank starts laughing, but I don't say anything. I keep selling the fund. Many years later, Ramos reminded me of that. He said that what first impressed him
about me was that I could handle myself in a tight spot, that
I could coach under pressure. I guess so. Fourth and one, sauce
in my shorts—same thing.

However, that kind of initiative can also backfire on a
working stiff. That first season I also helped our coaching
staff make a training film for Planters Peanuts, figuring the
bucks could buy some Christmas presents. Guess what? They
paid us in peanuts. Literally. For six solid months I had a
garage full of peanuts. Every time somebody came to our
house, they went home with a jar. Pretty soon, everybody in
the neighborhood had peanuts.

"Peanuts" is a pretty good description of our benefits and
working conditions that first year. Today, teams have a dozen
assistant coaches. Back then we had four. We had me, Clive
Rush, Jack Donaldson, and Walt Michaels. We took care of
everything, from the scouting—checking out a college game
every Saturday before our Sunday pro game—to carrying the
equipment trunk.

Today, teams and local dealerships provide all NFL coaches
with leased cars. Makes things easier. Back then, no local
dealer trusted the Jets to bring the cars back. The Jets provided the four of us with one car to share. A station wagon,
of course. It was kept in the driveway of whatever coach was
living farthest from the office. He would pick up the others
on his way to work and drop them off on the way home. I
made certain right then I would never live farthest away. I
figured my life was hassled enough. Even today, I'll never
live far from the office. Once you've got that fear of the car-
pool in you . . .

At least there was one car. When it came to players, the
Jets had fewer than that. All the old Titans had been released, and the team had lost all of its 1963 draft choices
because of the bankruptcy. So my first pro training camp became two months of tryout camp. The Jets, to save money

on airplane tickets, brought in only those prospects who could get there in a day by bus.

> *Former Jets head coach Weeb Ewbank: We had three teams back then. We had today's team on the field, yesterday's team checking out, and tomorrow's team driving in.*

And all of this was in addition to our real tryout camp, held that first summer in Van Cortlandt Park, one of New York's toughest. It was like an unofficial welcome to the world of big-time, uh, wrestling. We were hoping for a few guys with some college experience. We got four hundred people. And man, was it an experience.

We got guys who had never finished high school, guys who were forty years old, who said they were twenty-three, who had gone down to the supermarket and bought a shirt with Notre Dame written on it, hoping we would believe they had an alma mater besides PS 99. We had the daggondest, motleyest, toughest crew of the characters there was. Some of the meanest guys I have ever seen, and I've seen some.

We were afraid to touch or even speak personally to most of them. But remember, this was a real tryout, and we really needed players. So we developed this system. Anytime one of the coaches saw a player with potential, he would shout, "Ruby! Ruby!" Then all of us would come over and watch. We were desperate for rubies. Today sometimes, during training camp, our players are confused when they hear Seahawk coaches shouting, "Ruby! Ruby!" Maybe if they read this, they won't be.

After camp ends, Weeb announced to the players, "Nobody call us, we'll call or telegram you. You got no phone, don't worry, we got your address, we'll get ahold of you if we need you." That's always the safest way to handle this sort of thing. But it doesn't always work.

Sure enough, next month two of the thugs show up at training camp, saying they never heard from us but figured we needed them and just lost their addresses. Huge guys, one who worked on a garbage truck and had the biggest arms I've ever seen in my life. It just so happens that I did remember both guys from the camp, but I also remembered that neither guy could run. For that matter, they could barely walk. Couldn't even finish the forty-yard dash. One said he was twenty-two and had to be at least thirty-eight.

A couple of us coaches went outside and told them to go home, but they wouldn't. They said, "You want somebody who's tough, we're right here. Bring some of those guys down from that dorm and we'll see who can whip who." I love that attitude. But not in guys who, if they couldn't find a fight with a football player, would settle for a piece of me.

Weeb and I finally call the cops. They come in with their lights flashing and all that business, and escort these guys home. Just another day of camp.

The Van Cortlandt Park tryout camp wasn't a total failure. A lot of it was for publicity, and thanks to a guy named Marshall Starks, publicity was something the Jets got. Even if that publicity wasn't quite accurate.

Here's what happened. Management was already committed to signing Starks, a top free agent cornerback from the University of Illinois, but they didn't tell him. They ordered him to show up at the camp, where he played like he was fighting for his bread money. Right there, with all the newspapers watching, they signed him, and he later became a starter, and this phony tryout camp success story made more front pages in a week than I made in my entire New York career. Worse than all that, we never told Starks. For that reason, I sort of hope nobody he knows reads this. Instant success stories, even fabricated ones, are hard to come by anymore.

Ugly preliminaries aside, on July 1, 1963, the coaches and I piled into the station wagon for the thirty-five-mile trip north to my first pro training camp. The site was the Peekskill Military Academy, five miles south of West Point. One difference, though. West Point is for men. Peekskill is for boys.

Pro football, huh? This place had tiny rooms with beds the size of sleds. One night during bed check, I tripped over one of our linemen, Dave Herman. He had taken his door off the hinges and was sleeping on it. But of course. I told him I didn't blame him and that I wouldn't report him. If that was my first official act as a player's coach, well, it was just eighth-grade Sewickley. Man has no bed, he invents a bed. I've done it a time or two myself.

If I really have this player's coach reputation, I must have first gotten it during those early years with the Jets. But under those conditions, any coach who had an ounce of human being in him would be considered a player's coach. There was no air-conditioning at Peekskill, which was no big deal because you could open the windows. Except there were no screens on the windows. Meaning, nobody could turn on any lights at night for fear of attracting bugs. The key was, you didn't go to bed until you were so tired you went right to sleep with the lights out, then the bugs went right to sleep, and it was cool enough so both of you could *stay* asleep.

Then came the worst part. Getting up in the morning and eating. In the Peekskill cafeteria, breakfast, lunch, and dinner all appeared to be hot dogs. To this day, I'm not sure what that meat was. Jars of white stuff in the middle of the tables appeared to be mayonnaise, except there was nobody to seal and refrigerate the jars, so after a couple of hot afternoons they could be used by the medical staff. Oh yes, there was corn, always corn, and for a reason. Legendary spendthrift Weeb used to brag that a man could make a whole meal out of corn on the cob.

After breakfast we would leave the dining room and go out and face our players, and increasingly this became the strangest part of all. Every day some player would be outfitted in old Titans' stuff. It made us wonder if the New York Jets really existed. Talk about an identity crisis. But it was really just another one of Weeb's little ways of saving money. I guess they were lucky to have clothes at all. I remember when a player named Will Rentzel came onto the field wearing an old pair of pants with no visible crotch. Turns out, they didn't have pants with crotches left in his size, and when Weeb asked him what he was complaining about, he came right on the field for fear of getting cut.

However, once we got on the field, I loved that team. I love all teams like that, teams that kind of remind me of me. We went 5 – 8 – 1 in each of my first three years there, but we were competitive when we shouldn't have been. I loved that.

Our first games were still in the old Polo Grounds. There would be about twenty-five hundred people in the stands, and half of those were there for free. Even after we started playing, nobody knew who we were. I'd come to the front gate and tell them I was a Jet assistant and they wouldn't believe me. I'd start trying to convince them and they would say, "Oh, what the heck, come on in, we need the people."

Our first star was created by a crazy public-address announcer. The player's name was Wahoo McDaniel, a Choctaw Indian linebacker previously known only because he nearly broke his neck one night sneaking out of a Peekskill dorm. As he climbed down a vine from a second-story window, unable to take the heat or the bugs or the bunk beds, the vine broke. All the players knew about it, but I was the only coach who did, and I wasn't telling. I figured a little sore neck was punishment enough.

During the first regular season games, when McDaniel made a tackle, the PA man would shout, "Guess who?" and the crowd would chant, "Wa-hoo, Wa-hoo." It was all very cute, until the PA announcer began starting the chant for every tackle, every play, no matter where Wahoo was. He could be five yards away from the tackle, totally beaten by a blocker on the play, totally out of it, and the crowd would start chanting "Wa-hoo, Wa-hoo." That's the sort of silliness we were up against.

Or how about the halftime show that considered itself more important than us or the football? One of our first games, there was this drum-and-bugle corps; they had fifteen minutes for a halftime show, and man, there they were, parading up and down that field, up and down, strutting like peacocks. But then their show goes fifteen minutes, sixteen minutes, seventeen minutes, eighteen minutes. Our business manager runs out and screams at the marjorette, "Get off the field, we've got a second half to play!" She looks at him and says in her most dainty majorette voice, "You go to hell."

That's what we were up against.

The saving grace in all this was that when it came down to taking the field, the Jets still had a football team, and I still had my offensive linemen. Those linemen weren't just five foot eleven like I was, so they didn't fight as much as I used to, but they were still offensive linemen. They were still me. I learned in this first pro coaching assignment that I had a soft spot for that position. Even today, on the sidelines, I catch myself talking more to those guys than anyone else, even the quarterback. Just habit and heart.

Take Winston Hill. Nobody else would, but the Jets did. He was a rookie tackle who had been cut from the Colts. He was as raw as dirt. But he wanted to play, *wanted* to be a pro. He retired thirteen years later with eight all-Pro awards. He'll be in the Hall of Fame, you watch. We took him that first year and gave him the chance to believe in himself.

Former Jets tackle Winston Hill: Chuck was telling people I could play before I knew I could play. He told me I could be a star, and I laughed at him. I never knew what I could do until he showed me. And how he would show me. When he got mad, he would look at you with those cold blue eyes. His freckles would pop out. All of his energy would be collected, and you'd hope something would break through before he exploded.

I remember when he'd say, "There are no dumb football players." He would tell us that learning was a question of concentration. Any player who could concentrate could learn, period. And remember, this was at a time when all linemen were considered big and dumb. He actually made us big guys feel good about ourselves.

I tell my players today what I told them back then: You're
smart enough to learn if I'm good enough to teach you. Blanton Collier's advice.

Go back to our one big win in that first year, 17–0 over
the Kansas City Chiefs, our major rivals. They came out with
a 3–4 defense, one of the first teams to do that. We had never
seen it before. We had guys running around during the first
half wondering who they should block. We had guys running
into and over each other. At halftime I got them in front of
a blackboard and changed our scheme. They listened, and in
a span of about ten minutes, they learned. After the win,
they began to realize any of them could learn anything.

Back then everyone in football thought that IQ was important in determining one's ability to learn. No way. It's not a
question of IQ, it's a question of concentration. Anyone who
can concentrate can learn. Lots of teams give IQ tests. Not
me, never will. All an IQ test does is give some coach who's
not a good enough teacher an excuse not to teach his player.
"He can't play, he's too dumb. Look, his IQ is eighty-five." I
don't use tests because I don't want to give my assistant
coaches that excuse.

Winston Hill was the beginning of some great good fortune
that came to the Jets in the form of offensive linemen, mostly
the same linemen who eventually won a Super Bowl. To this
day I feel that if I hadn't had some of these guys, I might
never have gotten to be a head coach anywhere. Anybody
who says I made them, well, it's probably just the opposite.
They made me.

In my second year, guard Dave Herman showed up, a free
agent from Michigan State. For his tryout he drove all the
way in from a farm in Ohio. Man wanted to play bad. And
there was the tackle we converted to a center, John Schmitt.
He was a free agent from Hofstra, meaning nowhere, who at
first played with us only during the week, on our taxi squad.
Because he wasn't eligible for Sunday's game, he played for
the semipro Jersey City Bears on the weekends, making fifty
dollars a game. Talk about hungry. These were my kind of

men. In my third year, 1966, came another unknown, a tight end named Pete Lammons, an eighth-round draft pick from Texas whom I had accidentally spotted in the Orange Bowl game while scouting Joe Namath, then of the University of Alabama.

On January 12, 1969, Hill, Herman, Schmitt, and Lammons made up the bulk of the offensive line that kept the pressure off Namath and led the Jets to the 16−7 Super Bowl victory over Baltimore in what must be one of the most important games in modern professional football history. I was there that day, but I wasn't there. I was in the Orange Bowl, but in the stands as a member of the Detroit Lions coaching staff. Two years earlier, I'd gotten an offer to coach in the established league, a chance that was too great to pass up.

Yeah, I felt funny. Good for them, bad for me. No matter what anybody said, they were no longer my line, no longer my guys. You move on, you get new guys. I was history. Closest I ever came to a Super Bowl, and I still missed it by two years. I didn't go down to the locker room to see any of them after the win. It was their time. I had already used up my time.

Former Jets lineman Dave Herman: We remembered Chuck. Hell, linemen never forget. All we said the whole Super Bowl week was, this is Chuck's line, this is Chuck's team. It was wrong, but that year we sort of ignored anything different our coaches would tell us, and we'd do it Chuck's way. We remembered that when we were nothing, Chuck was there.

But I'm getting ahead of myself. I had one other favorite player that first year with the Jets who, like me, didn't stick around for the Super Bowl. Name was Sherman Plunkett, a tackle who was so heavy we weighed him at a feed mill. I liked Plunkett because he fought so hard to stay so fat. Don't laugh. It doesn't matter what you are fighting for, as long as you fight.

He had to be kept on a constant diet during training camps. Every night at dinner, before sitting down to eat, he would smile and show Weeb his near-empty tray. After my nightly line meeting, he would go straight to bed, still smiling. But I noticed that every night a rookie would follow him to his room. Always a different rookie. One night I followed the rookie. Turns out, inside his shirt the kid was stashing a grocery sack full of hot hamburgers. Every week during his weigh-ins, when we discovered he was losing no weight, Plunkett would only shrug those big ol' shoulders and say it must have something to do with metabolism.

We began fining him twenty-five dollars for each extra pound. One time he requested that we donate the fines to charity. We said great, and asked where we should send the checks. He gave us an address that, we later learned, belonged to his wife.

I used to use Sherm to demonstrate stuff. I always pick out one big, hardworking guy and demonstrate techniques with him. Even though I can do it alone, I think when I use another player, the other guys respect more and understand better what I am trying to teach them. Remember, I'm just a coach, and coaches just coach. Players play, and players win. It's eighth-grade Sewickley.

There were a bunch of things I had to teach the Jets linemen in those first years. One of those things was a pass-protection technique that involved extended arms with open hands. It didn't quite go along with the letter of the NFL law, but in time the higher-ups saw its value and put it in the rule books.

Weeb Ewbank: A lot of people don't know it, but Chuck was the first person to teach linemen to block with their hands. Everybody does it now. In 1978 a rule was passed that reads: "Extended arms and open hands are permissible in pass blocking." There should be an asterisk at the end of that sentence. It was Chuck Knox's rule. He was the first person in football to even out things between of-

fensive and defensive linemen. At the time, the defense could do just about anything short of killing you. Chuck changed all that.

I guess I was one of the first guys to get linemen to block with their open palms. My reasoning was simple: Act like you are guarding a guy man-to-man in basketball. Just like you should always stay between your man and the basket, you should stay between your man and the quarterback. The motivation was also simple. Pass blocking is an alley fight. I still tell my linemen to think of themselves as the only person between the defender and a loved one.

Back then, defenders were allowed to grab and shove and twist and everything. They were even allowed to head-slap, which forced me to spend practice time beating my offensive linemen over their heads with rubber baseball bats so they would learn not to flinch. Nowadays that's probably the only thing most of them remember me by, those damn baseball bats.

Anyway, I figured we would do just what we did at the University of Kentucky when our big rival Tennessee would come in and give us hand shivers. I taught my Jets to keep their elbows in and hands out and give the defense less room to grab, partly because we were grabbing them first. And it worked. The Jets quarterback that first year was a six-foot-five guy who'd had six knee operations, named Dick Wood, a man who so feared for his life he wouldn't get on the team plane for road trips until he saw that Plunkett, his protector, was getting on that same plane. Yet he was kept alive.

Then Namath came along, with the knees of an elderly woman, and he was kept alive. Even the referees finally gave their silent approval. In 1966 Namath was sacked just three times, and the offensive line was called for holding just eight times. I don't feel anything special about their finally changing the rule. Should have changed it a long time ago. But there again, nobody understands an offensive lineman but another lineman.

Maybe I taught the players too much that first year. I must have worn them out. By the time the season ended in Kansas City, all the players' wives had gone back to their home-towns and all the players had brought all of their bags and belongings to the ballpark. They were ready to go home for the winter as soon as the last gun sounded. This was my first experience of what is known as a "running for the buses" game. Kansas City beat us 48−0, and I vowed it would never happen to one of my teams again.

Now I talk of every game as a business obligation, no mat-ter what the situation, no matter how far you are out of it. Many years later, my players in Buffalo were stunned when I gave them each a game ball after beating Baltimore in a meaningless last game of the season. On each of the balls was printed "We Didn't Run for the Buses."

The second season with the Jets started out great, we went 3−1−1, but we knew we still didn't have the talent. I will always talk like we can win, but you can't fool football play-ers or coaches. Sure enough, we lost six of the last seven games, partly because we had to play them all on the road. The schedule was designed with the understanding that no-body wanted to come to New York in December. Too cold and no fans.

Ironically, I still coach in a place where nobody wants to come later in the year—Seattle—but the reasons are differ-ent. A domed stadium and too many fans. Funny how things work.

And funny how things were working at home. Shirley had become the boss. After a couple of years in New York, she realized what a drain this pro coaching business could be. And just like that, she took over. The house, the day-to-day upbringing of the children. Then came that time just before my third year in New York, in February of 1965, when she had to deal with the birth of our fourth and final child, Chuck.

Daughter Chris: During the time Dad was working in the city, Mom always had to be the strong one in Cress-

kill, where we lived. At one point she was so busy being strong, she wouldn't even tell us she was pregnant with Chuck. I was twelve, Kathy was ten, and Colleen was six, and she didn't want us worrying about her being burdened with another one.

Pregnancy being what is is, Mom started getting sick. It seemed like all the time she was sick. Finally I called my sisters together for a meeting up in our little bedroom. We decided that Mom was dying. We spent a week trying to figure out what we'd do with just Dad around the house, until one day Mom let it slip. We heard her tell someone on the phone that she was pregnant. We nearly cried with relief.

I did my best with the girls. You know the bit about quantity of time versus quality of time. I always felt like I gave them the quality part, but then I'm sure they have their own definitions of quality.

Daughter Kathy: When we were little, his quality time with us was bath time. He would step in and scrub our ears until they were raw. Quality ears, you'd call them. He also enjoyed playing with his girls in the public swimming pool. He'd jump in and start acting like a shark and we all would jump out screaming bloody murder. My mother would shout, "Chuck, they're just girls, just girls." He would agree, apologize, and then try to bribe us back in the water with promises of ice cream later. My father.

I'll say this much: We all knew how to swim, because as soon as we were old enough to hold our breath, he would throw us—just little kids—into the shallow end of the pool and order us to try to get out. Darn, if we didn't always manage to do it.

He gave us quality time, yes, especially if you consider that quality to be independence and toughness.

If those girls told you those stories, I'm sure they told you about how, even though the junior high was right across the railroad tracks from our Cresskill house, I made them walk a half mile south to the regular crossing. They constantly complained—until one day a kid in one of their classes was killed by a train as he ran across at just that spot.

We came out the third season with the Jets in about the same losing pattern as in the first two, going 0–5–1. It was now that I realized just how many things can distract a football player from his job. First it was things like getting sent bad game film of next week's opposing team, with all of the weird formations deliberately cut out. That happened to us a lot back then. Or there was that exhibition game in Birmingham's Legion Field, when even the bus drivers turned against our team. We had scheduled a 5:00 P.M. departure time from the hotel, but the drivers became confused and arrived outside the lobby at 5:00 A.M. It wasn't so bad until the fools started honking.

I made up my mind then that I would never let any off-the-field problems like that stop my players. Since then my philosophy has been, Everything small, we'll take care of it. Everything little, we'll treat like it's big.

This philosophy helped me many years later, in my first year in Seattle, when we went to Miami to play the Dolphins on New Year's Eve in the second round of the play-offs. We were very much the underdogs, but as a reward to everyone who had worked so hard that year, we took the entire organization with us, chartering an Eastern Airlines L-1011, a huge plane. We arranged to leave Friday afternoon for the Sunday afternoon game, taking no chances of getting there late. But guess what? We get to the Seattle airport and they tell us that the little black box that has to go on all flights hasn't arrived for our flight. We are facing at least a four-hour delay. All these people, and a four-hour delay. That's a lot of idle time for a team that's getting keyed up for a play-off game. Four hours is a *lot* of time for things to get disturbed.

I got the team together and told them that no way was this

delay going to dictate the way we played in Miami. I got everyone a room at a nearby hotel, called in for some food, set that up in another room, and then we all ate and relaxed while waiting for this plane. We didn't sit around cussing and moaning and ruining ourselves.

The plane was finally ready, but we didn't get to Miami until 5:00 A.M. on Saturday. The game is at 4:00 P.M. the next day, but we still needed to practice in the meantime. Again I called the team together. This time I told them that we needed to put in some new formations, so they were to get a couple of hours' sleep, then show up for a team meeting at 9:00 A.M. I told them, "You're young and resilient—you'll bounce back." Then I made it quite clear to them: No team of mine would be bothered by a damned plane delay. There were more important things to worry about. There were the Dolphins to worry about. And somehow, they believed me. It worked. We practiced for an hour, got a little more sleep, then went out and beat the Dolphins 27–20 in what people call the greatest game in the Seattle franchise's history.

That's the main thing I learned in New York and from Weeb, not to let distractions become distractions. By my last season there, we had gone 6–6–2, and things were making sense.

One other thing I learned there: hard work works. Weeb was known for keeping his assistants twelve hours a day, but even then, I would stay longer. I would finish my work and wander over to the other coaches and learn about their work.

Back then, after twelve-hour flights from the West Coast, the coaches would unload the equipment truck late at night, enter the Polo Grounds locker room, and toss coins. The winners would sleep on training tables; the losers would curl up on the floor inside duffel bags. All of us would stay until morning, when Weeb woke us to warm projectors and sticky films.

Jets publicity director Frank Ramos: That's the one thing everybody noticed about Chuck—he would stay longer than the rest of us. And he would enjoy it more than the rest of us. And he was always prying into somebody else's business.

During meetings, no matter what formations the coaches were discussing, he had this goal: to be the last guy with the chalk. He wanted to draw his play or his technique on the blackboard so that it was the last play drawn that day, the play we would eventually use. Guys would be snoozing and he would be drawing. He would always say, "The last guy with the chalk wins."

Sure, the last guy with the chalk always wins. The last guy holding the chalk at the blackboard would have the last word on how to block this, or how to line up like that. His method would win. It's eighth-grade Sewickley. I know it makes me sound like a fanatic, but when you're twenty-nine and coaching pro football, you're interested in every bit of the game, every hour of it, you *never* want to put that chalk down. When you're twenty-nine years old, how can you be tired? How can *anybody* be tired when they're twenty-nine?

On top of our regular work back then, we also had to be like college recruiters, convincing guys to go with us in the AFL instead of the NFL. It was an unusual arrangement made more unusual when I realized I could only recruit like I coached: No frills. No soft shoe. No bull.

This was when I nearly got into my first fistfight as a coach. It was 1964, and the object of dispute was a defensive tackle from Utah State named Diamond Jim Harris. Both me and Joe Thomas of the NFL Vikings were in these tiny rooms in the office of Utah State coach Tony Knap. I knew what my high offer would be. I even carried a contract and a check in my briefcase to validate it. Weeb Ewbank never sent a man on the road without a high offer. Thomas, however, needed to call his boss, Norm Van Brocklin, at every turn of the negotiations, using a phone resting in a hole in the wall that separated the two rooms.

Diamond Jim was going from one coach to the other. I first made a low offer. Thomas then needed twenty minutes to call Van Brocklin and counter. Then I needed all of ten seconds to counter again. This went on, and because I was able to top his every offer immediately, Thomas suddenly accused me of eavesdropping on his negotiations. That did it. I was going to whip Thomas, physically.

I told him, "You say that again, and we're going to have the daggonedest fistfight there ever was. We're going to have it right here, in the office, not even going outside—right now!" The college coach jumped between us. The player jumped out into the hall. There wasn't any silly fight. And I later signed Jim Harris.

But that's what we were up against.

The fringe benefit for me in all this extra work was that somebody finally noticed it. After my third year, after my salary had gone from $11,000 to $14,000, the Atlanta Falcons and the Detroit Lions of the *other* league each offered me offensive-line jobs at $17,500. The only question should have been, which one? Back when I first began dreaming of coaching, teams like the Jets, and leagues like the AFL, were never for me. The NFL was what I wanted, where I belonged. Hell, I deserved this chance. I had earned that new money. But there was no question. I turned both the Lions and Falcons down and stayed in New York. Here's why.

After the calls, I visited Ewbank with an excited "What do you think?"

"I think," said Ewbank, "that when I brought you out of college coaching as a nobody, I was planning on you staying four years here. I would hope you would live up to that."

"Oh," I said.

I thought about what he said. I thought about what I had learned, about how he had put food on my table and made life a little better for my family. I sucked in my breath. "That's the way you feel, that's what I'll do."

I stumbled out of his office, called both NFL clubs to say thanks but no thanks, and then went home to a sleepless night.

Tough choice, but no choice. Growing up on the streets,

you learn there are things more important than money. Loyalty is one of them. If you are loyal to people, they will be loyal in return. Watch their back, they'll watch your back.

As soon as Weeb reminded me of the four years, I knew I couldn't take those jobs. I could only pray that I hadn't blown it and that I would get another chance down the road. Two days after turning those teams down, I was called back into Ewbank's office.

"Almost forgot," said Ewbank, handing me a new contract for 1966. "Here's your seventeen thousand five hundred."

I learned a lot about loyalty that year. Looking back, I'm glad I stayed. Usually life works that way.

But I'm especially glad I stayed, because I got to spend one more year with a guy named Joe Namath. In the winter after the 1964 season I had convinced the Jets to chase Namath out of Alabama, and they made me go and catch him myself. Once we got him, it changed the face of professional football.

When I first saw Joe, I could look at him only as a kid from the same part of the country I was from. We grew up within a few miles of each other, Beaver Falls being just down the road from Sewickley. We both spoke in that slow, thick sort of drawl found in the hills of western Pennsylvania. Despite Namath's trips onto Broadway and Hollywood, despite the playboy reputation, when the door is closed and the shoes are off, we pretty much cut the same kind of rug.

We first laid eyes on each other, naturally enough, beneath the cloud of a steel mill, on an Ellwood City High School basketball floor. Joe played on the Beaver Falls junior high squad. I coached Ellwood City junior high. I could see, even then, that Namath could be a great football player. Don't ask how I saw. Man can't explain everything.

We ran into each other later when I tried to recruit Namath for the University of Kentucky. Bear Bryant being an awfully good recruiter himself, I never stood a chance. Four years after that, in 1964 when Namath was a senior at Alabama and I was with the Jets, I talked about him in every recruiting meeting, in every talent evaluation session. The odds of our even getting his phone number were slim, but I wanted the staff to be convinced when that time came.

The AFL was just finishing its fifth season then, and both the league and the Jets were doing better. But unbeknownst to me, Sonny Werblin, the owner of the Jets, felt we weren't doing enough. Werblin was a former president at the Musak Corporation of America, a classy promoter kind of guy, a good guy, who threw us nice parties at the 21 Club, did things for the wives.

In 1964 though, we were still 5–8–1, and the crosstown Giants, even at 2–10–2, were still number one in New York. So the man who had signed everyone, from Andy Williams to Ed Sullivan, decided he needed a star just like them, a great quarterback. He wanted the kind of man who, when he slips into a crowded room, the crowded room slips into him.

So Werblin called us together and put out the cry for . . . Tulsa quarterback Jerry Rhome? Yes indeed. Rhome was who we had taken in a special redshirt draft that winter for players who had been in school four years but, for injury or other reasons, had just played three seasons. These boys could either stay and play another year in school or turn pro. Rhome had decided to turn pro. We decided we had to have him.

Before the regular draft, we brought Rhome to New York to woo him into a contract. What happened next was a faux pas that may have changed the course of professional football. During the visit, Werblin invited Rhome to take a ride in his limousine. Rhome said "Great." Not so great. Rhome jumped in the backseat ahead of Werblin's wife. Werblin glared at his associates. "I don't believe this!" he cried. "This—this is not star quality."

It was a bit of bad manners that the city of New York should be forever grateful for. We decided to trade Rhome's rights, picking up the phone and calling Houston, which owned the first pick in the regular AFL draft. It helped that in the other league, Houston's NFL counterpart Dallas had expressed great interest in Rhome.

Weeb said to the Houston people, "How would you like to

stick it to the Cowboys? We'll give you Rhome and a chance to sign him right away from Dallas if you give us that dumb little first pick of yours."

The Oilers agreed. The trade was made. Now it was my turn.

Weeb called me. "You know all this stuff you've been saying about this guy Joe Namath? It's time to put up or shut up. We're using our first-round pick for him."

"Joe who?" I asked, unable to suppress a chuckle.

We drafted Namath, but so did the NFL's Saint Louis Cardinals, ahead of the Cowboys, and thus began the most important fight in the Jets' history.

Weeb came to me again. "Now that we've drafted him, we need somebody to go out and find him. Any ideas?"

"Just one," I said.

I was on the next plane to Alabama.

Werblin wanted to meet with Namath before our next game, which was in San Diego, so I had to drag Namath to California, then sell him to the boss once I got there.

I get down to Birmingham on a Friday where Joe is attending an Alabama A Club banquet. He is supposed to meet us in the hotel lobby at six o'clock the next morning to fly to California. I get up early. I go downstairs and wait. And wait. He doesn't show. Turns out, he's not even in that hotel. I'm waiting down there with a buddy of his, an attorney named Mike Bite, of Bite, Bite, and Bite. That was their name, I swear.

As six o'clock passes, we're beginning to panic. I've lost Namath. We call all the hotels in Birmingham. We finally find him in some other joint, registered under his own name, for pete's sake. So maybe he wasn't hiding, maybe he was just confused—I still don't know. We get him and get to the plane just in time to carry on our luggage.

We're flying first class out there; and while Joe and I are playing gin, this Mike Bite comes up and asks me questions about the legal parts of the contract—asks questions about a contract of a guy who is so economically wise, he has a garage full of peanuts.

And why does he consult me about the fine points of a football contract? Because the only thing Mike Bite has ever done before is lawsuits for car accidents. Sonny Werblin is going to love this.

We arrive in LA in early afternoon and start negotiating back and forth. Before long we're talking about three hundred thousand dollars, which would make Joe the highest-paid pro athlete of all time. Suddenly Mike Bite of Bite, Bite, and Bite jumps up and says, "Gentlemen, we're talking about an awful lot of money here. I'd like to have a word with my client in private." Sounded like something he heard on "Perry Mason."

After they meet in this other room, Bite come out and gulps and says, "Gentlemen, uh, uh, the question we have is, is my ten-percent fee added to the contract, or does it come off the top? Ten percent of three hundred thousand is three thousand dollars, and that's a lot of money." Ten percent of *what* is *what?* We look at each other. These guys were as small-town as I was. These guys were unbelievable. Turns out, we give Bite his *thirty* thousand (although we should have given him what he asked for) on top of Namath's three hundred grand.

Just before Namath agrees, he asks for ten thousand dollars each for his sister and two brothers for three years. That was when I finally sat back and smiled. Bite may be small town, but not Joe. That was a big-city move right there. One of the best moves of his career. Werblin agrees even to that, putting Namath's family on the Jets payroll as scouts. With the salary, Bite's cut, and the Namath family's salary, the entire deal came in at around $425,000.

We were all impressed by Joe, and it had nothing to do with football. What other kid would come out of a tiny town, turn into a big star, and still take a buddy to be his lawyer, a guy named Mike Bite, and insist on salaries for his family? Think about it.

Me, I should have been paid as a baby-sitter. But my real baby-sitting days were just beginning. While Namath had given us his word, he still couldn't formally sign until after Alabama played Texas in the Orange Bowl, formally ending his college career.

That meant the Saint Louis Cardinals still had a chance. And we didn't want to leave anything to chance. Shirley and I were sent to Miami for Orange Bowl week with one instruction: Don't come home without Joe.

In Miami, Namath's mother, Rose, was staying at the Bal Harbour Inn. So that's where we stayed. Namath and the Alabama team were next door at the Seaview. All week we watched Namath and his mother. I took Joe to dinner. Shirley shopped with Rose. We were more like cops than babysitters. We had them covered.

But then the Cardinals came barging in with promises to Namath that they would trade him to the New York Giants to replace the aging Y. A. Tittle. We knew Joe wanted the big city and the bigger league. We sweated. I sat with Joe by the pool. Shirley took Rose to dinner. We sweated some more.

Then a couple of days before the game, the *New York Journal American* reported that Joe Namath had just turned down a $389,000 offer from the Saint Louis Cardinals. My bosses immediately called me, asking if it was true. I had just checked it out. It was.

"You fellas up there had better believe it!" I shouted through the phone.

I don't shout much, unless my hat is on backward and an offensive lineman is in my face. In fact, I don't think I shouted that loud again until last year when the Seahawks learned we'd won the lottery for Brian Bosworth.

We had gotten Joe. And part of it was because Joe had believed in me. I decided, if I could do that with one, I could do it with 45. And I decided, fate would have to give me a chance. One day. Not now, but one day.

| *Joe Namath: Chuck was definitely a factor in my coming to the Jets. He was the first one who whispered my*

> *name to them. He came from my neighborhood. He spoke*
> *my language. I was comfortable with him. He was no bull.*
> *It's funny how people from Western Pennsylvania seem to*
> *stick together, but that's what it was. I was going to a big*
> *city, but with Chuck there, I knew I would be taken care*
> *of.*

I had helped bring Namath to New York, but now came the hardest part. I was the one who had to keep him there. Weeb, anyway, thought that was my responsibility. Hardly a day went by when he didn't remind me that Joe's being there was mostly my idea, and how did I plan on keeping him out of trouble. Any time anything went wrong, Weeb came running to me.

At first I tried preventive medicine. I escorted Namath into his first training camp. I introduced him to his offensive linemen, most of whom were already grumbling about how cocky he was. I told the linemen one thing: "This is your new quarterback. He gets hurt, you get fired."

But taking care of Joe couldn't be accomplished in one speech. It was an everyday event. Take the first half of his first game as a Jet, against Kansas City. He was struggling and, as is often the case with kids, the harder he tried, the worse it got. At halftime the coaches were giving the standard directives about concentration and reading the coverages. After the speeches, I called the kid over.

> *Joe Namath: Chuck told me not to worry anymore about*
> *reading any damn coverages. He told me just to go back*
> *to throwing the damn ball like I always had. That's the*
> *way he talked. He said, "Pick a guy and let it fly." That's*
> *all he said. No big strategy. Just throw it. One of the best*
> *halftime talks I've ever heard.*

Whatever I said to him must have worked, even though we lost that game 14–10, because just a week later he threw for 287 yards against Buffalo and his career hit stride. He was picking guys and letting it fly. Eighth-grade Sewickley.

This convinced me that to deal with Joe off the field, you needed the same eighth-grade Sewickley. One night we're in Denver a couple of days before a game, and it's eleven o'clock and Joe misses curfew. Weeb comes running to me like always. "What are we gonna do, Chuck, what are we gonna do?" I make some calls and send out Bill Hampton, the equipment manager, and sure enough, we find Joe at some bar.

I call him there and say pleadingly, "Joe, you got to get home."

Joe says, "Now wait a minute, Chuck. If I come in now, it's gonna cost me a five-hundred-dollar fine. If I come in two hours from now, it's still gonna be five hundred. So what's the use? Why not get my money's worth?"

He's right, of course. And although Weeb is standing there, I can't argue with my quarterback. I tell Hampton to stay there with Namath and make sure he makes it back in one piece. In a couple of hours Joe comes home, and he's fine. So fine, in fact, he is carrying a very messed-up Bill Hampton.

It was always one thing or another. Joe lived his own life; he was a man's man, and there wasn't much anybody could do but keep him pointed in the right direction. A man has to be what he was meant to be—so long as he can show up on Sunday.

After I'd been four years with the Jets—two of them with Namath, and one year after the Lions and Falcons had offered me jobs—the Lions called again. Joe Schmidt, the new head coach, had a vacancy for a line coach. He offered it to me. Before I could say anything, he floored me.

"How much money will you need?" he asked.

I had been coaching more than ten years, and it was the first time anyone had ever asked me how much I wanted. Until then, I had never had the power to negotiate salaries. I had always been assigned them.

I did some quick adding in my head, picked a number, added

more to the number, and more again, and then blurted out, "Twenty-four thousand a year."

"Fine," said Schmidt.

"Fine?" I said.

5

Detroit

Let's cut to the chase. I took the Detroit Lions job.

There's no use trying to build up any suspense here. You read the part where the man from Detroit asked me how much money I wanted, so you will have figured out by now that I immediately joined his team as an assistant coach in charge of the offensive line.

I said good-bye to New York, attended a party in my honor in some joint down in Harlem, and headed off to a place in eastern Michigan called Cranbrook College. That's where this chapter will start. Late summer, 1967.

Me—at an NFL training camp. Yes, sir! I *had* arrived.

Former Lions guard Bob Kowalkowski: First day of camp, and here comes this new line coach, doesn't so much walk as strut; stocky guy, says his name is Knox.

I miss an incidental block in an incidental drill, and then I hear this foghorn. "Know something, Kowal?" he asks in a voice that could shut down an auto assembly line "You're a sissy."

I look up. I stare. This was my second year, and nobody had ever talked to me like that. I want to fight the son of a gun. I get ready to charge—hell, he's not much older than we are—but a teammate grabs me. After practice, I turn my anger on someone else. During the first of these insane one-on-one drills Knox dreamed up for the reserves so they could get in their licks, I attack some kid named Frank Penney. Blocks become punches and soon we're rolling around in the dirt. I beat him bad, but I don't quit until the kid's face mask comes off his helmet. I look up again and I see Knox. This time though, he's smiling. I'll never forget that smile.

I didn't hate Frank Penney. I hated Chuck Knox.

I'd waited a good part of my life to be in the NFL, but now that I was, I felt out of place. Because I was just thirty-three years old and from a league that nobody considered much worth a damn, I had to prove myself all over again. Haven't we heard this somewhere before?

This Lions team had produced two NFL championships and twelve NFL Hall-of-Famers. Joe Schmidt, the head coach, had been a Hall of Fame linebacker. Most everyone else on the staff had either played or coached in the NFL. And then there was me. Once again, the new kid. The outsider.

One difference this time. This being my sixth coaching job, counting high school, I had grown weary of being the new *anything.* When I got to Cranbrook College for my first training camp, I decided I wouldn't try to play their games. I wouldn't try to prove myself at all. I would just be myself. I figured either they'd understand or they wouldn't. Call it the start of the rest of my life. Or something like that.

Former Lions tackle Rocky Freitas: It's the second day of camp. I'm a rookie just cut by the Steelers and scared anyway, when suddenly Knox is leaning over into my face. "You Rocky Freitas?" he asks.

"Uh, yes, sir," I say.

Then Knox says, "In Pittsburgh they said you wouldn't hit."

I hear Knox saying this, and I can't believe it. I say to myself, Couldn't do what? *I don't even know him, and I want to kill him.*

My limited experience be damned. I knew what I was doing. Four years with the Jets had taught me how to push some buttons, how to kick the butts that needed kicking and pat the backs that needed patting. Through the Jets I had realized that my teaching methods *would* work, that I *could* get the job done, and that the players would eventually understand that. I knew the acceptance factor would be there; they would accept me when they realized that what I was doing was right. Until then, I couldn't suffer those who didn't give me everything. I didn't *have* to suffer them. This was the NFL, the pinnacle, remember? There were plenty of guys in steel mills waiting to take these players' places.

The angry part of me that only insiders see anymore, the hat-thrower, face-mask grabber, stare-and-dare-to-hit-me coach—it was in Detroit that I discovered that. The offensive line there was in shambles. They had the great defensive players—the Mike Luccis, the Wayne Walkers, the Alex Karrases—but on offense, they had one good lineman, John Gordy, and he was hurt.

Couldn't I ever get a team handed to me? I wondered. Maybe just once? Just a little team?

The year before I arrived in Detroit with coach Joe Schmidt, the Lions had achieved their worst record in seven seasons (4–9–1). In fourteen games they scored just 206 points. Only twice in the previous twenty-one seasons had they scored fewer points, and in both instances (1948 and 1959) they had played only twelve games. Shambles. Life on the end of football's earth.

I came from an eventual world championship line in New York to one where, for the first and only time in my career, I knew even less about my players than they knew about me. I wondered how some of these Detroit linemen were going to react to this adversity. I wondered if there was any fire in them. I had to find a spark.

I knew the biggest guy there, Freitas, has already been cut by Pittsburgh and was on the verge of going home to Hawaii and eating himself to death. With his personality and build, my biggest question about Freitas was whether he was a football player or a throw pillow. I knew Kowalkowski was the veteran of the previous Lions season, but that only counted against him. While a 240-pound guard can survive if he knows how to block, Kowalkowski was as familir with blocking as I was with easy living.

I thought I knew all about Chuck Walton, a rookie guard, until I found out the man wasn't really a rookie at all but had played the last four years in the Canadian League, where they blocked with a different accent. Then I saw another rookie named Bill Cottrell, who came not from a different country but a different world, the Richmond Rebels of the semipro Continental League. Just my second job, and already I led the business in semipros and castoffs.

Cottrell was also unusual in that he was black. Some officials told me that this might be a problem because he also wanted to play center.

I may be dumb, and this may have been suicide, but I politely asked them, "What the hell does that have to do with it?"

> *Former Lions center Bill Cottrell: There was an unwritten rule back then: no black centers or quarterbacks or middle linebackers. Nobody had them. Nobody thought they were smart enough. Until Chuck. He walked in and said the best player would play. Told me I didn't know how smart I was, or how good I could be. Didn't care what other teams did. Back then, nobody would have taken that chance. He did. Looking back, I'm not so sure he ever did notice I was black.*

There is no black or white or green on the football field. Just like there's no rich or poor or Italian or Polish. Just equipment and body and brains. And I swear I don't know what the big deal ever was about my playing a black center or, when I got to Los Angeles, a black quarterback named James Harris. I played them because they were the best. That's all I can ask of a player. I can't ask him to change his color or nationality. I can only ask him to be the best he can be, and if that best is good enough to start, he starts. Eighth-grade Sewickley.

Later in Detroit, the blacks on the team started calling me "Dolomite." I had no idea what they were talking about until some guys down at one of my taverns told me that Dolomite was a fictitious character from a soul song by an artist named Rudy Ray Moore.

In the song, Dolomite is the baddest dude in the whole world. It was like a rap song. This singer talked about him swimming through crocodile-infested rivers and getting out without a drop of water on him. Talked about all kinds of jungle fights. Mostly, he talked about him kicking every white's butt. You see, Dolomite was black. But that's what they called me.

Former Buffalo Bills guard Reggie McKenzie: After Chuck left Detroit, the word got out that the Lions had called him Dolomite. Then all the blacks around the league started calling him that. I'm certain there are other ways to illustrate the black players' respect for Chuck. This one just stands out.

The only player on the Lions who had a chance of gaining my respect from the git-go was Ed Flanagan, our third-year center. He had experience. He had smarts. But he also had a gut. He was 270 pounds. Unlike other people then, I had a theory that centers needed to be lean and quick in order to find the middle linebacker in the 4–3 defense scheme that was so popular. That theory caught on later, but at the time, Flanagan needed some convincing that he needed to drop the weight.

In shaping these Detroit Lions into what some people eventually called pro football's best offensive line, I figured this was where we had better start. So I didn't call him Flanagan; I called him Fluff. In front of everybody. He had to lose twenty pounds, but he was always fighting me about those twenty pounds, so I ordered him to lose *thirty* pounds. Ordered him in front of everybody.

Tacking on the extra ten pounds is a tactic I use on players today. You see, I knew that as soon as he had weighed in on Friday night, Fluff would go out and have a big pasta dinner, then eat his way to game time and gain those extra ten pounds back.

With the new rule he'd always weigh about 250 at game time, which was perfect.

I don't know if he knew what I doing. Don't care. He got it done.

> *Former Lions backfield coach John North: Hell, Chuck knew what he was doing. The one thing that stood out about Chuck back then was his ability to feel talent when talent wasn't there. He got a great deal out of players who I thought couldn't play. Knox thought different. He knew he could make mountains out of moles. Don't let him fool you.*

So we have all these lousy linemen, and who do we play in my first game in the NFL? We play an exhibition with the AFL's tough Denver Broncos. It's the first-ever interleague exhibition game. The whole week in meetings, I'm warning everybody. I'm telling them, "I coached over there, those guys in that league are better than you think they are." Nobody was listening. Even the veterans were laughing at me. I was still just some kid coach from a second-rate league. Who wanted to hear him?

Even Alex Karras stands up in the middle of a meeting and says, "If Denver beats us, I'm walking home."

How do they put it? The rest is history?

Denver wins 13 – 7 and we're the first NFL team to lose to an AFL team. It was so bad, I didn't even need to say "I told you so." Last I looked, on the plane ride home Alex Karras was riding way in the back.

It is one thing to lose ugly. It is quite another to lose un-
prepared. By the time that plane landed, I had decided that if
such a loss happened again, it wouldn't be because we didn't
take it seriously.

So I mapped out several ideas pertaining to the way my
football teams would practice. They were ideas that I developed into principles that I follow today.

For example, the best practice sometimes happens before
practice.

The practice field at Cranbrook was surrounded by trees
and would have been a nice place to relax in isolation while
the coaches were back in the locker room getting everything
set up. Except that when I came through the brush about
twenty minutes prior to practice, my linemen had better be
on their feet and ready to work. Right then.

We would do one-on-one pass-protection drills and other
prepractice things, so when the rest of the team came through,
we were that far ahead of everybody else.

> *Rocky Freitas: There was never any set time; we started
> when Knox showed up, so we all had to be there early and
> wait for him. If he came through the woods and we were
> sitting down, no matter how early, he would scream at
> us. After suffering through one summer of this, we figured
> out a solution. Every day we would station a rookie up
> the path to serve as a lookout. When the kid saw Knox,
> he would run to the field ahead of him and rustle all of
> us to our feet. It worked. But I still sweat thinking about
> it.*

What they didn't know was that I knew what they were
doing. I knew there had to be a kid on lookout, because there
was no way they could always be on their feet every time I
came down. But that was OK because they were there, weren't
they? They had figured out a way to get themselves ready.
That was all I could ask.

By the time we got to our first game that first year, our

preparation showed. We took a 17–10 lead on Green Bay after scoring off an onside kick that we had noticed would work by watching their films. They eventually tied us 17-all on a seventy-five-yard touchdown run by Elijah Pitts. But I hate ties. I think a man should always play to win, that's why we're out there. Life is lived to win. But it was a moral victory. And my players still remember those little prepractice sessions, don't they?

Another principle I adopted was that perfect practice makes perfect. In other words, only by getting fired-up in practice can you understand how to be fired-up for a game. Sometimes I had to illustrate this principle myself.

> *Rocky Freitas: I remember one practice where there had not been a fight among linemen for, oh, at least five minutes. Nobody was charged-up. Nobody but Coach Knox, that is. There's this pile-up and we see him running toward it, then we see his clipboard fly, and . . . suddenly, all we see are the bottoms of his shoes. He jumps right into the damn pile and starts head-butting people. What a crazy son of a gun.*

Getting into the action, doing stupid things like blocking people, that's just me. I couldn't help myself. I would lose my head. I just wanted to show them how much all of it meant to me.

I still have problems today with putting my life in danger like that. Before every season I tell myself that it's bad for my heart and my noggin. But a couple of times every season I still jump in there and try to shake somebody up. I don't know if it's because I want to be a player, or because I want *them* to be players, real players with heart. Maybe it's a mixture of both.

Another practice principle involved what I considered the heart of my offensive line: the reserves. Few coaches believe more in reserves than I do. Few work them harder or test them more. Thus, when practice ends for everyone else, it does not end for them; it *can't* end for them. Subs are often asked to win games for you on Sunday, but how can anybody excel in a game that he hasn't played for a couple of weeks? It's not fair. If your reserves fail, then you as a coach have failed.

So I try to simulate game conditions after regular practice and make sure my reserves know what they are doing when the real time comes.

> *Rocky Freitas: Us subs knew what we were doing. We just didn't know what the hell Knox was doing. He would set us in the kind of one-on-one drills where we would kill the other guy just to make the starting lineup and avoid repeating the drill. In the middle of one after-practice drill, it was ninety degrees and I was dying. He came up to me and he stuck his head in my face and said, "This is the life, eh, Rock? You get to be on this health farm and you get three hots and a cot and all for nothing. Boy, you can't beat it, can you?"*

I would tell Rock, Hey, would you rather be here or in some steel mill or on some pineapple farm? He didn't know how lucky he was.

The biggest problem I had with those postpractice things was the weather. Specifically, winter weather. Half of my time would be spent looking for an unfrozen place in Tiger Stadium with enough footing to enable men to knock each other's heads off. Sometimes that space would be the size of a batter's box. But as long as it could hold two men, it would be enough.

Another practice principle was, only through admitting your mistakes can you profit from them. Even if that means admitting them over and over and over again. I'll admit I was a tough guy before practice in the film room. The hardest part for some of my players was not getting beat, but listening to me break down the film of that game, marking up each of their mistakes.

The Old Man, Charlie Knox.

My mother, Helen, in 1965.

With my brother, Billy, outside a house on Walnut Street in Sewickley, 1938.

My Sewickley High School team. I'm number 21, kneeling in the front row.

At the age of sixteen,
I joined the National
Guard.

My senior high portrait,
1950.

As a freshman player,
Juniata College, fall
1950.

With Mother, Billy, and
my first daughter, Chris,
in 1954.

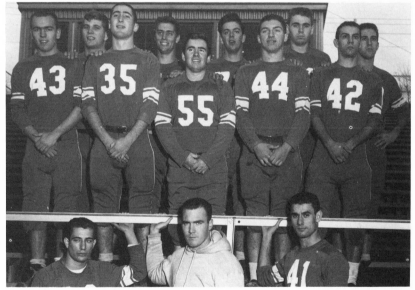

The seniors I coached at Ellwood City High School in 1956.

Cheering an Ellwood
victory.

At the University of
Kentucky in 1962 with
head coach Charlie
Bradshaw (on my left)
and assistant Dave Hart
(on my right).

With Blanton Collier, my
University of Kentucky
mentor, and our wives
in 1970.

The New York Jets coaching staff in 1963. Clockwise from center: Weeb Ewbank (kneeling), Jack Donaldson, George Sauer, me, Clive Rush, and Walt Michaels.

Trying to earn a little extra money selling blankets on TV during the years with the New York Jets, when my salary was lean.

With Alex Karras in 1967, when I was the Detroit Lions offensive-line coach.

With LA Rams owner
Carroll Rosenbloom
in 1976.

With Buffalo Bills
owner Ralph Wilson
(on my right) and
Pete Rozelle in 1980.

In 1983 I was awarded an honorary doctorate from my alma mater, Juniata College.

In 1984 Merlin Olsen presented me with the NFL Coach of the Year award.

Showing a Seahawk
how to do it.

Sometimes you've
got to make sure they
let you play the hand
you're dealt.

> *Rocky Freitas: On the good parts, Chuck would praise us. Great. But on the bad parts, he would stop. And play again. And stop. And play again. Then maybe turn on the lights, fix the projector, and blow the image up life-size, bringing a man's failures to the size of an average chalkboard.*

I could tell my players weren't too thrilled by all this. They would wait until the last minute to enter the room, and then occupy the last couple of rows of chairs, almost circling them like a wagon train.

> *Former Lions guard Chuck Walton: We were so strongly affected that we would judge the severity of each session by the size of the sweat rings on the underarms of our T-shirts. We'd come out of a session saying, "Oh, this was a bad one, the sweat goes all the way down to the tits." Frietas was the only one who figured a way out of it. Before coming into the room, he would take off his shirt.*
>
> *In general, there was no use trying to keep cool in there. If you did, you were in even more trouble. Once, Knox thought this top rookie tackle wasn't paying attention. Knox stopped talking, raised his hand, and pounded a school desk so hard it popped three inches off the ground and nearly hit him in the chin. We all turned white, but it didn't even faze the kid. The next day, the kid was gone.*

All I'm doing in a film session is pointing out the proper way of doing things. We teach technique, the right way of doing it. Our method is tried and true. If you're good enough to do it another way, fine, but it better get done. Film sessions are good because I have the proof right there, and there is nowhere the player can go. There is nothing he can say. He is forced to learn. And isn't that why we're here?

You know what is a little unsettling? I still look at films with players, but not all the time. And never in the small,

cramped rooms with the stress and the sweat. The bureau-
cracy surrounding a head coach has become so thick that every
year you can get farther and farther away from the guys you
are coaching. I've been very lucky to stay close, considering
I never played pro ball. Maybe I'm close *because* I never played.

I will say this: I get tired of people thinking coaches have
to be ex-players. Many of the best coaches were never players. They are guys who didn't have the skills necessary, and
as a result had to develop an understanding of how to play
the game, how the intricacies worked. Joe Gibbs, Bill Parcells, Bill Walsh—all are Super Bowl coaches who never played
a pro down.

Coaches who weren't great players have the patience to
work with people who aren't good either, and turn them into
good players. A lot of ex-players don't have that patience.
The guy with great God-given athletic ability sometimes expects that, because he was able to do it, everybody who steps
onto the field should be able to do it. He was so gifted, he
was able to get it done without being fundamentally sound,
so he doesn't worry his team about fundamentals. As a result
his team fails.

There remain, of course, a number of ex-pros who have
paid the dues and who have become very successful NFL head
coaches, guys like Don Shula, Chuck Noll, Tom Landry, Mike
Ditka, and Dan Reeves. But there are more who have failed.

Good coaches are those who had to learn how to teach,
motivate, stimulate, and be fundamentally sound, and who
feel that all those things are necessary just for basic survival.
Those coaches coach champions. Look at me. Not that I'm a
champion, or even necessarily an outstanding coach, but
through longevity alone I am an example of how coming up
through the coaching ranks can help you as much as coming
from the playing field.

I've heard guys complaining because they had to wait eight
or nine years for a head coaching job. Poor babies. Remember, I had to wait nineteen years.

While other guys were *playing* the game for the big money,

I was *learning* it at the high-school and college level, learning about organization, about disciplining yourself during your workday, about allotment of time. A player almost never concerns himself with these things.

While I was directing kids to the practice field, then to films, then back to the field, bang, bang . . . players my age were still being told what to do. A lot of ex-players have failed at coaching because, one, they didn't understand how many hours they would have to put in, and two, they thought they'd make a lot more money than they actually did. Very few players want to step out and work for thirty-five thousand dollars, which includes fifteen-hour workdays during the six-month season, and regular hours the rest of the time. No way. It's too much of a change.

People wondered if, as a result of this attitude, I resented Joe Schmidt because he was an ex-player who walked right into the job as a head coach. No sir, not one iota. He taught me a lot about the psychological highs and lows of a player. On the other hand, he allowed me to help him with the nuts and bolts of coaching. He took a lot of my input and in turn gave me freedom to shape my offensive line and, eventually, my future. Under anyone else, I might not have learned to become my own head coach.

> *Rocky Freitas: Shoot, there were times we thought Knox was the head coach. Let me tell you about training camp Saturdays, when everybody's family was invited to the field to see their boyfriends or dads or husbands who'd been gone all week. Usually a real festive time, like a picnic. Knox would bring his two teenage daughters. It turned out to be the most pressure any of us felt all week. Somebody would say, "Who are those cute girls?" and somebody else would say, "Coach's daughters." From then on, we'd all be afraid to turn our heads sideways. If he ever caught us looking at them, he'd surely kill us. On Saturdays, we were afraid to move.*

Yeah, I knew they were scared of me. They were so scared,

if I said boo they would leap over the daggone building. But I think it was based on respect. I really think—I hope—they respected me. That's what I was trying to get, and sometimes the starting point is fear.

About those Saturdays. The reason I brought the kids was that I needed to see my family whenever I could. My time away from home became greater and greater. The kids were getting older. And it was getting harder.

> *Daughter Chris: No matter how Dad tried, there was one thing we learned in Detroit: even our holidays revolved around football.*
>
> *In Detroit, you know, they play every Thanksgiving. So for six straight years we would eat Thanksgiving dinner after a game. For six years it was always the same: if we won, great meal; if we lost, it was inedible.*
>
> *It wasn't Dad's fault; he never said anything. In fact he always put on a good face. It was us. We felt so rotten for him, we ruined it for ourselves. I guess from those years in Detroit, we learned that holidays aren't dates or events, but states of mind.*

When you mention Thanksgiving Day, the first thing that comes to mind is not turkey, but turkeys, as in, the teams that have to play in Detroit and Dallas on those days. Because of the short work week and travel time, I think those two visiting teams that day face the biggest disadvantages of any team, in any game in football. That is why most everybody is trying to break up that tradition—in vain.

Back when the NFL wanted to schedule another Thanksgiving game along with Detroit—which had been around on its lonesome since 1934—nobody wanted to take it. Until the Cowboys boss Tex Schramm, shrewd businessman that he is, suddenly stepped forward and said not only would he take it, but he would promote the hell out of it. However, this was under one condition: the league must assure him of that Thanksgiving Day game at home *forever*. The league agreed. And before I brought the Seahawks down there in 1986 and beat them on Thanksgiving, they had racked up a 19–3 record on that day. Incredibly smart man, Tex Schramm.

As hard as I worked those first years in Detroit, I began to wonder how incredibly smart I was to take this job. In the beginning we didn't seem to be learning anything. The first year, 1967, we went 5–7–2, and then 4–8–2. But in 1969 it was like we suddenly got smart. We went 9–4–1 and ended the season by beating the Bears 20–8. Hard work does pay off. Sometimes you just have to wait a couple of seasons while you live by that principle.

I had this final principle that I tried to live by: If my linemen didn't mess with me, I wouldn't let anybody mess with them. We could rip each other, but heaven help any outsider who tried to rip us.

Bill Cottrell: You played for Knox, you were his baby. Nobody else on the team could say anything to you. No coach do anything to you. When the special teams coach came up to yell at the linemen, Knox was always right there, getting in the last word on that coach and you. You were his.

I guess sometimes I took that support stuff too far. There was still some street in me, and it often came out when I thought all my problems could be solved with eighth-grade Sewickley. One night at a restaurant in downtown Detroit, a buddy and I encountered three men who really believed that sad old story about the Lions defensive line being far superior to the offensive line. Without knowing who I was, they tried to convince me that the Lions offensive line stunk.

It shouldn't have mattered. Those should have been just liquor words, not fighting words. But all of a sudden one of the guys took a swing at me and it was fist city.

As if my fist belonged to someone else, a young street kid from Sewickley maybe, I leaned back and let it go. I hit the guy back, in the face. I hit him again. Now he's hitting back again. I turn around for a second, and there's my buddy running out the door. Now it's one on three.

I just kept throwing punches, figuring the odds were good they would land on *somebody*. I was crazy. Thank goodness they thought so, anyway. In fact they thought I was so crazy, trying to fight all of them, that they eventually just got the hell out of there. So call it a draw. It cost me eight stitches above my eye, and a broken watch, but at least I was alive.

The biggest problem I had was the next day at practice, when I put on sunglasses and tried to hide the shiner.

> *Former Lions center Ed Flanagan: He is in the middle of a chalk session, when he leans over and the glasses fall off. Bam. Mouths and pencils are dropping everywhere. It's a shiner, our thirty-five-year-old coach has a shiner. We all howl. Later in the day, we find out what happened. If anybody had doubted Chuck's affection for us, they didn't anymore. Knox stands up for you like no other coach will ever stand up for you.*

I only got in one other big fight while I was in Detroit. It was a couple of years after my first fight, after an exhibition game in nearby Ann Arbor. I duked it out with some guys in a parking lot. That's all I remember.

> *John North: I'll tell you what happened. We were riding back to Detroit in a van with some acquaintances of mine whom Chuck had just met. We stopped at a hotel to make dinner reservations. I'm on the phone in the hotel, when all of a sudden I hear a bunch of noise. I come outside and there's Knox and this guy slugging it out. Then there's Knox and all the other guys slugging it out. I grab Knox, his wife screams and grabs him, and while we're holding him, the guys jump back in the van and leave us. We take a cab home.*
>
> *Apparently, one of the guys said something about the offensive line and didn't know what he was talking about. Knox didn't like it, and then the guy sucker-punched him.*

| *I don't know what Knox was madder about, the offensive-line comment or the sucker punch.*

I do remember one thing. I fought because of the sucker punch. Whatever you do to me, do it honestly. That's all I ask. I can't handle a sucker punch, whether on the streets or in the business world. I have a tendency to lose my mind.

There was, and still is, another good reason to go fist city for my guys: usually it means they will go fist city for me. There was the time in Detroit when I was running a substitute offensive squad against the first-team defense. We weren't supposed to be blocking real hard, just kind of going through the motions so the defense could learn our next opponent's offense.

After one play, linebacker Wayne Walker shouts, "Who's supposed to block me?"

I tell my guys to ignore him.

Four plays later he yells again, "Who's supposed to block me?" This is a direct affront to my coaching, to my blocking scheme. This is a hotshot taking a potshot at a nothing assistant coach—me.

So now in the huddle I tell the guy who was blocking him, "Go down and get him this time; somebody knock him right on his big butt. I don't want to hear any more of this stuff. He's embarrassing us. Somebody kick his ass."

So somebody does. All of them do. They run down there and cream him, and I guarantee you, he knew then who was supposed to block him.

I carried this attitude over into my dealing with the referees. Still do. I won't fight them, but I will get between them and my players and make sure they understand just what my players will be doing. Before every game in Detroit, I would meet with the refs and explain to them how our guys were taught to block, and how it was legal. Sometimes I would have to grab a ref by the collar to demonstrate. Even today I meet with the refs; only now it's more for trick plays and things like that.

This doesn't mean I won't try everything within the outer limits of the rules to win. You *have* to try everything—at least I do. I've come from too far down to afford Sunday nights where I have to admit to myself that I did not do everything I could to win that day's game. And I mean everything.

> *Bob Kowalkowski: The week before a Dallas game in 1969, our first good year, Knox started getting off about Cowboy defensive lineman Jethro Pugh. Because Pugh was an All-Pro, Knox spent the whole week before the game telling us, "This Pugh is on the glory train and you ain't on nothing. He thinks he's better than you. Everybody else thinks he's better than you. You got him right where you want him." Knox would always talk this way about the great and decorated players. Because he always felt like an underdog, he made us play like underdogs, too. During the game, Pugh starts beating me, beating me bad. I get back to the sidelines and Knox is nuts. He comes over and says, "I don't care what you do. You kick. You bite. You scratch. You tackle the son of a gun. But you don't let him touch our quarterback. Do what you got to do. But do not give me a sack."*
>
> *Of all his talking, this last talk worked. I had the game of my life. I finally realized what Knox had been trying to tell us. Of course, the next week in films, he found the plays where I was beat and ran them. Blew them up. Over and over and over.*

In 1970, my fourth year in Detroit, we finally did it. We took that city to a football play-off for the first time in eight years. That was when I learned just why we were working so hard, and how the rewards can be so sweet. And I think it was that year, standing next to Joe Schmidt as we went through more ups and downs and excitement than I had previously experienced, that I realized I could become a successful head coach.

Start with November 8, 1970. After seven games we were

5–2 and playing weak New Orleans in Tulane Stadium. We're leading 17–16 with the Saints stuck in their own territory. Time is running out, and it looks like we've got it locked. We'll soon be 6–2—our best early-season record in years.

But with time enough for one more Saints play, out runs their kicker, Tom Dempsey, and he's lining up to try a field goal. A sixty-three-yard field goal. Nobody in pro football history had ever come close to kicking one that far before. Now Dempsey has a big butt, a huge butt, man must have weighed 260 pounds. Joe Schmidt turns to me and says, "If he makes this field goal, I will kiss that big butt in front of Hudson's Department Store in downtown Detroit, and I'll give him fifteen minutes to draw a crowd."

I smile. Then Dempsey hits that ball and it sounds like a gun goes off. We stand there watching, and watching, and it seems like the ball is in the air forever . . .

And it's good.

It's good.

How can it be good?

I don't know, but it was good. A sixty-three-yard field goal. A record that still stands. Game's over and we lose.

With nothing left to do, I turn to Schmidt, shrug, and say, "Joe, that's a lot of butt to kiss."

The next week it gets worse. We travel to Minnesota, a team that has just beaten us 30–17 two weeks earlier. A good learning experience, right? The defense had learned so well they repeat the lesson: in our second meeting the Vikings get another thirty points. But my offensive line, after playing well early, loses its script. It stinks, allowing eleven sacks. We lose for the third straight game and our record is now a very common 5–4. Afterward Joe comes up to me.

"Charlie, Charlie," he says. (He's the only one besides my father ever to call me Charlie.) "Charlie, what are we going to do about it? We've got to make your line aware of what they've done. *We* have to do something. And if we don't do something, it's our fault, not theirs."

He was right. I had to think of something that would blow

my linemen away. They had already seen me do just about everything, so I had to come up with something special, a speech containing the unexpected. I think in listening to someone talk, the listener remembers three things—the first thing the speaker says, the last thing he says, and anything unusual. So I decided to get unusual.

> *Rocky Freitas: We're one of the league's best lines, yet we allow all those sacks against the Vikings. The roof caves in, and we're in deep trouble. We get back home and go into the Monday film meeting. Walton and I are a little scared, so we wait until everybody else has gone in, hoping maybe Knox will be all yelled-out by the time we get there. We sneak in last. But you won't believe what happened next. Nothing. He didn't yell. He didn't scream. He barely said a word. Just, "I'm leaving. You guys watch this damn film, I can't stand to look at it anymore. When you're done, somebody burn it."*

What could I say? Sometimes saying nothing is the loudest thing you can say.

> *Rocky Freitas: But the burn-the-film speech was just part of Chuck's plan. After that he orders us back to Tiger Stadium the next day, our off-day.*
>
> *We get there on a cold November Tuesday afternoon, while the rest of the team are enjoying time in front of the fire with their families. He turns on all the stadium lights and pulls out the blocking sled, the most disgusting of all instruments, used for the most monotonous and exhausting of drills. Some say sleds build muscle and technique. I think they just build anger.*
>
> *He grabs guys from the stadium grounds crew to hold either side of the sled. Then he jumps in the middle and shouts at the players to start hitting. Around the field, in the frozen gray, we hit.*

After several guys are close to dropping, Knox jumps off the sled and finds a piece of dry earth for one-on-one pass-protection drills. It's crazy. It's awful. We fight. A few more drop. We finally stop. But we never forget.

I wanted them out there on that frozen field as a way of telling them, "Don't ever again tell me how rough the waters are. Just bring the ship in."

Not once during my career in Detroit did we have to go back out there. We win our next three games, putting us in position to go to the play-offs. Well, sort of in position. All we have to do is beat the Los Angeles Rams of Merlin Olson and Coy Bacon and Deacon Jones, beat them in Los Angeles, beat them on "Monday Night Football."

We arrive the Tuesday before the game and set up camp at Long Beach, complete with guards because we are certain George Allen, LA's head coach, will be spying. We're real tense. Every day in practice there are fights. By the final meeting before taking the field Monday night, the players are so nerve-scraped that one reserve actually closes his eyes and appears asleep.

"When the sucker wakes up," yells Schmidt, "somebody tell him he's cut."

I've got my own worries. Kowalkowski has a bad back and is unable to practice all week. So we can't plan on playing him. But then tackle Jim Yarbrough's sore knee is reinjured and somebody is needed to take his place. We've got just one guy, Kowalkowski.

I corner him in the locker room a day before the game.

"Can you go?" I ask.

"At *tackle?*" Kowalkowski gapes. "I've never even played tackle. And against Coy Bacon? An All-Pro?"

"I know who he is," I said. "Can you go?"

I always hoped that I was coaching my players not to play a specific position, but just to play. Everything I taught them about the winning edge, I hoped could be applied anywhere.

I hoped I had spent four years teaching Kowalkowski not to be just a damn good guard, but a damn good football player. His answer told me I had succeeded.

"I'm going," he said.

The next night Kowal gets his butt beat on the first play. But he doesn't get beat again. We win 28–23, and Joe Schmidt is ecstatic and Howard Cosell raves over this young offensive-line coach named Knox. But afterward, there's only one person I want to be with.

> *Bob Kowalkowski: Knox runs over, and with all the television lights on all the big heroes, he gives me the game ball. Just me. I've got plenty of game balls, but none ever meant more.*

Afterward we party all the way down the interstate to Long Beach. Schmidt stops the bus at a liquor store and orders cases of beer brought aboard. Later he dances on a table in a bar.

I understand that there are a lot more important things than football: family, religion, feeding hungry children, peace, a lot of things. But because coaches and players have chosen to be in pro football, because it is the source of 98, 99 percent of their income, we have to spend our lives giving it every bit of our respect and attention. If your family matters, then nothing else but supporting them can matter.

That's why nights like that 1970 night against the Rams make it worth it. That's the payback. It doesn't last long—it lasts maybe only that night—but it does exist. That night, and on many nights since, I told the guys there are two great things about pro football: winning and getting paid. If you're lucky enough, you can experience both.

We traveled home the following Sunday to defeat Green Bay 20–0, ending the 1970 regular season at 10–4, with five straight wins since that wild Tuesday afternoon at Tiger Stadium. Most important, we qualified for the play-offs against Dallas.

A week later, in one of the most frustrating defeats in play-off history, and my history, we lost to Dallas 5 – 0. Ironically, it was the score by which my Buffalo Bills defeated the Cincinnati Bengals eight years later. When that happened, all of the Buffalo reporters rushed in and asked me, "Have you ever in your life heard of a five-zero score? Who has ever heard of a five-zero score? How strange can you get?" I just looked at them and said, "Why yes, I have heard of a five-zero score. As a matter of fact, I've been involved in a five-zero score." Then I laughed and they didn't.

My final two years in Detroit were nothing like that play-off feeling. We went 7 – 6 – 1 and 8 – 5 – 1 and didn't play after the regular season, even though that final year we had the best record that didn't qualify for the play-offs. But those years were memorable for a couple of reasons, one of them not so nice. On October 24, 1971, playing at home against Chicago, for the first and only time in my life, I saw a player die. Wide receiver Chuck Hughes went out for a pass and never came back. Just collapsed and stayed there. We all knew something was wrong when we could see, from a distance, our team doctor pounding on Chuck's chest. Usually the first thing some doctors do is give a signal to the public-address announcer, to show what part of the player's body is hurt. But he didn't do it this time. All I can remember is the doctor pulling up the man's jersey and pounding on his chest.

After the game we found out he had died of a heart attack. At first it made me sad, and then it just made me want to hug my wife a little longer, tell my children how much I loved them, stay at home for a few more minutes in the morning. Made me realize something my mother always said in that Scottish brogue of hers, that we are on this earth for just a wee minute, only a wee minute.

Of course, this was also football. Chuck Hughes was buried and we played the next week. And the week after. Sometimes I think, To hell with football. But I know I don't mean it. I'll always be there the next week. And the week after.

Following the 1971 season, I received my first call for a head coaching job. It was the Saint Louis Cardinals, who were looking to replace Charley Winner. I didn't get the job, but I got an interview with the team's co-owners, Billy and Stormy Bidwell. Looking back, that story alone was worth all the trouble.

The two Saint Louis bosses were at odds with each other, and I couldn't meet them in the same room. I couldn't even meet them in the same city. So I met them in two different places in Florida, two separate interviews. They told me they couldn't agree on anybody, so they would pick three finalists. Those finalists would be interviewed by an industrial psychologist in Chicago. This psychologist, not they, would choose the new football coach of the Saint Louis Cardinals.

This is not a fabricated story.

I wasn't one of the finalists. I don't want to sound sour, but thank goodness. The winner was Bob Hollway, who lasted two seasons.

But by then, for completely different reasons, I figured my time was coming. The way I see it, you first become head coaching material when your players start imitating you and making fun of your mannerisms behind your back. This is what eventually happened in Detroit. I would hear them talking about the way I threw my cap when I got mad. I would hear them talking about my hair falling out, and what hair was left falling all over my head. Actually, I am quite easy to imitate, from my funny walk to my clichés. The Lions were the first ones to get good at it.

Chuck Walton: You knew Knox was the most influential coach on the staff, because every time he threw his cap, another coach would throw his cap, too. But the funniest part was when Chuck put his hat back on. He was losing his hair even then, and he had just one strand left across his forehead. When he put his cap on quick, that string of hair would get caught in the back. After a bad series, he'd be over there in your face, but you couldn't

*keep a straight face because the man chewing your butt
had a six-inch pony tail.*

Yeah, those guys all laugh at me now. But look at how
some of my misfits turned out. Look at fat Ed Flanagan. He
wound up a four-time All-Pro. Wound up playing during my
final Lions season with a back so bad, he couldn't practice;
he couldn't even sit in a chair during film sessions. He had
to lie on the linoleum. But he played, how that man played.

And look at lumpy Rocky Freitas. He also eventually made
All-Pro. Funny thing about all of those misfits. The combination of Flanagan, Freitas, Walton, Cottrell, and Kowalkowski ended up playing a combined forty-eight years in the
league—more than double the average of four years per man.

*Bob Kowalkowski: After Knox called me a sissy, I
couldn't stand to talk to the man. But in the winter after
his second season there, he heard I was a good fisherman
and invited me with some other coaches north on a fishing trip. I was stunned but I thought, What the hell.*

*Once we got there we baited and drank scotch, baited
and drank beer, then threw away the bait and just drank.
Finally, when we were alone and pretty sauced, I cornered
Knox. I told him, "You know, a couple of seasons ago I
wanted to clean your clock. I wanted to kill you, literally
kill you, for calling me a sissy."*

*"Really?" Knox said. "Why didn't you tell me then? I
could have explained it to you then. I could have explained about patting some guys on the back and kicking
other guys on the butt, and about how I had to check
each guy for an inner flame. Calling you a name was the
best way I knew how."*

*I thought about it awhile and decided, Yeah, I under-
stand.*

In the winter following the 1972 season, while at a coaches'
convention in Chicago, I was paged over the loudspeaker. I
had a phone call waiting at the front desk. It was Shirley.

She told me that back in our Bloomfield Hills house, she had just received two phone calls: one from Joe Schmidt; one from Jack Teele, an administrative assistant with the Los Angeles Rams. I had a pretty good idea about both of them. Joe Schmidt was going to retire, damn him. And the Rams head coaching job was open because they had fired Tommy Prothro.

I returned the calls in reverse order. First I called LA. I reached Don Klosterman, the Rams' general manager. He said they had gotten permission to talk to me. He then asked if I could come to Los Angeles for a job interview under an assumed name. *Assumed name?* I told Don, "Call me anything you want, just call the airline and get me out there before you change your mind."

Face it, this was a dream job about which I had no business dreaming. I told myself even Shirley was not going to find out about this. I didn't tell her every joke I heard at the office, why should I tell her this one?

After I got off the phone with Klosterman, I flew back to Detroit. I called Joe.

"Charlie," he said, "I'm leaving, I'm retiring."

That's what I thought he'd say. I had already thought long and hard about what this would mean to my future there—I would be next in line to replace him as the head man. But suddenly I couldn't even think of that. All I could think of was a guy who had spent the last six years growing with me, a guy who had made this the best place in the NFL to be an assistant, a guy who treated me like a head coach already. And this guy was going.

"Joe, you can't," I said to a man who had become a great coach. "Look what we've built here, you just can't!"

I insisted that he unlock his front door, and in the middle of the night I went to his house and met him in his den. We stayed up the rest of the night drinking beers and talking about it. I figured, if nothing else, maybe he'd be too sick to make the announcement.

He wasn't. The next morning he resigned.

By then I had decided, OK, this is my shot. I've given six good years to the organization. I think I should replace Joe. And Joe thinks I should replace Joe. But before I can get in to see Lions general manager Russ Thomas, he comes out in the newspaper and says none of Schmidt's assistants will even be considered for the head job.

Comes out in the newspapers before even telling the assistants. Nice.

I'm sitting at my kitchen table. I read it, read it aloud, read it again, and finally say to no one: "How can he say that? All I've done, all the grunt work and loyalty work and plain hard work—how can he *say* that?"

In a moment, my career had been snapped in two by somebody from a different world, somebody with a coat and a tie and a knowledge of football that was not worth as much as either one. Just like that. I was genuinely angry and disgusted and, well, hurt is probably the best word.

I finally get in to see Russ Thomas.

"The new coach might rehire you as an assistant," he says, "but we can't even promise that."

I leave with a different sort of anger. I'm not mad at Russ, I'm mad at myself: how dare I think anything would ever be *fair!*

Oh, yeah. In the middle of all this the Rams call back and set up the airplane flight. Sure. When they called earlier, they were calling a successful assistant coach. Now they were calling an *unemployed* assistant coach. And they were supposed to hire me? When a team that had seen my work for six years wouldn't hire me? If I had absolutely no chance in Detroit, I certainly didn't have anything better in Los Angeles, where they were reportedly interviewing up to twenty coaches.

Before I flew to LA, I finally explained it to Shirley, the whole story, everything. My last words before getting on the plane at the Detroit Metro airport were "This won't take long."

6

Los Angeles

Chuck Mills.

If I ever get rich and famous, maybe that would make a pretty good trivia question.

On a warm Tuesday night in January 1973—I can see all of this as though it happened last week—I get off the plane in Los Angeles, fresh from an all-day flight from Detroit. I take a cab to the Century Plaza Hotel. There it is in the guest books, plain as ink. My pseudonym, Chuck Mills.

I find it funny that during my job interview the Rams were so afraid of somebody finding out who I was. Eventually, when everybody found out who I was, they still didn't know who I was.

So here is Chuck Mills down at breakfast the following morning with Rams owner Carroll Rosenbloom (C. R. is what everybody called him) and the general manager, Don Klosterman. C. R. is asking all the questions, and Klosterman is taking notes on this big yellow legal pad as Chuck Mills is baring his soul. After all, I don't have a chance here anyway, right? So I figure, play no games, be honest, give them eight-grade Sewickley.

I tell C. R. I can win. I tell him that I know how to win. I tell him I am absolutely certain I can get the job done. C. R.

replies, "I need to run over to Le Bistro to check out the plans for a Super Bowl party I'm having tomorrow night. Want to come along?"

What a sense of humor, this guy. I kept telling myself that as we piled in the back of his car and headed for this place called Le Bistro. We get there and C. R. walks up to the maitre d' and they start talking about what kind of wines to serve. Then they decide that they will have only two entrees. C. R. calls me aside to explain why.

"If you have any more than two entrees," he says, "the food lines get too long because people can't make up their minds. Don't forget that."

"No, sir, I won't," I say.

Then C. R. whisks off to another corner, trying to decide where the band will set up and how long they will play and hey, let's check that wine list again.

This is how you hire an NFL coach?

We finally go back to the Rams office, where we meet again that night, and then the next day I fly home and with not even the promise that anybody will get back to me.

On that flight home, I read in the paper that there really are twenty coaches being interviewed for this job, and that the leading candidate is a guy who used to coach for Rosenbloom when he owned the Baltimore Colts just a year earlier, a guy named Don McCafferty.

Oh well. The trip wasn't a complete waste. Next time Shirley invites a thousand people over for dinner, at least we'll know how to serve it.

When I got back home, I had two calls waiting for me. One was from Don Coryell, who had just taken the head coaching job in Saint Louis. He wondered if I would be interested in coaching his offensive line. The other call was from George Allen of the Redskins. He was wondering the same thing. I told them both, "I will join one of you, but I can't say which one yet. Foolish as it sounds, I want to wait on the Rams."

One night about a week after my interview, I get a phone call. It's Don Klosterman. The Rams want me back for a second interview. Suddenly it seems real. It seems crazy, but for the first time it seems real.

> *Shirley Knox: Chuck runs in and says, "Honey, I am going back out there for a second interview and if I get the job, I will want to look good at the press conference. Honey, pick out my best suit."*
>
> *I say, "That won't be too hard, Mr. Big-Timer. You only have one suit."*

I flew back out, only this time there happened to be six or seven of my friends on the plane. They wanted to know what the hell I was doing. I made something up.

I was picked up at the airport by C. R.'s son Steve and his cousin Eddie. I stayed at the Century Plaza again. I was Chuck Mills again. I was interviewed the next morning, and then I was told to wait at the hotel for a phone call around five o'clock that afternoon.

I wait and wait, and about four forty-five Don Klosterman calls and tells me to be out front in a few minutes. I run out front and Klosterman pulls around in a big car and I jump in.

"Congratulations," he says while making a right turn. "You are the new coach of the Los Angeles Rams."

Before I can say anything, he adds, "But it didn't come from me; I'm not supposed to tell you. We're driving to the Rams offices right now. C. R. wants to be the one to tell you."

Looking back, that makes sense. C. R. always did insist on being the bearer of good news, while somebody else in the organization always had to deliver the bad news.

We get to the offices and C. R. calls me in, tells me to sit down, and says in this fatherly voice, "You are my new coach, congratulations. We will pay you fifty thousand a year, with a three-year contract."

Those were his exact words. You never forget the first time you hear words like that. The date was January 24, 1973. You never forget a date like that either.

I grabbed his hand and told him, "I'm going to win. We *will* turn this around."

He said, "Do you want to call Shirley?"

I said, "Please."

He dialed the phone, and when she answered, he told her, "I have a man here who has very important news for you."

I nearly climbed down the handset.

I had coached nineteen years, ten of them as a pro assistant, four of them as a college assistant, five of them at the high-school level. I had just recently been slapped in the face and cast out into football oblivion by an NFL general manager, Russ Thomas, who thought he would never hear from me again. I had never played pro ball. I had not played big-time college ball. I had no big-league connections, and I had more friends in Sewickley than in any NFL town. And suddenly, here I was, the head coach of the fastest team in the fastest lane in America.

Former Rams assistant director of college scouting Tank Younger: We had been without a coach for about a month, and there was all kinds of speculation. It seemed like every day they would sneak a candidate up in the back door. Everybody had an idea and none of us had an idea. Then our personnel guy, John Sanders, called Bucko Kilroy, the player personnel director of the New England Patriots, a guy who knew everything. Bucko said, "Tell everybody out there to quit worrying. Your new coach is going to be a good one. He is going to be Chuck Knox."

Sanders put down the phone and ran in to tell everybody. No sooner did he get out the words "Chuck Knox" than he stopped. And we stopped. And all together we said, "Chuck who?"

I remember the press conference that afternoon at the Beverly Hills Hotel. I went there with C. R. in a limousine, got out, answered more questions than I had ever answered in my life, and then the next day I woke up and read where Jimmy Murray of the LA *Times* had written something like this:

"A press conference was called yesterday to announce the new head coach of the Rams. A limo pulled up, the passenger door was opened, and nobody got out."

At first it hurt, but then like most things that hurt, it just made sense. Why should anybody know me? What had I done? Where had I come from? But really now, isn't it better when nobody knows you? On the streets, you can always sneak up on somebody better that way. That's eighth-grade Sewickley.

I'm not sure what happened after that press conference, only that it happened fast. I know I went back to the Century Plaza to let it all sink in. It is no coincidence that since I left the Rams, both my Buffalo and Seattle teams have always stayed at that hotel.

Shortly afterward C. R. called me there and said I would be starting immediately. I would not be going home. I would be staying at his house in Bel Air. Maybe I could fit into some of his sweaters? He ordered Jack Teele to answer all my mail. He told me not to worry about anything but lining up a coaching staff.

In fact, C. R. told me a lot of things in those early days. If you have read closely, you will have realized he even gave me an order on the one point over which it is reasonable for employee and boss to haggle: my salary. C. R. told me what I would accept. Think about that.

At the time, none of it seemed like much to get disturbed about. C. R. was The Man, and The Man wanted to take every possible pressure off me so I could concentrate only on coaching. Besides, he knew I would have taken this job for free; he knew this was the break I had been waiting two decades for.

It was the start of five of the most successful and difficult years of my life. I laughed the most, and I cried the most. I did something only one other coach—Paul Brown—has done: win division championships in his first five years.

And my reward five years later was a mouthful of pride.

First things first: I had to get my family out there with me. They couldn't come until June, after school was out. But some of them weren't sure they wanted to come, period. They were getting older now, and moving meant leaving friends. I flew back to Detroit my first weekend and we had a talk.

> *Daughter Kathy: Usually he would come in all diplomatic and everything, sit us all down, and say, "This is what I'm considering doing, I want your opinion on this job possibility . . ." You knew he had already made up his mind, but he was at least going through the considerate motions of hearing our input.*
>
> *But the Rams thing was too big. He didn't have time to talk to us first. Even though it was supposed to be hush-hush, we all knew he had taken the job. I was a senior in high school and had heard rumors on the radio at a girl-friend's house. Colleen had heard about it on the school bus. So this time he used a new approach—bribery.*
>
> *He walked in and said, "OK, so we're going to California. Before you say anything, I promise you kids I will get a house with a pool."*
>
> *We said, "Put it in writing, pal." But he did, he got us a pool.*

I decided immediately to treat this new job as NFL head coach like I had treated everything else up until now. You want something done, you push on it until it gets done. You treat it like a blocking sled.

My first training camp comes, and I see this team coming off a 6-7-1 record, a team upset and confused and, more than anything, a team looking right at me. I had all these fancy plans before I walked into the meeting room that first day, but when I looked into their eyes, I changed all that.

I decided, Hell, I'll be myself. A football coach can fool a lot of people—the fans, the media, the owner—but he cannot fool a football player. So I didn't try.

Former Rams defensive back Steve Preece: I had been cut by three teams in the previous four years when I was picked up by Knox. I thought I had seen it all, heard it all, until Chuck walks in on that first practice and announces, "The best twenty-two guys on this football team will play for me. I don't care who is making the big money, I don't care who the high draft pick was, the best twenty-two guys are going to play." That was the first time I had ever heard a pro coach say that. Usually it's not the best twenty-two, but the top twenty-two in the owner's checkbook.

On the spur of the moment I decided I was going to keep it simple. I was going to treat them the way I used to pray I would be treated. Growing up, all I ever wanted to hear was that, yes, no matter who I was or how poor I was, I was going to be given a chance to succeed. I decided my new players should hear that, too.

So we made moves.

We traded quarterback Roman Gabriel, who had been with the club for eleven years, to the Philadelphia Eagles for, among others, wide receiver Harold Jackson, who starred for us for the next five years.

We traded defensive tackle Coy Bacon, who had been with the Rams five years, to the San Diego Chargers for quarterback John Hadl, who became the NFC Most Valuable Player with us.

On defense we gave Jack Youngblood, Jack "Hacksaw" Reynolds, Fred Dryer, and Larry Brooks their first real starting opportunities. And on that poor defensive backfield we got rid of three starters and replaced them with two waiver picks, Steve Preece and Charlie Stukes, and a rookie fourth-round draft pick named Eddie McMillan. That defense wound up leading the league. And on not one play did it involve a Deacon Jones, a Lamar Lundy, a Coy Bacon, or any of those great players I supposedly inherited. Like I had promised: everybody who wanted a chance got a chance.

Former Rams running back Lawrence McCutcheon: Chuck called everybody into his office those first couple of weeks, every player, and told them if they were good enough, they would play. We couldn't believe that.

I had just finished a tough rookie year on the inactive squad, and he told me, "You haven't had a chance before, but I'm going to give you one now. I don't care what anybody says. You've got the ball until you drop it."

I said, "Who, me?"

That season I gained 1,097 yards, the most of any Ram running back who came before me. My career was started, and all because Chuck Knox wouldn't listen to anyone but himself and the ability of his players.

The thing with McCutcheon was so simple, it was funny. Everybody was asking me where I would get somebody to run the football, and I just said, "What's wrong with right here?"

All I tried to do that first year was treat the players like men, and let the rest take care of itself. I thought about what Blanton Collier had said about the acceptance factor, and how it doesn't do any good to tell them two plus two is four if they believe it's five. You have to get them to believe *you*, and with that acceptance comes learning and respect.

Such belief is never easy to obtain, and after my first four preseason games with the Rams, it seemed all but impossible. Of those games, we lost three and tied one. This was what is known in the football business as disaster. I had brought in new people. New coaches. New clichés. I had been there for a month of games. And we had not even had a *moral* victory.

I went home the Saturday night after the fourth preseason game and told the coaches to meet me back at camp at one o'clock Sunday afternoon to return to the drawing board.

Former Rams lineman Merlin Olsen: It was so tough, so quickly, for Knox. The first newspaper story about our de-

> *fense, for example, was headlined, "Merlin Olsen and the
> 10 Question Marks." And then we go 0–3–1, and the
> newspapers are already tying the knot around Knox's neck.
> They're asking, "Who is this guy?" They question every-
> thing about him. We could all sense the pressure.*

At nine o'clock on the Sunday morning after we fell to 0–
3–1, the pressure officially hit. I was called at home by Don
Klosterman. He told me C. R. wanted me to meet him at his
house in Bel Air at eleven. Since that was far out of my way
to training camp, I would be late for the one o'clock coaches'
meeting. This meant I had to call the coaches and tell them.
But I didn't want to tell them. Assistant coaches can smell
the house burning before the match is ever struck. Once they
pick up that smell, they get on their survival suits. They start
thinking about where they will be working next, instead of
concentrating on their job at hand. You can't be insecure and
successfully coach at the same time.

The last thing I want to do is scare them into thinking I'm
getting fired, even though, quite honestly, that is what I am
thinking. So I fib. I tell them that C. R. and I are going to
discuss a trade, and that they should go ahead and start
breaking down the films without me.

I drive to C. R.'s and he invites me inside. A shrewd man,
C. R. He doesn't ask me what's wrong. He turns it around
and makes himself into the good guy, and me into the child.

He puts his arm around me and says in that deep voice of
his, "Chuuuck, what can I do to help you?"

Both of us knew darn well, about the only thing an owner
can do to help his team, other than increase the budget, is to
replace the coach. I knew where he was coming from. This
conversation had to change direction. And quick.

"C. R.," I tell him, "there's nothing wrong with what we're
doing. We're just going to have to do it better. We have to
stay the course. Just give me time."

For whatever reason, he believed me, and he sent me on

my way. Good thing, because I also believed me. Now I had to get the rest of the operation to believe.

I walked into the prepractice meeting that Sunday after meeting with C. R., and even though I had given the coaches an alibi, they knew something was wrong. And they were scared. They knew that some people above us in the organization were starting to wonder whether C. R. had made the right decision on me. They knew everyone was starting to doubt us.

I could tell from watching the players at meetings that they were uneasy, too. You could feel it. Even the equipment manager sensed something was wrong. I remember asking him for something and he gave me this sympathetic look like, "Here, I'll do anything I can for you because you aren't going to be around here very long."

I thought, I have to put an end to this. If we don't all have the same fine focus, we're never going to see our way out of this mess. So after that day's light workout I called a team meeting. I gave them what, looking back, was probably the lecture of my life. Probably because it had to be.

Merlin Olsen: I still remember what he said and what it took to say it. He stood in front of us and shouted, "OK, all of our well-wishers have turned to Doubting Thomases. Outside this locker room there are thousands of Doubting Thomases. The boat is empty; they have taken not only the life preservers but the oars. Even the rats have deserted us. The only people who will keep us afloat are the ones in this locker room. It's us against them. And we will not let them win. We will keep it afloat."

It was quite a speech, considering everybody knew that this guy's job had to be in jeopardy.

I told the team the only thing I could think of, the only thing that made any sense. I told them there wasn't anything wrong with what we were doing; we just needed to do it

better. I told them we *would* do it better. We *would* get the
job done. Even if we were the only ones who believed it.

I explained to them that while some of our practice drills
may have seemed unusual, we weren't just spinning our
wheels. I told them I understood how ballplayers could tell
when a coach was bullshitting them. I said I hoped they
understood I wasn't bullshitting.

Finally I told them, "Don't dare put the full accountability
for your performance on me. Don't dare say, well, there's been
a change of coaches so we're missing some intensity. Be a
man about your job and yourself. While our job is to prepare
you, your job is to execute. So don't blame us when things
go bad. There will be no alibi Ikes in here."

Whew.

Call it a pep talk, call it the drawing up of a covenant between an unsure team and its rookie coach. I don't know
whether the players listened to me, but we won the next two
preseason games. We won the opener at Kansas City. Then
in came the cocky Atlanta Falcons, and unwittingly I sealed
my part of that covenant.

> *Former Rams quarterback James Harris: We were get-*
> *ting ready to play the Atlanta Falcons, who had won big*
> *in their first week. Their coach, Norm Van Brocklin, had*
> *made a statement that he didn't know anything about*
> *this new Knox coach, never heard of him.*
>
> *We're quietly sitting around the locker room before this*
> *game when Knox comes in. He's wound up like a spring.*
> *"Look," he says, "this game doesn't need a show at half-*
> *time. Let's have it right now, a fistfight, me against Norm*
> *Van Brocklin at the fifty-yard line, man to man." This*
> *was a head coach talking. We were stunned. We beat the*
> *Falcons 31–0.*

After everything had settled down, I guess I had as wonderful a rookie season as could be. We won the next two after
the Falcons game, making four straight. Then into our home

rolled Dallas, with many of the same Cowboys who had won the Super Bowl two years earlier. We were still feeling our way. We felt outclassed. But we won. We defeated them 37 – 31 on four touchdown passes from John Hadl to Harold Jackson. It shocked the football world. Shocked me a little bit, too. I really wasn't sure how I would react in game situations as a head coach. A couple of series into the game, I found out.

Former Rams quarterback John Hadl: Early on, I noticed the Cowboys' defensive backs slinking off Harold Jackson. I get this crazy idea. I run over to the sidelines and ask Chuck about a play that would send Harold one-on-about-four, all alone deep in the Cowboys' secondary, with our only chance being that he outrun the defenders and that I outthrow them. We had never practiced the play. Barely even had it diagrammed. Reason being, it was a crazy play. It was a Hail Mary that shouldn't have had a prayer. But my gut instinct told me it could work.

Chuck thought for all of thirty seconds. "Do it," he said. We hit Harold for about a fifty-yard gain. On a thirty-second commitment.

Right then I learned I was willing to adjust maybe more than I thought I was. I learned that my survival instincts went with me right onto the field. Whatever it takes, whoever thinks of it—if it can work, do it.

On my teams there's never been exclusivity. If a ball boy diagrams a play on the dirt with his foot, and I happen to glance down and see that it might work, I'm using it. If it works, the ball boy is getting the credit. If it fails, I'm accepting the blame. I guess that's what some would call my management style. I call it coaching.

After that Dallas game we had a dinner party for the coaches and their wives. On the way home I told my wife, "Honey, this is working. I believe I can coach."

She smiled. "For the last nineteen years, isn't that what you've been trying to tell them?"

And the rest of that first season—I'll say it again—is history. Rams history. We went 12–2, the winningest team since the franchise began. The only games we lost were by one point to Minnesota and two points to Atlanta.

The boy from Sewickley was voted Coach of the Year. Great. But more important even that that, I think I established respect among my team. I could tell that when they started making comments about my hairdo.

Former Rams guard Tom Mack: Get him to talk about his hair. He only had one long tuft of hair left on his head. He comes to LA and decides to get it dyed and waxed and spread around so it looks like he has a whole head of hair. He walks into a meeting one day wearing these tailored clothes and that wild hair, and one of our running backs, Jim Bertleson, stands up and starts shouting, "Earl Scheib! Earl Scheib! The coach got his hair and clothes at Earl Scheib!" Chuck just smiled. In case you didn't know, Earl Scheib runs a chain of auto body and paint shops.

The only thing bad about the 1973 season was the way it ended. In Dallas. In the first round of the play-offs. The Cowboys beat us 27–16. But remember, everyone had been talking earlier like we never should have been there in the first place. In fact, I allowed my players to revel in that notion. I told them afterward, "You guys can look anybody in the eye, you played hard."

I know you're thinking, What does playing hard matter when you can't win the big game? You're thinking, How many times did Chuck Knox have to give those Los Angeles Rams that playing-hard speech? Let's get this over with now. In my five years there we won five division championships. In the regular season we won everything you could win. But I gave that speech, or some variation, all five years there because we ended every season by losing our most important game.

Three of those years, we lost an NFC championship one step from the Super Bowl. Surely, some sort of record. It's certainly become a permanent mark on my record. In life every man has a cross; in football every man has a rap. And in LA I gained mine: Chuck Knox can't win the big one. Chuck Knox can coach a team to the edge of greatness, but then they slip, and in grabbing for their leader, they all tumble backward. I hear that. Hear it all the time.

I don't listen—I don't think you should listen to anyone but yourself—but I'll face these comments. Sometimes only in facing others can you truly face yourself. I want to discuss my failures so everyone knows how I view failure. So everyone knows, at least for this man, how it can hurt. And I guess I especially want my old players to know that, as haunted as they may have been by the championship losses, in the years since, compared to me, they have slept like babies.

Tom Mack: Let's face it. I have to hold the record for the most play-off appearances without going to the Super Bowl.

Twelve games. I counted.

I think Chuck must hold the coaches' record. I hung in there with Chuck, but for three of five years, all of our Super Bowl plans for rings and money vanished at the last minute.

The bad thing about it was, we were physically beating teams in the play-offs, really beating up on Minnesota twice. Yet we could never get over the top. I retired when Chuck left, and what happened? Ray Malavasi comes in the next year, and two years later they go to the Super Bowl.

Like I said, a record. And yeah, it makes you mad. And it makes you wonder. Nobody would ever blame Chuck, but I still could never figure out what was wrong.

I am not sure there is an explanation. Losing those three championship games is certainly the one thing I cannot explain, even in the manner which I normally use to explain things—even through Knoxisms.

That word "Knoxisms" is somebody else's. I've just always thought of them as my little messages. They are derived from my experiences, mostly from the streets, and are used to simplify an ideal or value. I didn't so much begin using them as they began using me, spilling out of my mouth when I was trying to make a point. Like my western Pennsylvania dialect, they came naturally. Although they have since become a staple of my management style—one of my assistants once collected a list of 248—I first tried them out on my first Rams team. If they had laughed and not listened, I never would have used them again. Some of them laughed. But it turned out most of them listened.

> *Merlin Olsen: At the time, we called them little homilies. All these little sayings. Some players would write them in their playbooks, and then every time Chuck repeated them, they would put check marks next to them. At last count, the most-used Knoxism was "The faint heart never won the fair lady." But through all the jokes and homilies, Chuck was the first coach I had who would look me in the eye and relate to me with gut-level instincts. It was like, "If you don't like it, come to my office and we'll talk about it. If you still don't like it, let's go out back and settle it."*

You've read some of the homilies earlier in this book. You will read some new ones later. One of my favorite ones I pulled on the Rams that year was that old Italian proverb "He who lives in hope, dies in crap." That means if you want something, you can't sit and wait. You have to go out and work. Work will win; wishing won't. And I would tell them, watch your six P's—proper preparation prevents piss-poor performance. Mistakes are usually made in games by players who do not prepare properly during the week. And I don't know how many times I told them, "There is no guy in a red suit with a white beard down to his belly button who will give you something for nothing—either on the football field or in life. If you want something, you have to go earn it."

Steve Preece: Chuck was always saying the same things, so much that we knew what was coming.

Of course I repeat myself. I will repeat myself in this book. It will be on purpose. My little sayings, any little sayings, are effective only through spaced repetition. It's like, if you throw enough mud, some of it will stick. If you tell somebody something over and over—Play the hand you're dealt, play the hand you're dealt—soon it will become internalized. Soon your players will not only be thinking like that, but talking like that. Listen to my players after games, even today. If they sound like me, it's because they are supposed to.

The players listened to me that first year and, I hope, respected me. And not because I gave them every damn thing they wanted, or told them only what they wanted to hear. It was a matter of letting them know I would do everything possible to let them worry about just one thing—kicking butt.

It was in LA that first year that I formed an executive committee, something I have kept ever since. I won't announce the members' names to the public, or even tell the press such a thing exists, but I'll take five or six of our team leaders and appoint them to an advisory board.

Once a week I'll bring them upstairs to my office to discuss how things are being done. It's not a gripe or complaint session—I tell them that right off. But we'll discuss things like what kind of food they want on the plane, why I made this certain deal, why our practice schedule is changing, why we are running certain plays. I will listen to their opinions and explain my various points of view in the hope that, through the committee, the rest of the team will feel like they have a say, and feel like they know what the hell is going on.

Of course, not all things could be solved by the executive committee.

That first year, Merlin Olsen informed one of my rookie coaches, Jim Wagstaff, that when he stepped onto the players' floor at training camp, or went through our hotel for bed checks, the rule was that he had to yell, "Coach in the hall, coach in the hall." Wagstaff, who didn't know any better, followed this so-called rule and took to shouting "Coach in the hall," giving the players plenty of time to stop their shenanigans. Finally somebody told him there was no such rule.

But I never reprimanded Olsen for making it up. Darn good idea, if you ask me.

My second season, 1974, begins, and we win three of our first five games. This would be fine for most teams, but it meant that we had already lost as many games as in all of 1973. And in the public's and management's eyes, that meant trouble.

At the same time, Coach Dan Devine of Green Bay calls. He sounds as desperate as I'm starting to feel. He says he needs a quarterback. Bad. He needs our MVP, John Hadl.

You laughing? Me too.

But I talk to Devine because I also understand desperation. I understand what it can make a man do. I say, Fine, Dan. You want John Hadl, you give us two first-round draft picks, two second-round picks, and a third-round pick. In other words, give us the immediate future of your franchise, and ensure the immediate future of our franchise.

In football terms, I was making an outlandish request. In street terms, a predictable one. I had something Devine badly needed. I knew this because he told me so. The more somebody wants something, the more he will pay. Thus, if what he wants belongs to you, the more you should ask. Eighth-grade Sewickley.

So we make this unbelievable trade. It's so unbelievable, we keep the terms of the deal hush-hush. Well, we try to keep everything hush-hush. But it's so unbelievable that our administration can't keep their mouths shut and they leak the particulars to the press. Suddenly all these draft choices are being written up in the newspapers, and the deal is being called the NFL rape of all time.

Hadl sees this and thinks, Hey, if Green Bay is willing to give up that much for me, then they better pay me for it. So he says he won't report until he can get a huge raise.

Now C. R. calls me from New York and wants to know whether I will take John Hadl back. I tell him a deal is a deal. So we end up throwing a bunch of money at Green Bay to help pay for a new Hadl contract. Ah, what pride and ego can cost people who can't keep their mouths shut.

But now for the bottom line of this whole story: this is how my Rams quarterback came to be James Harris. You may remember Harris. If you followed the Doug Williams stories surrounding the 1988 Super Bowl, you certainly have heard of James Harris. He was the NFL's first black regular quarterback, which didn't mean a thing to me. However, he was the first quarterback that I developed, which did.

James Harris: Usually, if you've been around the game long enough, like I had been, for four years before that 1974 season, you can see things coming. But I never saw this John Hadl thing. I was shocked. I never had any idea. Knox comes in one day and tells me I'm the starter and I think, Does he know what he's doing? Remember, although I was the backup quarterback, I am black. I had just spent three years with the Buffalo Bills, where it didn't pay to be black. In Buffalo, when you passed the white players—your own teammates—in the shopping mall, they wouldn't even look at you.

It was obvious from his first day with the Rams, Chuck Knox was color-blind. But to make me the starter, in that day and age, he was being color-foolish.

I really liked James Harris. It was obvious he had the ability and had never gotten the chance. And look, the stats proved me right. Harris took over in game six of 1974 against San Francisco and led us to a 37 – 14 win, the start of a four-game winning streak. Overall he took us to seven wins in our last nine games. We finished the season 10 – 4, and James Harris led everybody in quarterback statistics.

As we entered the play-offs that season, things were going smoothly. We're rolling. And it looks like James Harris is going to be our quarterback for a long time.

Or at least until the 1974 NFC championship game. It's in Minnesota. We're down 14 – 10 late in the game, when we move the ball deep into Viking territory. It's second and goal from the six-inch line. I call a quarterback sneak. Harris is big enough to get in by just falling over the goal. Minnesota veteran defensive lineman Alan Page anticipates this and jumps offside. He knows that if he is caught, big deal; it will just halve the distance to the goal, which in this case is six inches. Good veteran maneuver. The line judge sees him and throws a flag.

But the umpire, who also throws a flag, doesn't see it that way. The umpire gets to the referee first and says that guard Tom Mack, who lined up opposite Page, has moved and drawn Page offsides.

By that time the line judge gets to the ref, hears their conversation, and doesn't want to cause any waves. So he goes along with it, and we get pushed back five yards with a call that changed the face of that year's Super Bowl. To this day, the worst big-game call in my experience.

They say that officiating evens itself out. Bull. What are the chances of getting the same officials even twice in a season, much less every week? None. And what if that official's call cost a coach his job? Even itself out? Life doesn't even itself out, why should officiating?

Now we're back at the five-yard, six-inch line. We run John Cappelletti a couple of yards, and then try a surprise pass. The ball is tipped, then intercepted, and the ball game is blown.

> *Tom Mack: I come running off the field after that bad possession and Chuck is screaming, "What the hell did you do? What the hell did you do?" I scream back, "I didn't do anything, and I bet you the game check I didn't do anything!"*
>
> *And as Chuck and I later find out on film, I was right. To this day, he owes me a five-thousand-dollar game check.*

This game, my first of those three big-game losses with the Rams, did teach me one thing. Losses can't be treated like wins that didn't happen. Losses must be treated differently, or they won't do you any good. They must be accompanied by soul-searching, self-appraisal, looking at the man in the mirror. Losses must make every individual think, How could I have done better? Only then will losses be worth something.

It was after this loss that I started a postgame practice I sometimes use today.

> *Former Rams lineman Phil Olsen: I remember after the games, Chuck would stand by the locker-room door, waiting for everyone to come through. He would stare into everyone's eyes, one guy at a time. If you had done everything you could do, it was like a touching of the souls. If you hadn't, you could barely get through the door.*

I have put that Minnesota loss behind me, but it's one of those things that you still see, that I'll always see. Over and over, Tom Mack has not moved. Damn it.

And what that loss did to James Harris . . . instead of blaming the referee, or even Mack, the fans and some media had the audacity to blame *him* for that call. Blamed it on what they thought was his sometimes offbeat signal cadence. Said it was Harris who drew Mack offsides. Can you imagine that? Maybe by then fans had realized that James Harris really was our starting quarterback, and was going to be our starting quarterback until he lost the job. Since they didn't like him, they had to find something against him. And that's how it started.

I hate to call it racism. I firmly believe that except for a few isolated pockets, our society has risen above that. But what do you call it when a coach like myself gets threatening letters filled with racial slurs about his quarterback? What do you call it when the coach gets *dozens* of letters like that? During the 1975–1978 seasons, I received them almost every day. And how about Harris himself? I thought I had it bad. He received a ton of nasty mail addressed to both of us through my office, much of which I never let get to him.

> *James Harris: Those were supposed to be the happiest times of my life, but looking back, I don't know how I got through them. He said he held my mail? He sure didn't hold all of it. I would get terrible letters on a regular basis. I remember one letter contained a drawing of me and Knox in a toilet, being flushed down together. I would get two or three letters like that a day.*
>
> *Then came the longest night of my life, in the Beverly Hills Hilton Hotel before one of our home games. Somebody called me and said that if I went out on the field that day, something bad would happen to me. Of course, I didn't tell anybody. If I told somebody, that might mean I didn't play. And if I got benched once, it might be forever. So I kept my mouth shut.*
>
> *I got on the field and finally told the story to Ron Jaworski, my backup. Then I kept my head down the rest of the game. Nothing happened, but I guess just getting the threat was something, wasn't it?*

James Harris's life was threatened? He never told me, but I'm not surprised. What does surprise me is why he just told Jaws. And why did he tell him on the field, during the game? A lot of good Jaws could have done.

Harris came out and had a great year in 1975, leading us to that 12–2 record, but our critics thought that anybody could have led the club to a 12–2 record. The only ammunition anybody had to nail James Harris with that year came later when—well, sit back for another big flop.

Harris hurt his shoulder and was forced to miss our first play-off game. We give the ball to Jaworski, and he leads us to a 35–23 win over Saint Louis and into the conference championship. So Jaws is now the hot hand. And the week of the championship game, nobody wants to talk about anybody else. By virtue of his play against Saint Louis, he had surely earned a start against the Cowboys. But James Harris is looking better and feeling better. And by virtue of his play *all season long*, Harris is more worthy of the start.

I don't go by one game; I don't go by a flash; I go by durability, longevity, history. Flashes may appear better, but history inevitably works better. It's the same thing I've done my whole coaching career, and just because this Dallas game was a little bigger than some of the others, I wasn't about to change it. You change something like that, you change yourself, and then if it fails, you don't know who to blame.

So Harris started. And history failed. Miserably. We got smashed, 37–7. Harris started slow and was hurting, and once our defense let up early, he could never get us back.

It failed. I failed.

Afterward you could hardly see me for all the fingers. The media and fans and fate pointing at me. I've rarely felt worse. But did I make a mistake starting Harris? No. Did I feel like I'd just eaten seven different varieties of crow? No. I've got news for those newspapers, the same thing I told my team: Harris didn't play defense, Harris didn't block, Harris didn't play special teams. This game was lost far outside the field of James Harris's influence. We couldn't stop them, and if you can't stop somebody, you have no chance. It doesn't make any difference who your quarterback is.

I made the decision and could live with myself. Loyalty

wouldn't mean so much if it didn't come so hard. Who knows if Harris could have led us so well during the regular season if he hadn't known I was behind him all the way?

If I live by somebody, damn right I'll die by him. I know this sounds like rah-rah bullshit, but loyalty will make a man more remembered than any win. Sometimes that feeling has cost me, but in the long run I've been repaid many time over.

> *Steve Preece: I know we never went to the Super Bowl, but when a lot of us think about the things Knox did for us, sometimes it doesn't matter. After I had played four years for Chuck in LA, I came into the option year of my contract. At the time, I was sitting the bench. I decided all I wanted to do was to finish my career near my home-town of Portland, meaning, I wanted to finish with the Seattle Seahawks. Under normal circumstances, that would have been impossible. The Seahawks would never have picked me up, because that option year was too expensive for a part-time player. So I was stuck. But Chuck called me in one day and said, "You've played hard here. You want to go home? Go home. We're giving you your re-lease. Your contract is void. The Seahawks can pick you up for next to nothing."*
>
> *When you see Knox, tell him I've never forgotten that.*

Not that loyalty doesn't hurt. At the time, I thought all the critics were picking on me for playing James Harris. I later find out they were turning on both of us. I find this out quick. Like, that off-season.

In the winter after the 1975 season we picked up Pat Haden, local guy, USC Rhodes Scholar, dearly loved by all. For what-ever reason, James Harris was in trouble. And there wasn't anything I could do about it. To this day, I swear, nothing was ever said directly to me. C. R. never ordered me to bench Harris. It was never on a billboard or in blazing lights or any-thing. But it didn't have to be.

It started innocently enough the winter we acquired Haden. C. R. invited Shirley and me to one of his infamous dinner parties at his house in Bel Air. I forget the names of all the celebrities who were present that night—I think maybe Jonathan Winters and Ricardo Montalban were there—but I do remember what happened after dinner.

We all gathered in C. R.'s living room. With this spark in his eye he said, "Let's play a game. Let's vote on who we want for President this year, and then, just for fun, we'll vote on who we want for Rams quarterback. No big deal, fans play these games all the time."

So he passed around these little pieces of paper and everybody voted. I don't remember who won for President. But in the quarterback race, Shirley and I were the only ones to vote for James Harris.

I went home that night, looked in the mirror, and realized James Harris was in trouble.

It continued into the next training camp, when C. R. would come down at practice and say, "Hey, Haden looked good today, didn't he?" and "You know, maybe we'll need to make a change here one of these days, huh?"

You could hear things, feel things. I fought through it at first. I started that 1976 season with Harris, and in our first eight games he leads us to a 6–1–1 record. But then he loses in a bad one to Cincinnati, 20–12, and I'm hearing the talk again. It's getting louder and louder.

James Harris: I remember playing poorly in the Cincinnati game in 1976 because I had bruised my thumb knocking it off somebody's helmet. But I thought I could play the next week. Then on Thursday before the game, Chuck called me over. He told me that he had all the confidence in the world in me, and that I was his quarterback, and that I could still be one of the best in the league. But he said he was going to have to play Haden. Said it was out of his hands, and that was that. For the last six games of the 1976 season, I was benched.

Yeah, I told him that. It sounds like it came from somebody else, but that was me. To this day I think James Harris
could have been one of the NFL's all-time great quarter-
backs. But sometimes it just doesn't happen. As big as you
are, sometimes it's never big enough.

> *James Harris: Mentally, it ruined me. I couldn't handle
> it. As a quarterback I had done all I could, more than
> most people could, and it still wasn't enough for the Los
> Angeles Rams to accept me just as a quarterback, not a
> black quarterback.*
>
> *The beginning of the next year, I was traded to San Diego.
> Chuck called me and told me again that it wasn't his de-
> cision. After that I was never the same. The motivation
> was no longer there. Like I said, it ruined me.*

I was being torn smack down the middle. I wasn't secure
enough to fight my owner. I had not been around long enough.
The problem was, C. R. flat thought his judgment was better than anyone else's judgment, period. Most of the time I
would agree, fine, no problem. Then I would go out and do
what I thought gave us the best chance to win. But some
times just giving him lip service was impossible. Sometimes
I had no choice but to follow him step by step down a road I
thought could lead to ruin. I look back on it now sometimes
and shudder, but there's no regretting what you had no choice
about. You must move on. Life must move on. I just told
myself I was going to coach my butt off and get secure so I
didn't have to put up with compromising myself again.
I was mostly disappointed because of what I felt—and had
not expected to feel—from the Rams organization. I could
handle the open nastiness coming from the fans, but not the
subtle nastiness from the ownership. I'm not saying C. R.
was a racist; he was not. He was just the type of owner who
would always make suggestions about whom to play. He did
the same thing when he owned the Baltimore Colts. Race or

religion didn't matter to him, only winning, and winning in show-biz fashion.

Then C. R. came out and told the media that the James Harris benching was totally my decision. How totally untrue.

About the only positive thing in all this was, my team believed me. We fought through it.

I never really verbalized any of these problems to anyone, not even Shirley, until after I resigned from the Rams following the 1977 season. Then it so happened I had occasion to talk to a man who was interested in the vacancy. It was the Grambling coach Eddie Robinson, a black man who had coached Harris. I called him and told him, "Come out here, interview with C. R.; you're a street guy, you'll know whether he's being sincere about hiring you. Right away, you'll know the score." He knew what I meant. This was my way of getting the word out.

The middle of the 1976 season marked the beginning of Pat Haden's career as the Rams leader, the end of James Harris's, and for an increasingly frustrated coach it was both—the beginning of the end.

Pat Haden started the last five games of 1976, going 4–1 to help us finish our regular season at 10–3–1. We win the first play-off game in Dallas, and we're back in Minnesota for another try at the Super Bowl. I'm thinking, *Now* is the time.

It was the time, all right. Time for our third big-game flop.

During the heat of this championship game, on third-and-two from the Viking two-yard line, we ran a reverse with Ron Jessie. He dove and landed in the end zone, but the officials say he bounced first. So we don't score, and stopped inside their five-yard line on third down, we wind up going for a field goal. The kick is blocked, Minnesota's Bobby Bryant picks it up and runs ninety-nine yards for a touchdown, and we lose again, this time 24–13.

And now everybody is asking, How come you didn't go for the touchdown? I answer, How was I supposed to know the kick would be blocked? How did I know that a little mistake would occur? I went for the field goal because earlier that year in Minnesota, we went for a touchdown on fourth-and-one from the *one-yard line* and did not make it. You go for a touchdown, any number of things can happen—fumbles, interceptions, anything. Football not being an exact science, a field goal is about as exact as it gets. Either you make it or you miss it, period.

Like I've said before, I live a lot by history. I lived by it that day and it cost me. And it hurt. I was getting tired of being second-guessed. I was getting tired of having no answers. By this championship game, the criticism was coming down on me like bits of hail.

What hurt the most, though, was that after our third championship loss I knew my players were having some of the same doubts as everyone else.

> *Merlin Olsen: If making it to the Super Bowl is the only measure of a man's career, that's sad. If that is the only method by which Chuck is judged, that's criminal. But I'll tell you what we thought he did back then, and what some people say he does now. He considered it his first responsibility just to get our floundering team to respectability. He put in a risk-free offense designed not necessarily to win, but to not lose. This worked fine until play-off time, when we faced teams as good or better than us.*
>
> *He wasn't willing to take the chances you have to take to beat teams like that. Therefore, we couldn't get what we needed to win the big ones. In big games, our risk-free offense turned on us.*

I offer no apologies. Considering what I took over in LA, that philosophy only made sense. I had to teach some of these young guys to go to war with themselves before they could go to war with others. We had to worry about ourselves first. Without that confidence, we never would have advanced to any championship game in the first place. And I can guarantee one thing: those guys were a lot happier losing in the NFC finals with me than never playing past Christmas with other coaches.

And I do feel the players were happy then. I was even able to throw annual Christmas parties and give out gag gifts, something I don't do anymore because players make too much money to come to Christmas parties. I liked our parties because somebody would always make fun of my hair by giving me an Afro wig. Whatever hair I had, the more we won, the more unafraid I was to let it down.

Tom Mack: After one Pro Bowl game in Tampa, all of the Rams were out drinking and hell-raising. We got back to the hotel at one o'clock in the morning and called Chuck and the other coaches and their wives. They were all in bed, but they all got up. We met in somebody's suite and partied all night. No matter what any critic may say, I'll go to war with Chuck anytime. You win the war and it's a blast.

If they would go to war for me, I feel it was because I was not afraid to treat them like real people. That's what this game is. It's just plain people, real faces that sometimes get dirty and don't always come clean.

It's guys like tackle Doug France, a 1975 first-round Rams draft pick from Ohio State. He was a big, nice, innocent kid who came to LA and got completely lost. Shirley heard about him and suggested we help. Before I could comprehend what she meant, she was allowing Doug's wife to use our washer and dryer, she was baby-sitting for them, and I was counseling him in my office when I wasn't trying to head-butt some meanness into him on the field. He turned out to be a pretty good player, but more than that, he served as an example of what I might expect in the way of players' personal problems. He served as an example of how, try as I might, something in me can easily drop all pretense of coach and slip back into daddy.

Some of my players have had domestic quarrels that have turned into police reports. At the request of the players and the cops, I have gone to their houses to help. It's eighth-grade Sewickley. Your neighbor down on Walnut Street throws out his wife, you take her in for a few days.

Bill collectors have called and asked me to pressure certain players. I will not. I tell them I am not in the collection business. It's not my duty or responsibility. I have enough trouble pressuring the guys into pressuring the opponents.

Judges will call me and tell me they are going to throw one of my players in the slammer for thirty days following the season for missing child-support checks. I tell them jail is fine; missing child-support is one of the most gutless things a man can do. But I ask them, Why not put the guy on work release, maybe spending weekends in jail, so he can earn the money to pay the support checks? Usually, judges will agree.

I don't do anything for my players that the common man wouldn't do for his neighbor. I don't like people making a big deal out of it, especially the players I help.

Well, OK, in LA and Buffalo, there *was* one player who maybe brought out the uncommon in me. As in, the uncommonly stupid in me. Because of this player, I am no longer such an easy mark for troubled minds. His name was Isiah Robertson. He was called "Butch." He was a linebacker. And he was a handful.

> *Former Rams linebacker Isiah "Butch" Robertson: I recently celebrated my thirty-eighth birthday. I think if it wasn't for Chuck Knox, I wouldn't have made my twenty-eighth. No other coach could have coached me. Believe me, some others tried."*

My Butchie? Trouble?
Understatement.

Butch was an example of how, as hard as I coach them, a lot of times I flat-out don't reach them. Let me tell you about one lovely Christmas Eve in Los Angeles. For some reason Butch was eating at a restaurant this night, eating clam chowder. Bad chowder. It had a bug in it. He wouldn't pay for it.

The waitress told him he had already taken a couple of bites, he had to pay. Poor waitress. You don't tell a guy like Butch that he has to do anything. Even I knew that. He poured the chowder over the cash register, and then went outside and threw a brick through the window.

Have you ever received a phone call from a troubled employee who is in jail on Christmas Eve? Shirley loved this one. I was still young and dumb then. I went down and bailed him out, the first of several times.

> *Isiah "Butch" Robertson: Cops would always want to talk to Chuck alone. He would always say, "No way. My player and I win together and lose together, and anything you say to me, you can say to him."*
>
> *We'd get it all worked out and he would grab me and say, "Butch, let's get the hell out of here." And that would be it.*

How I tried to reach Butch. I would sit him down—I had this one special chair in my office just for him—and he would sit there looking like an angel, very apologetic. Then he would leave my office, and two weeks later he'd be back in that special chair. I'm sure he meant well, but the road to hell is paved with good intentions. I later traded for him when I went to Buffalo because I thought he had matured and learned his lesson. Once there, he gets into a bar fight and bites off a piece of teammate Jim Haslett's finger.

Oh well. I'm not Super Coach. I got where I am by being just another man. That's something I remember now when problem players come into my life. People say I've always been so good with them—Winston Hill once said I make men out of rogues. But really it all comes down to what a man wants to make of himself. I've learned that I'm just there to hold the compass.

Obviously, hindsight being what it is, I might have done some things differently. I knew after a few seasons in LA that nothing would be easy. As it turned out, the criticism of my big-game offense and Butch Robertson's police reports were to be the least of my Rams worries. By the end of my fourth year, the pressure from C. R. was starting to get to me.

The best way to describe how I felt would be to describe how Weeb Ewbank used to feel. Weeb told me that one morning when he was coaching the Colts—owned by C. R. at the time—he got up, went into the bathroom, shaved, came out, got dressed for work, and then went into the bathroom and shaved again.

Now that's feeling pressure.

Here's how much C. R. wanted to win. Just before our first play-off game in the 1974 season—in Washington, against the Redskins—C. R. had a heart attack. We won the game 19–10. Afterward there was a big argument in the locker room over who should take him the game ball. His son Steve, Don Klosterman, Jack Teele, all were fighting. I was the compromise guy—I was always the compromise guy in LA— so Shirley and I took him the ball. We get to the hospital and the first thing C. R. says, all hooked up to machines and stuff, is, "Hey, it was worth it."

I look at him.

"*What* was worth it?" I ask.

"The heart attack," he says. "If my having a heart attack helped us win this game, then it was worth it."

I nearly had my own heart attack. He meant it, he believed it. There will never be a football man with more dedication and desire.

Problem was, he believed a team could only win *his* way. He believed this even when he had Weeb Ewbank in Baltimore. In 1963, three seasons after Weeb led the Colts to two straight NFL titles, he was gone. C. R. then hired Don Shula, who like Ewbank became a great coach there. But seven seasons later, in 1970, shortly after leading the Colts to the most infamous loss in Super Bowl history, that beating by the AFL's New York Jets, Shula hightailed it to Miami just before C. R. could fire him. Tough boss, C. R. If he didn't trust anything but his own judgment in Baltimore, my rookie judgment in LA didn't stand a chance.

During my five seasons with the Rams, every Thursday was "Heads Up Day." Not because of any special drills or anything, but because at any time, dropping from the sky would be C. R. He flew over every Thursday in a helicopter, landing the damn thing on the field, getting out, and sitting on the sidelines in a director's chair with his name on it.

Afterward we would meet. At first, when he expected us to struggle, he would talk only about team play and nice things like that. But the more we won, the more he became engrossed with *how* we won. He would talk about throwing the ball down the field more, showing more flash, pasting on more glitz. In particular, he hated it when I ordered the quarterback to fall on the ball at the end of the half. Now, I've seen coaches lose their jobs because a last-second handoff was fumbled and run back for a touchdown. Didn't matter to C. R. He said he wanted our quarterback to throw the ball deep, whether we needed to or not, and regardless of the risk.

"If he just falls down, the crowd will boo," explained C. R. "But if he throws it deep, those boos will turn to ooohs."

I thought, Welcome to Hollywood. At times I thought, Welcome to hell.

Shirley Knox: I think the whole LA scene just really wore on us. And the pressure, not only to win, but to look good. Once in late 1976 I wanted to have a Christmas party at the same time a boat parade would be passing by our house, which was on the waterfront in Huntington Har-

> bor. *Problem was, it was on the day of a regular season game.*
>
> *Chuck told me he could be no part of the party; he was washing his hands of it because he couldn't stand partying if the Rams didn't win, or didn't win big. Said he might not even come home. I said fine, I'll do it. I invited a hundred people. I set up valet parking, outdoor heaters— the works. Then I went to the game and sweated, really sweated.*
>
> *A happy ending. We win 59–0, Chuck is the hero again, and the party is the greatest.*

Although I had to play along, I don't think C. R. realized that this game only went Hollywood on Sundays.

> *Ken Meyer: C. R. wasn't around much, but with his big voice and his power, it seemed like he was everywhere. Chuck loved to have these hamburger buffets on Saturday nights before the game, a kind of team-as-family type thing, where the players relaxed and mingled. C. R. was always at those with his movie-star friends, pumping hands with players and pushing Chuck to the background.*
>
> *Chuck knew going in that it would be tough coaching for C. R. The man did have a reputation. And there were times Chuck felt like he couldn't take it anymore. But remember, there are only twenty-eight of those jobs. A man will do a lot of things to get one, and even more things to keep one.*

An example: One day in the middle of the 1976 season, C. R. is shocked by something he sees in a TV game. The Washington Redskins are playing the New York Giants. The Redskins make a field goal, but the Giants are called for roughing the kicker; so Redskins coach George Allen decides to take three points off the board and go for the touchdown.

His team fumbles, the Giants recover, and the Redskins lose the game by the exact three points of that field goal.

This so unsettles C. R., he takes me aside the following Thursday and decides to teach me a little football. Tells me, never go against that old maxim, never take points off the board, look how stupid George Allen was.

A couple of weeks later we're playing Dallas in the first round of the 1976 play-offs. We're down 10–7. We line up to kick a field goal, the kick is good . . . but the Cowboys are penalized for roughing our kicker.

Understand that by now I've just about had it with C. R.'s overbearing direction. I've taken so much in four years, I'm having trouble swallowing.

So what do I do? I take the three points off the board, regain possession of the ball, and go for the touchdown. I know C. R. must be feeling faint, but I do it anyway. And what happens? We score the touchdown to go up 14–10 and win.

I felt like dancing.

After the game I get C. R. and Don Klosterman aside and say, "OK, tell me the truth, when I took those three points off, what were you saying?"

Here C. R. smiles and says, "Don was saying you should go by the old maxim and keep the points. I tried to tell him, throw the old maxim out the window, play this game to win. I told him you were doing the right thing."

Klosterman just looks at me like, *You're not going to believe that baloney, are you?*

Of course not. But I kept my mouth shut because I knew C. R. was unafraid to wield power.

I remember when Shula left Baltimore in 1970. It happened while his owner, C. R., was out of the country. Bad timing. C. R. was so mad when he came back, he coerced the NFL into giving him a first-round draft pick from the Dolphins as recompense for tampering.

I saw this power again in 1976, in one of the strangest games I've been associated with. We're heading down to play Miami in a game that's scheduled for the Jewish holiday Yom Kippur. The game is being played at a time that, according to Jewish law, is supposed to be devoted to worship. It's happened before, and actually it happens all the time.

But C. R. was mad at the league office about some other things and decides this would be a good way to pay them back for his anger. Out of nowhere he raises all kinds of hell with Commissioner Pete Rozelle about not honoring a Jewish religious event. It makes the national newspapers, and Rozelle gets to feeling very uncomfortable and intimidated. C. R. has made his point.

Of course, we play the game anyway, and after being down 21 – 7, James Harris throws for more than five hundred yards and we come back and win 31 – 28.

Afterward C. R. is right there and, in a big show in the locker room, kisses Harris on the cheek and says, "Great job, from one member of a minority to another."

Five games later Harris is benched.

I think what contributed to my leaving LA as much as anything was that I was caught in a lifestyle with C. R. that made me realize, hey, this was definitely *not* eighth-grade Sewickley. Everything had to be show biz, from the long passes at the end of the first half to the Friday night appearances in Bel Air.

I'm not show biz. I'm not anything, really, but a western Pennsylvania football coach. The LA experience made me realize this.

After that 1976 season, I was emotionally finished. With C. R., with the Rams, with the whole southern California mess. Then I heard that Lions owner Bill Ford might be looking for a new coach, and even though I had one year left on my contract, I remembered C. R. always telling me, anytime I wasn't happy I was free to go.

I walk into his office and tell him I'm not happy. He stares at me. He says, "There are ways to make you happy."

I tell him he doesn't understand me or where I'm from. I

tell him my kind of happiness can't be found in his kind of ways.

So he agrees to talk to the Lions owner about giving permission for me to talk to him. Ford and my old "buddy" Russ Thomas fly out to Los Angeles and they all sit down. C. R. tells them they can have me—but on one small condition. He wants to give them a list of his fourteen most coveted Lions. In exchange for my contract, the Lions must give the Rams seven of those players.

Now, who in the hell would make a deal like that? I would never make a deal like that, and if Bill Ford had made a deal like that, I would have considered him such a poor owner that I wouldn't have wanted to coach for him in the first place.

So C. R. had made it impossible for the Lions to talk to me.

I was upset. C. R. had told me I was free to leave anytime, yet he wouldn't let me leave. I went home, lay in bed, turned out the lights, and decided to myself and no one else that 1977 would be my last season with the Los Angeles Rams.

Former Ram and Seahawk tight end Charle Young: C. R. flat-out punished Chuck by not letting him go to Detroit. We all saw it. And we all saw how that last year Chuck was trying to keep his sanity and survive. We all knew 1977 would be it.

That last season actually wasn't any big deal until, guess what, we finally get Minnesota on our turf in a first-round play-off game and blow it. Again.

It rains like hell, mud everywhere, the field is ruined— which suits Minnesota just fine because they are missing their injured scrambling quarterback Fran Tarkenton. We lose 14– 7 and don't even make it to a conference championship. All around me, I can feel it crumbling.

> *Tom Mack: After that last play-off game, he comes up to me and says, "What am I going to do? I win five division titles and I'm not exciting enough! Tom, what am I going to do?"*
>
> *We knew then, either they were going to fire him or he was going to quit. We hoped for his sake he would quit.*

Behind my back, I could hear C. R. talking.

Talking about how I bored the fans. Whispering about how, in this entertainment capital of the world, his football coach wasn't doing much entertaining.

I hear it, but I don't see it, because by then C. R. never says anything directly to me, just stares right through me like I'm an old dollar bill. But I listen from behind the doors that are closing around me, and I hear it.

I hear it and decide, finally, Carroll Rosenbloom should stick it. We're 10−4 and I feel like I've had a terrible year, and damn it, I don't want to coach where 10−4 is a terrible year.

A couple of weeks after the season, I sign a new five-year contract because my old one is up and neither of us wants to get left in the lurch. But both C. R. and I know it is paper only.

Relations are strained, and I realize my decision to make 1977 my last year there was a sound one. Now I just have to find a way out before I'm thrown out. I wasn't going to let them fire me. I wasn't going to let C. R. tarnish five division championships in five years because they weren't Hollywood, because they were eighth-grade Sewickley. Somehow I was going to find those twenty-three steps.

The final days of 1977, my life came down to a simple Q and A.

Was C. R. planning to fire me? You bet.

Was I going to give him the satisfaction? No way in hell.

Where would I go? Anywhere. Siberia. Buffalo.

7

Buffalo

Late December 1977. I'm sitting at home, and it's a brown, brown Christmas. I smile though I'm not happy. My family smiles, though sometimes they hate me for letting football ruin their favorite holiday. The tree is half dead. I'm half crazy. I'm spending half of my time gazing out the window, looking up at the sky as if another NFL head coach's job—anyplace but here in Los Angeles—would hit my backyard on the fly.

It's funny I should wish for something like that now, when I never much wished for anything as a kid. I never looked to the sky for anything, never hoped for any miracles, nothing. There was no luck, only work. But I guess the longer you work, the more all of your accomplishments come as a direct result of work . . . the more you come to expect a little luck. Please?

I get this phone call. It's from Melvin Durslag, sports columnist for the Los Angeles *Herald Examiner*. Darn.

"Sorry, Melvin," I say, "but I'm pretty much finished answering questions about the season, and I'm not sure I'll be the one giving answers next year, and besides—"

"Chuck, Chuck," Melvin interrupts, "this call is not for me; it's for you. I got somebody I'd like you to meet." That somebody was a Detroit businessman named Ralph Wilson. Within a month of that phone call, because of the phone call,

I would leave LA. But it was to be via the underground railroad. And it was to Siberia.

> *Sports columnist Melvin Durslag: We all knew Chuck was about to be let out by Carroll, who said his offense was putting this town to sleep. Entertainment capital of the word, Carroll said, and Chuck is making them yawn. Chuck was a goner.*
>
> *Well, I am pretty good friends with Ralph Wilson, the owner of the Buffalo Bills; and while Ralph and I were talking one day, the subject of coaches came up. He had just fired Jim Ringo and was looking for another one. His team had won only five games in the previous two years, and he needed a guy who could completely reconstruct. I told him, "Hey, this may sound like a long shot, but I think you can get Chuck Knox."*
>
> *He tells me, "No, I can't."*
>
> *I say, "Why not?"*
>
> *He says, "Because to get Chuck, I first have to get permission to talk to him from Carroll Rosenbloom. And me and Rosenbloom aren't talking."*

Get a load of that. My big chance to get away from C. R. almost ruined—once again, by C. R.

> *Melvin Durslag: The reason the two owners weren't speaking had something to do with Carroll trying to steal O. J. Simpson from the Bills. I tell Ralph, "This is silly, Knox is a damn good coach, you want me to talk to Carroll for you?"*
>
> *Ralph says, "Would you, please?"*
>
> *I call Carroll and he says fine, if Ralph calls, he'll talk to him. So I call Ralph. And Ralph calls Carroll and gets permission.*
>
> *Then I call Chuck to tell him what's happening. I tell him what a good owner Ralph is, and how he doesn't*

meddle with his coaches and—Chuck stops me in mid-sentence.

"How soon can we meet?" he says.

All I remember, of that first phone call from Durslag are the words "head coach." I remember something about Buffalo, but I didn't think of it as a city or anything. All I saw was that vacant head coach's office, big and bright, falling out of the sky.

Ralph Wilson calls me and I still don't hear anything but the words "head coach." I try to sound coy, but those words get my blood moving for the first time since the season ended. A new chance. A new environment. In, uh, Buffalo.

Buffalo? The thought of actually having to go to Buffalo to make all this happen never once crossed my mind.

Melvin Durslag: So Ralph calls Knox and they make a date to have a talk. Ralph flies out here, I pick him up at the airport, we drive to Huntington Harbor, where Chuck lives, and they meet. I think Ralph offers him the job, but something funny happens. Chuck, who I thought was desperate, says, "I don't know, I'll give you a call tomorrow."

I was set to sign a contract right on the spot, right on my dining-room table. Ralph was offering me a raise from $123,000 to $200,000 a year. He was offering me a five-year contract. He was offering to make me vice president of football operations, something I desperately wanted, ensuring that I would have final say over who was signed and who wasn't, who played and who didn't.

It was all there in front of me, and it was all great. But I told Ralph to wait a night. I had to think about it. I didn't want to jump into this and take whatever was tossed to me the way I did in LA. As an NFL head coach; instead of 0–0–0, I was now 55–15–1. I could negotiate.

As I was sitting at home that night thinking about it, my

son, Chuck, and a couple of little sixth-grade friends came tumbling into the den. He knew nothing about this; none of my family knew anything about this. I looked at him giggling and roughhousing, and a thought hit me: These are nice kids, but he's only known them a couple of years. He doesn't really have any permanent friends. He doesn't have a Mook or a Bummy—he's never been around one place long enough.

For me, for head coaches, it's easy. Friends come with the job like a weekly television show or use of a car. There are people who make a career out of being friends with head coaches. You know what I think about some of those people, but nonetheless, they are there if you want them.

For a sixth-grader, it's not so easy. Kids don't care if your father is the head coach. Most times you're embarrassed to tell them, especially if it means you have to be the school's best football player because of it.

Shirley Knox: In LA, when our son was playing Little League baseball and had "Chuck Knox" written on the back of his uniform, friends would ask him if his dad was the coach. He would tell them no.

For a transplanted sixth-grader, making friends is about as easy as making money. And as soft as my son has had it— and sometimes I think he's been spoiled rotten—at least when I grew up I never had to move. Part of the reason I was able to step forward in life was that during those years I always knew where I stood. Chuckie didn't. And at that one instant in the den, looking at him and his buddies, I decided I couldn't keep putting him through this. I decided that through him I was going to make it up to the three older children, who never had a choice.

I called Ralph. Told him I needed *six* years on the contract. Told him, if I was going to take Chuckie to Buffalo, I wanted to be able to promise him an entire four years at the same high school there.

Lucky me. Ralph agreed. So I verbally accepted the job as head coach of the Buffalo Bills.

Now we had to meet in secret and get this signed before anybody else found out about it—not an easy thing in Hollywood.

Melvin Durslag: Day after Ralph gets there, I think he's going to fly back home, but instead he tells me Chuck has called and accepted the job.

Then he tells me that he and Chuck and their two lawyers are going to need my dinner table to get the agreement hammered out. It's the only place nobody will find them. And besides, we have a pretty big table.

Ralph flies his lawyer in from Buffalo, and they both sleep at my house, so I'm feeling a little like a Holiday Inn. The next morning Chuck and his man come in, my wife makes them all breakfast, and they begin working.

She makes them lunch and they keep working. Finally in the early evening they are done. Chuck is going to be the new coach of the Buffalo Bills.

"Ralph," I say after Chuck has gone, "I just want to tell you, Chuck got in trouble with ownership here because his offense was not exciting enough."

"In Buffalo," says Ralph, "they are happy if you win 3–2."

On January 12, 1978, I was gone. C. R. didn't put up much of a fuss, except he demanded a sixth-round pick from Ralph, just to get the last turn of the screw. Ralph never gave it to him, thank goodness, and that was that. C. R. was already happy because he had controlled where I went.

Chuck Knox in Buffalo. I still didn't realize what that meant. All I saw was *Chuck Knox out of LA.*

Until we made the announcement. Until I saw the shock in everybody's eyes. Until I realized how nobody could believe I would leave a division champion for the worst team in the worst city in professional football.

Then it hit me: what had I done?

> *Former Bills vice president of public relations Budd Thalman: I heard the news and I'm thinking, what have we done? I was stunned.*
>
> *The Buffalo Bills had gotten the hottest coach in football. We had gotten a coach that had never done anything less than win a division championship.*
>
> *I had not heard we were even talking to Knox. And if I had, I would not have believed it. Nobody moves from Los Angeles to Buffalo. Nobody.*
>
> *To show you how unprepared we were, the hiring of Knox resulted in a very bizarre press conference. Our new coach was in Los Angeles, I was in Tampa for the Pro Bowl, and the press was in New Orleans for the Super Bowl. We made three different conference calls to three different cities. It's a wonder anybody ever found out about it.*

Chuck Knox in Buffalo. It finally hit me as I stepped off the plane in that city for my first formal appearance, a couple of days after the announcement. Hit me like an arctic wind. This was not a city, it was Ice Station Zebra. The temperature outside couldn't have been more than zero. *Chuck Knox in Buffalo.* Nobody, but nobody, could believe it.

> *Longtime Knox assistant coach Tom Catlin: I was on his staff in Los Angeles at the time, and all of us knew we might be going elsewhere, so I made a list of other NFL places we might go, and ranked them. But instead of ranking them in terms of where I would like to go, I ranked them in terms of where I would not like to go. First on that list was Buffalo.*
>
> *I wrote it down and laughed, thinking, Ha, don't worry, that's the last place we'll go.*

You know what everybody thought? They won't admit it, but they thought my going to Buffalo was a victory for C. R. They thought it was C. R. who was getting the last laugh. They thought it was the young coach being forced into exile at the last outpost of coaching civilization because he had crossed the old master. "Yeah," everybody was saying, "C. R. sure showed him."

About an hour after that first Buffalo chill, I thought they were right. Not only was the town barren and forbidding, the organization was a disaster. An absolute disaster. At times, those first few days, only Shirley's perspective saved me.

Shirley Knox: People were asking me, "How can you leave LA for Siberia—how?" I would look at them and say, "Easy, easy."

Excuse me, but at first it was hard to think about how lucky I was. What I found in Buffalo was nothing. There was no morale. No direction. Nobody was thinking about doing anything to help the coaches and players win football games. I was actually surprised that they had won five games in two years—as in, surprised they had won *that many.*

Their scouting department was run out of a shoe box. Literally. All the college prospects' names were crammed in there on little index cards, with little ratings of each player but no names of the scouts who had rated them. There were no files on any of the current players. No properly edited film. We scoured the hallways to find people who would go out and watch future prospects, because our assistant coaches, who normally do that stuff, had to stay in and go through this film and figure out what to make of our *own* guys. Ralph Wilson was a nonmeddler all right. He had ignored this team right to the edge of chaos. Correct that. They had long since passed chaos.

Not only did we not have any players, we had no players coming. In the years since O. J. Simpson was the Bills'

number-one draft pick in 1969, look at some of the other
guys they took as number one—Al Cowlings, Walt Patulski,
Tom Ruud. Cowlings lasted eight years, but with five different teams. Patulski and Ruud each played five years, with
two different teams.

It got so bad, during the 1977 draft, the year before I arrived, everybody was saying you could bet money the Bills'
number-one pick, the big guy they pinned all their hopes on,
would be some Joe Dokes. Guess what? Their number-one
pick was Phil Dokes, a defensive tackle from Oklahoma State.
He lasted two seasons.

OK, maybe this job did fall out of the sky. But it fell like
Dorothy's house in *The Wizard of Oz*. It landed right on top
of me.

What's a chief executive officer to do? This one decided to
treat it like a street fight: Surround yourself with people from
your own turf, people who have been around you long enough
to know how you fight, and how to help you win. I decided
to begin a tradition that has stuck with me like my belly—
bringing in people from my old job. That job being the Rams,
I went to Los Angeles and invited everybody from my staff
to join me. Five of them accepted—Tom Catlin, Ray Prochaska, Jim Wagstaff, Elijah Pitts, and Kay Stephenson. Plus,
I made Norm Pollom, the Rams director of player personnel,
the personnel director in Buffalo.

Everybody thought that method was old-fashioned. With
newer and brighter minds entering the game every year,
everybody thought it was weird that I would stick with old
friends. I thought it was so weird, I did the same thing when
I left Buffalo for Seattle. I took six coaches with me then.
They call it loyalty; I call it street smarts. The guy who knows
my old neighborhood is the guy I want walking with me down
the streets of my new neighborhood.

*Tom Catlin: I guess that shows my feeling for how Chuck
takes care of his coaches. Buffalo was my least favorite
place, and yet I went. You worry you will never find a*

head coach who is less like a head coach than Knox. So you follow.

Now, for my next move as Bills head coach, I decided to be a little more subtle. I decided that we had to trade O. J. Simpson. The great running back had lost several steps to injury and age. His record-setting 2,003-yard year was four seasons ago. In 1977 he had gained only 557 yards. But those weren't the biggest reasons to trade him. The biggest, pure and simple, was that he wanted to be traded.

Now, I'm not suggesting that you should trade every guy who wants out. If you did that, sometimes you'd end up with an empty locker room. But when a man of O. J.'s stature and clubhouse influence wants out, you listen. When a man could cause an attitude problem for younger players if he stayed, you seriously listen. And if, when a man stays, a whole lot of bitterness and unproductiveness might stay with him, you think about saying good-bye.

And then you say good-bye. Even to O. J. Simpson.

It's called addition by subtraction. And the three years remaining on O. J.'s contract, at $700,000-plus per year guaranteed, were definitely pushing hard on the other side of that equal sign.

I wanted to trade O. J. so bad, I did it even before I started receiving my mail in Buffalo. Even though I saw right away that this was not going to be easy. Simpson was already out in the newspapers asking for a deal. The papers ran a picture of a moving van taking his stuff out of the house the club provided for him in Buffalo. He was really sticking a gun to our heads.

I figured I better talk to O. J. So one weekend in Huntington Harbor—I was still living in California then, commuting every week to Buffalo for work—I called him in Los Angeles, introduced myself, and asked him to drive down and see me. He sounded hesitant, as I guess anybody would who was invited to the house of somebody he didn't know. When O. J. walked in my door a couple of hours later, he had this very stern look on his face, as though he were not going to listen to any of this bull about how much I wanted to coach him and how much I needed him.

"Juice," I said flatly, "I *want* to trade you. I *want* you gone as bad as you want you gone."

"What?" he said.

"You heard me," I said. "Problem is, you are making it very difficult for us to do anything about it."

"What are you talking about?" he said.

And then I explained to O. J. the three things he must do to increase his value enough so we could make this trade and still keep our shirts.

I told O. J.:

First, publicly say you no longer want to be traded. You have changed your mind; you want to play in Buffalo. Since Coach Chuck Knox likes to run the ball, you have been given new life and want to finish your career here. Tell everybody that.

Second, publicly say you want to play for at least three more years. That is the length of your contract, and nobody is going to want to eat that baby. So what, if you don't feel that way now. You might feel that way in two years. Don't cut off your options, or ours.

Third, accentuate in public the fact that your knee is 100-percent recovered from that latest surgery. Tell the world how healthy you feel. Always talk about how healthy you feel. Don't outright lie, but if you do feel the least bit healthy, let everyone know.

O. J. listened to all of this quietly and then finally said, "Fine, whatever it takes."

Sure enough, the next day he came out with a big statement saying that having Chuck Knox in Buffalo had given him new life. It was printed in all the newspapers, bigger and bolder in the cities whose teams needed running backs. It was flat-out perfect. It's a wonder that when O. J. retired, he never became a great actor. In the winter of 1978 with the Buffalo Bills, he was Oscar material.

So when O. J.'s future employer called—Joe Thomas, general manager of the San Francisco 49ers—I had the gun to hold to his head. I met Thomas in one of those red-carpet rooms at the San Francisco airport (his membership, not mine), and by the time we walked out, in exchange for O. J. Simpson we had received a first-round draft pick, two second-round draft picks, and a third-round draft pick.

It gets better. I also got Joe Thomas to pick up the entire three years of O. J.'s contract, thereby saving the Bills $2.1 million in guaranteed money. Most Bills officials thought we were going to have to eat some of the salary, but I guess they forgot that I used to make deals like this all the time when I was coaching in college. Of course, millions of dollars weren't involved back then, but in recruiting for Wake Forest and Kentucky I learned a million-dollar skill—one that I used in that room with the red carpet in San Francisco.

If you research who it was the Bills later acquired with those four draft choices—either by using or trading them—you'll come up with former running back Joe Cribbs and, get this, current Bills quarterback Jim Kelly. The current Buffalo rage owes his presence there to the politicking of the last Buffalo rage, one O. J. Simpson.

The Simpson trade has been ranked up there with the Hadl trade as one of the best in league history. I don't know about that, but I do know I've had a hard time coming anywhere near repeating the kind of deal I made with Joe Thomas. Few NFL teams make blockbuster trades nowadays, in case you hadn't noticed. It's not quite like baseball. In order to make an NFL trade, both sides must feel the trade is an unqualified success. They are worried about the media, worried about failure. Because of that, some management teams want that trade to be 90 percent in their favor before they will make it. They want something for nothing. And so 90 percent of the time, they can't make the deal.

And as our O. J. Simpson trade later proved—by giving Buffalo both Cribbs and Kelly—when talking about draft choices, there is always a chance you could be trading away the future of your team and your career without even knowing it.

That spring, a few days after the O. J. Simpson trade, I had my first real business meeting with Ralph Wilson. First thing one of his buddies from his insurance company said was "Couldn't you have gotten Delvin Williams in that deal, too?" I nearly fainted. Choosing a calmer option, I simply said, "You guys have no idea. You guys just have no idea."

That's something I should have understood by now but never do. Is my profession so simple that people who don't know whether the ball is stuffed or pumped can tell me how to do it? I didn't run over to their company and tell them how to sell insurance, did I?

What my businessmen critics have to realize is that when I get angry with them, it is not because of their criticism. It is because they feel they can criticize in the first place. This sends a message to me that they don't think much of what I do, that they think anybody—namely themselves—can coach a professional football team.

How should that make me feel? I've spent my life doing one thing, and then up in some owner's box, after spending their life doing something entirely different, these guys are telling *my* boss how I can do *my* job better. But damn it, my job is not that easy. No pro football coach's job is that easy. I'm sorry, but it's not.

When I walked into my first training camp with the Buffalo Bills, I saw something I'd never seen before—wide eyes, open mouths. The players were looking at me like they had been stuck on an island—an arctic island—and I had just gotten off a boat that would take them home. They did everything but reach out and hug me. Funny, because up until then I'd always felt like it was me on the island, the rescuers were my players.

Former Bills defensive end Sherman White: You know how players are, as soon as we heard Knox was going to be our coach, all of us called out to California to see what he was like. The word we heard was that we were lucky dogs. They all said Chuck had the Midas touch. They said he could turn anything to gold, even us, and that was saying something.

We had an owner who didn't care about football. We had no defense. We were coming off a coach, Jim Ringo, who during one halftime in Seattle threw a chalkboard at us. He was so mad, he yelled, "You pricks, you put your shoes up my ass today, well, someday I'll be wearing those shoes and walking up your ass." Nice motivator.

It was so bad, I had been trying to get out for a couple of years. But his former players all said Knox was all right, so I decided to stay. But in changing my mind, I decided I should get more money out of it. So I held out of that first camp. Usually, with a new coach, that's suicide. But Chuck told me, "Do what you have to do. Come in only when you're satisfied you've taken care of yourself and your family." Sure enough, when I finally came in, he never said a bad word. Told me, in future negotiations, if I played hard for him, he would be the first one in the owner's door for me. So I played hard.

That's the way I've always been with players and contracts. No big thing. A man has a right to earn all he can earn. The more one man earns, the better it is for all men. I learned this from my father and his various Sewickley unions.

I will never fault a player for trying to get more money. For *holding out* to get more money if his contract is up. I will never fault anyone for trying to take care of himself and his own.

Now here's the catch: Once he comes to play, that man better come ready. Once he's on the field, he better give me every ounce. He better not *back up* to the pay window. That way, he and I will get along just fine. This was the case with

Sherman White. He worked hard, so I backed him. I guess in the long run, because he was a team leader, that helped me with the other players.

And man, the other players. Compared to the other players, Sherman was ecstatic. I'll never forget one of the first days of practice. Afterward Reggie McKenzie, this big guard, a holdover from O. J.'s Electric Company, came to my office. Walked right in. He said, "Coach, I just want you to know, everybody who is supposed to be on your side here is not on your side." I just looked at him. You couldn't find morale in that place with a dictionary.

> *Reggie McKenzie: You know what Chuck said to me?*
> *He said, "If I had known how bad it was here, I would*
> *not have come. But I'm here. And I will turn it around. I*
> *will."*

The morale on my home front wasn't so great either. I could tell that sooner or later we would end up loving it in Buffalo—Shirley had found a house on three acres of suburban Orchard Park, with a pond in the back and everything—but not all of us were on the same page.

> *Daughter Colleen: I loved Los Angeles; what's more, I*
> *had just graduated from high school and was all set to go*
> *down with my friends to San Diego State. Then Dad gets*
> *the job in Buffalo and tells me what he's told my sisters*
> *and my brother before and since: while I was still in col-*
> *lege, I had to go with him.*
>
> *He never likes anyone in the family far away from home,*
> *if he can help it. He told me he'd pick up some enrollment*
> *forms at Penn State University, which is not far from Buf-*
> *falo. He told me I'd love it there. I didn't tell him any-*
> *thing. I ran out of the room, crying.*
>
> *I spent that entire first summer in Buffalo crying, mop-*
> *ing around the house, hating what my father had done.*

> *But then I got down to Penn State, got going, and I liked*
> *it. I liked it so much that I stayed all four years.*
> *There was a lesson for me in all that. Today I know,*
> *whatever the situation, I can adapt. Sometimes you don't*
> *understand the things my father teaches until after you've*
> *learned them.*

It's ironic that today, while I live in Seattle, I've got children scattered all over the country: Chris is in Denver, Colleen is in Hartford, Connecticut, Kathy's near Los Angeles,
and Chuck is at the University of Arizona in Tucson.

Yet back when they were growing up, it was so important
to me to keep us close. Even when they were in college, I
wanted to be near them. In doing that, in a funny way, I
guess I taught them to be adaptable and independent. And
though I wish they all lived in Seattle, I'm glad they don't
feel they have to. Even though I kept them close to me all
those years, I didn't make them dependent.

My first year in Buffalo was going to be a long one not only
for Colleen. With no outstanding players and no young talent, I knew it would be no day at the pond for the Bills either.
With the team coming off a three-win season, I knew it would
take a minor miracle just to double that. So I decided to play
it cool.

You know what happens when you run before you can walk,
right? You might have a couple of nice bursts, but in the end
you land on your face. And nobody asks if you're OK. They
ask, "If he ran for a few steps back there, how come he's not
running now? Does this mean he will never be able to run?"

That's how I viewed my first Buffalo team. I flat-out told
my coaches we did not want to win before our personnel
were capable of sustaining winning. We did not want to trade
top draft choices for veterans who would only be able to play
for us one year. We would not look for short-term solutions
to long-term problems. Once we were on the edge of winning, we could always get veterans to push us over the top.
But before that . . .

So we started out safe—and sorry. Counting preseason, I didn't get my first win as a Bills coach until we had played six games. We finally won a couple, then lost six of our next seven.

In the end we won five games equaling the number of franchise wins in the previous two years *combined.* We got beat by 31 in New York against the Jets. We lost by 21 at Tampa Bay. Still, I put on my best face. I told everyone we were doing things right.

If a head coach looks distressed, his assistants are going to look distressed. And how will that look to the players? Keep the face, walk the walk, talk the talk. Steady as she goes. "There's nothing wrong with what we're doing. We just have to do it better." Yet after that first fall in Buffalo, I barely believed it. Inside, it was killing me. But I kept telling myself, We're building, we're building.

We did have the cornerstones to prove it. Three of my selections in my first Buffalo draft made All-Rookie teams— running back Terry Miller (Oklahoma State), defensive tackle Dee Hardison (North Carolina), and linebacker Lucius Sanford (Georgia Tech). It wasn't much, but it was enough to allow me to tell myself to settle down.

And we weren't building just a football team, we were building a lot of things, things you've got to have to have a football team. Like fan support. I'm not beyond pounding the pavement for fans. You know me, I'm not beyond pounding the pavement for most anything, but particularly not fans— considering that for the most part they are guys pretty much like me.

When I got to Buffalo, I cringed when I discovered we played in this huge eighty-thousand-seat stadium in the suburbs. In my mind the important thing has never been how many fans you draw, but how many empty seats you have. Give me a sixty-five-thousand-seat, sold-out-every-Sunday stadium any day.

But we had a ton of empty seats. In our inappropriately named Rich Stadium, the Bills had not had a sellout—common in the NFL—in two and a half years. The year before, they had averaged just forty-one-thousand for seven games. Out in Los Angeles we'd get double that amount for *one* game.

If there was ever any promoter in me, now was the time to show it. I began caravaning through the city. I went to its power brokers and its beer drinkers. In the process I discovered that this team could be sold, and, surprise, Buffalo was a pretty good city to sell it to.

Budd Thalman: Chuck brought with him a reputation as a winner. And following Jim Ringo, people in Buffalo had to look at him like some kind of savior. With his personality, he could really play the part. He took the town by storm.

I don't know if I took the town by storm, or if it was the other way around. Although I always knew the place was a lot like western Pennsylvania, I never knew how much I'd go out to pump the team and end up in ethnic neighborhoods where everything was strangely familiar.

After a couple of months I realized that Buffalo was like me. It smelled like me. It felt like me.

But first things first. I had to get the big money behind the team. So I started a Quarterback Club. I know it sounds juvenile, but isn't that where anybody's real love for football begins? In the part of his heart that is always like a kid's? I set up the Quarterback Club to be held every Monday after home games down in the Memorial Auditorium. One difference between my club and other clubs was that I insisted on going down there every meeting and talking to the guys. My man Thalman would tell me I was crazy, but that was my format. There would be about three hundred people at the meetings, the real movers and shakers in town, the big businessmen. I would bring in guest speakers, guys like Pete Rozelle and Ahmad Rashad and some of my old football buddies, and everybody would have a heckuva time.

But I also had to get the common guy behind the team. So I started forcing my mug onto the newspapers and television. I began my own newspaper column and appeared in several weird commercials. One of my most cherished memories of Buffalo, in fact, is of a commercial I did for Malecki Meats. They got a nice camera shot of me grilling sausages in the backyard of our house out in Orchard Park. Some years later I did a commercial for a financial firm in Seattle, where I sang while shaving, but I liked the one with me and those wienies better.

> *Shirley Knox: At least he told me about the wienie commercial before they shot it. He didn't tell me about the singing commercial in Seattle until after the film was in the can. I told him, "But honey, you can't sing!" He smiled and said, "They don't know that."*

You laugh, but by the end of my first year, the average Bills' attendance had risen 6,269 per game, up to 47,185. Sausages or not, that's a lot of butts in the seats.

> *Budd Thalman: It was amazing, because in a very short time he became the most recognizable man in the city. He may not have been as popular as O. J. was, but he wasn't far behind. And this wasn't just with the prominent attorney. This was with the parking lot guy.*

The spring after that first season, as we prepared for the second phase of the building program, something awful happened that made me forget about my problems. On April 2, 1979, Carroll Rosenbloom drowned off the Florida coast. It bothered me terribly. As tough as it was with him, we were still friends. We both had an amazing ability to leave business out of socializing, and so we still talked.

The last thing he said to me as I was leaving him in LA

was "Maybe we'll have a chance to work together again." I like to think he meant it. And I like to think that maybe one day, when bygones had become bygones and all that, I would have been able to take him up on it.

After that first season in Buffalo we had a growing community interest, we had a couple of good young kids, and then that spring we fell into the draft of a lifetime. As the number-one pick in the draft, we got Ohio State linebacker Tom Cousineau. Next we got Clemson wide receiver Jerry Butler, then Boston College defensive tackle Fred Smerlas, and then, from Pennsylvania, little-known Indiana College linebacker Jim Haslett. At the end of the 1979 season, Butler won AFC Rookie of the Year, Haslett was named Defensive Rookie of the Year, and Smerlas made several All-Rookie teams. It was one of the best drafts I've ever been associated with.

Check that. It *should* have been one of the best ones.

We're forgetting one Tom Cousineau.

I still shudder when I hear that name. He became a thorn that I'm still trying to pull loose. Just when everything seemed to be working my way in Buffalo, just when it was obvious things were going to be turned around, Cousineau proved one thing to me: In football, as in any other business, you cannot let the bean counters decide what you are going to do. The bean counter thinks getting the job done cheaper is better than getting the job done right. The bean counter does not realize that winning generates the revenue that will pay everyone's salary, including his own.

Remember, Cousineau was the first pick in the entire draft. Not only our first pick, but number one in the first round. He was the front pages, the huge photos, the big interviews. Not to mention, he had the reputation as an impact player, a big-ticket item for our growing defense. He promised to be the player who would, in two or three years, direct us right through the face masks of the NFL's upper echelon.

And we never had a chance to sign him. Not even a chance.

I was initially confident we'd be able to get his name on a piece of paper, because his agent was Jimmy Walsh, an old friend of mine who used to be Joe Namath's agent. With me, this guy would play it straight. Everything would be up front and on the line. Right away he said high-spending Montreal of the Canadian Football League was very interested in Tom and ready to make a serious offer. I shook my head: Cousineau was already the property of Hamilton, a smaller, low-budget Canadian team that had picked him in their league's draft but would never sign him. Jimmy was straightforward, all right, but here he was blowing smoke. I left the negotiations to our lawyers and went on a little June vacation.

I was visiting my daughter Chris in Denver when I got a call from Stew Barber, our vice president of administration; he told me that Cousineau had just been waived by Hamilton and picked up by Montreal.

I said, *"What?"*

I called Walsh and he said, "That's right, Montreal is making a very big offer. And by the way, I told you so."

Now we were in trouble. Huge, Tom Cousineau-sized trouble. On top of it all, Cousineau was pissed off at us. Turns out, on draft day, when he and Walsh came to town, our front office people did not entertain them as planned. After the press conference, Cousineau and Walsh were left on their own. They ended up having dinner at a bar. They ate chicken wings. Now I know Buffalo has good chicken wings, but give me a break. Give our first-round draft choice a break!

I suddenly realized that I had better get involved in these negotiations, and quick. I called Ralph Wilson and told him Montreal was very, very serious. I told him we shouldn't even have come *this* close to losing our first-round draft pick.

Let's sign him now and get it over with. Please.

"But I've got this good source," says Ralph.

"Good *what?*" I ask.

"This good source up in Canada. He says Montreal doesn't have the money to pay Cousineau; they are just throwing up a smoke screen. We don't even have to worry about their offer."

"Who's your source, Ralph?"

"Just a source."

Oh.

Jimmy Walsh was my man from way back, and my men don't lie to me. I still believed him. I called him and begged him to give us a final shot at whatever Montreal was offering. He said fine, said he would fly to Buffalo from Montreal right before training camp. He arrived, and though I later felt bad about it, I checked the flight records. Indeed, he flew in from Montreal. There really were serious negotiations going on.

A source, huh? We're dead meat.

Walsh and my people argued over a contract for a couple of days, but it was obvious that Ralph wasn't going to release enough money to get this guy—he still thought they were just jacking us around. So Walsh left, headed back for that smoke screen known as the Canadian border. We started our training camp without Tom Cousineau. And of course everybody was wondering why. And once again, I was caught in the middle.

After a couple of days, and no word from Walsh or Cousineau or Montreal, I started thinking maybe Ralph was right. Maybe they were ready to come back on their hands and knees.

Maybe, just maybe . . . then one afternoon at camp a short time later, I got a phone call. It was one of my scouts: "Chuck, there's a press conference tomorrow in Montreal . . ."

That's all I heard before losing my cool.

Damn it! Damn everything.

I grab Norm Pollom and Bud Thalman and run back to our dorm room and jump on the phone. Damn, if we aren't going to get at least one more shot at it.

> *Budd Thalman: How important was Tom Cousineau to our franchise? How about, important enough for Chuck*

> *and Norm to stay up all night trying to talk Jimmy Walsh out of going to Canada. And I mean all night. They were on the phone constantly, calling Walsh, calling him back, calling him again. Then they were waking me up, having me call UPI, AP, all the wire services to find out any information.*
>
> *This went on, literally, until eight o'clock in the morning, when it was time to go back to work. I think they would have passed out from exhaustion, but they were too mad.*

We left the room that morning exhausted but with just enough rage to keep us going through the rest of the day. We tried, Lord knows we tried. Even as early as two o'clock Walsh had told us it was a done deal, but we tried. He told us he was sorry, but it was strictly a business decision, a business deal, and there was nothing he could do. And still we tried. We called and called and tried to get anyone, anywhere, to listen to us.

> *Former Bills personnel director Norm Pollom: We were even calling Cousineau's coaches at Ohio State. We were even calling his relatives. Longest night of my life.*

Only money talks. So nobody would listen.

That morning, at practice, the anticlimactic news came down that Tom Cousineau was a Montreal Alouette. The nation was watching. The nation was laughing.

I know you play the hand you're dealt and all that, but this had a devastating effect on me. There we were, trying to build a program. We'd been promised cooperation and support and the whole bit, but now we couldn't even sign our top draft pick, a guy good enough to be considered the entire league's top draft pick.

Ralph knew how upset I was, even though I never yelled at him. As long as I have a boss, I will never yell at that boss. He's the man, he's signing my paycheck. But Ralph knew I was mad. I kept telling him, this was going to cost us twice as much down the stream as it would cost us now. Those things always do.

Cut to three years later, 1982. When Cousineau's Montreal contract ran out, he got an offer sheet from the Houston Oilers which included a million-dollar signing bonus, plus five hundred grand for five years. That's about double what we could have gotten him for earlier. Now we had to match that offer sheet or lose him for nothing.

When I got Ralph on the phone about Houston's offer, the line suddenly went dead. How symbolic. When I finally got back to him, Ralph said no way was he paying Cousineau that much money. I said fine, could we please start calling around and trying to trade him so at least we could get something for that first pick?

He agreed. I eventually arranged for the Cleveland Browns to take Cousineau if we signed him. Which we did, and got a couple of second-round picks and a couple of third-round picks in return. Not bad—for losers.

All's terrible that ends terrible. So we got a few draft choices. But we had lost the use of a Cousineau for three years, and we had retarded the development of our program.

That summer before the 1979 season, after we lost Cousineau to Canada, I was stumped: Even when I got lucky, why could I never get lucky? How does one get in the right place at the right time? Where *was* this right place, anyway? And was there ever such a thing as the right time?

We went 7–9 that season with the top rookies we had. But angry with the owner and the future, and resentful of the past, I made an off-season decision that changed forever the way I will be perceived as a coach. The winter following the 1979 season, I realized I didn't deserve squat. No man deserves squat. Things aren't deserved, they are *earned*. I had forgotten that. If I wanted to turn this thing in Buffalo around like I did in LA, I had to stop crying because I didn't have the talent and experience of LA. I had to stop crying because my owner didn't want to put the best players on the field.

Instead of weeping at my bad fortune, I had to start whaling on it. And instead of talking about the future and resting on the notion that five- and seven-win seasons were quite comfortable when the club was coming off two- and three-win seasons, I had to start thinking about now. Right now.

I decided that in 1980, on the field, I would return to the Chuck Knox that had brought me to Buffalo. I would resurrect him and wear him on my sleeve and flaunt him like a new piece of jewelry. I would change, and the Bills would change.

I would start with me.

> *Shirley Knox: Get him to tell you about his diet. He went on the most incredible diet in the winter after the 1979 season. He started talking about how he had to get leaner and meaner, and show an example for his team. He talked about how the next year was a turning point for the city and the team.*
>
> *You've never seen a little belly shrink any faster.*

For the first time in my career—and anybody who watches NBC television will know it wasn't the last—I had developed a gut. All the work and worry were settling around my belt. Those pretty sweaters I love, they began looking like pretty balloons. I was an otherwise well-proportioned man who appeared cursed with a basketball under his shirt.

So I dieted. I started eating only fish and chicken. And I only ate that stuff if it was cooked in a wok. Why a wok? I don't know. Maybe this was a diet dreamed up by people who make woks. I also didn't drink alcohol—nothing, not a drop.

And it worked. From January to April I dropped from 242 pounds to 178. I hadn't been 178 pounds since shortly after birth.

> *Shirley Knox: It was incredible. He bought all new clothes, but kept his old ones just to be sure. That is why today he still has three different sizes of suits.*

> *Once, we had some friends over for a weekend, and the man didn't bring anything to wear to dinner, so Chuck opened his closet and said, "Hey, there has to be something in here that fits you."*

Problem was, nobody saw me all summer until I was finished with this diet. I came back after vacation and scared people.

> *Longtime Knox assistant coach Steve Moore: Cancer. We were certain he had cancer. He walked into our first meeting after summer vacation and he was so drawn, so thin, we just knew he was sick. "No, it's the diet," he kept saying. We knew better. All of us whispered it. It had to be cancer.*

It was weird. People kept staring and saying, real funny like, "Boy, you're looking good." I finally said, "Hey, there are three stages in a man's life: *young, old,* and *looking good.* You're trying to tell me that I'm already in the last stage?"

That shut them up. I had a cancer all right. It was the cancer of losing, the cancer of complacency. I was going to fight it out in Buffalo until either I won or I retired at age forty-eight.

> *Steve Moore: As soon as we got through with the cancer bit, and we were convinced that he really did just give up the red meat and the sauce, he suddenly called me to the chalkboard one day. As the youngest coach, I was always getting called to the chalkboard.*
>
> *Chuck said, "Steve, I want you to write some words for me. I want you to write* lean, hungry, intense.*" I did. And then he blows his top. He screams, "That's what I want to see around here from now on, friggin' lean, hungry, and intense. Look at me! I want you to be like me!"*
>
> *We look at each other like, Wait a minute, that's the real reason he went on the diet? Of course.*

> *For the rest of the year, the Buffalo Bills became lean,*
> *hungry, and intense. And Knox was the meanest, rot-*
> *tenest s.o.b. there ever was.*

We went to training camp that year with the right attitude, me and the coaches. Although because of my new intensity, it wasn't always the happiest attitude.

I had been thinking all summer about our normal defense,
a standard 4–3 setup, with four linemen in stances and three
linebackers standing up behind them. I had this funny thought
about that defense, but seeing as I was having a lot of funny
thoughts with no booze and a stir-fried brain, I held off until
after the vacation. At our first pretraining camp meeting, I
called my coaches together and asked them to write on the
chalkboard a list of our best eleven defensive players, regardless of position. They did. Of the eleven players, there were
four, not three, linebackers.

That's what I thought.

"Gentlemen," I said, "we're going to change our defense
from four-three to three-four. We want our best eleven defensive players on the field at the same time."

They looked at me like I was crazy.

Then they looked at their playbooks, so finely tuned to the
4–3 defense, like they were going to be sick. Every defensive
page had to be changed. Every scheme had to be altered. It
was July 5 and regular training camp started in three weeks.

"Are you sure?" one of them asked.

"I didn't decide it," I said. "You were the ones who wrote
the names on the chalkboard. You just decided it."

That's my management style for you. But that's what kind
of intensity I was feeling.

> *Shirley Knox: I don't know if this had anything to do*
> *with that defense or not, but during that diet time, when*
> *he was being so tough and single-minded, I remember a*
> *bridge game. He was my partner, and we were losing. I*

looked over at him and saw why. He was diagramming that new defense on one of the napkins.

No matter how much the 3–4 defense surprised them, my coaches would later thank themselves, and me. In 1980 we turned one of the NFL's worst defenses into one of its best, allowing twenty points or more only six times in sixteen games.

They say I was one of the first coaches in the NFL to use the 3–4 successfully. I've always said it wasn't anything. As you can see, it wasn't.

Because of this and other last-minute changes, by the time the 1980 practice started, my coaches were lean, mean, and hungry. So were the players, perhaps because for the first time in Buffalo, we had the right players.

Sensing it was time for the big veteran push that I talked about earlier and have come to love so much—bring in the old horses to carry you over the top of the hill—I brought in some of the leanest, hungriest, most intense players I could find.

I picked up linebacker Phil Villapiano from Oakland, guard Conrad Dobler from New Orleans, and defensive back Bill Simpson and wide receiver Ron Jessie from the Rams. And all for practically nothing. Dobler, for example, came for an eighth-round draft pick.

When people talk about me as someone who brings in old players, as someone who brought Joe Namath to Los Angeles and Franco Harris to Seattle, they always categorize it as another example of my loyalty. I hate to ruin any romantic notions, but while I'm a very loyal person, that isn't loyalty at all. It's good business. Loyalty is what you use with guys like Midget and Mook. What you use with old, wise football players is business sense. Old players know the plays. Old players know the pressure. Old players don't have to be told twice. While you want the young horses, there comes a time when you need somebody to lead them.

Former Bills wide receiver Ron Jessie: I spent the last two years of my contract with Knox in Buffalo. I was the highest-paid receiver on the team, but during that time I caught only twenty passes. Chuck said it didn't matter. He said it was my job to come in and teach the young guys what it takes to play and win under the Knox system, that's all. And I wasn't the only one. He brought in Villapiano just to get excited and tear up meeting rooms.

The only part loyalty has in any of this is in my refusal to bring in *more* old players. I will not bring in guys who will embarrass themselves. I'm loyal to the respect they earned in their prime. If a guy doesn't know when to end his career, I'll gladly tell him his time has come before I will put him in a position where the rest of the world will tell him. Careers come too hard to end so hard.

So we got these good veterans, this good blood, and we got rid of one bit of questionable-type blood. That same fool who traded O. J. Simpson was so brash at the beginning of the 1980 season, he traded five-time All-Pro guard Joe De-Lamielleure. When I got there, DeLamielleure, who had been with the Bills since 1973, was the golden boy. He was one of the few guys who lifted weights and worked out in Buffalo in the off-season, a great hero, a man who epitomized the work ethic.

But he could have been better. I don't care what you win, winning awards should not stop you from getting better. It should not stop you from chasing whatever has driven you to be good in the first place.

I liked DeLamielleure, but I expected more of him. I didn't care how many awards he had won. Look here, if the team wins, more people will win those awards. More people will get pay raises. More people will get endorsements. If the team wins, there is enough for everybody. Winning creates the climate in which all good things happen. If the team does not win, there is nothing for anybody.

If just one guy wins, well, one guy wins and forty-four guys are left on the outside. The Pro Bowl wasn't enough. The Pro Bowl was, and still is, based a lot on reputation.

I told my team this. And then I told Joe D. he had to get better. That's all I told him.

But you'd have thought I'd just announced he had to wear a skirt.

For the first two years under me he went around whining and complaining. He criticized Ray Prochaska, my offensive-line coach, and he criticized me.

> *Reggie McKenzie: Players almost never trash Chuck in the newspapers. So when DeLamielleure came out and trashed him, we all wanted to see what would happen. As usual, we were surprised.*
>
> *All Chuck said was, "In due time, in due time." That's all he ever says when somebody has wronged him. He says it relates back to the Sewickley days, when due time meant settle-up time, the time you settled your bills and other debts. Settle-up day was a big day in Sewickley, I guess. So Chuck relates a lot of things to that.*

Right before the 1980 season, Joe D. holds out through all of training camp, then demands to be traded. Nice timing.

By now I felt like fighting him, but he was too damn big, so I went over to his house with an olive branch and we talked. Finally I got him back into camp. He walks in the Monday before the first game, saying he's ready to play, even though Conrad Dobler has already taken his place. He even says he *expects* to play.

I say fine, get dressed. He does. He walks up the ramp to the field. Just as I see him step onto the field, I get a phone call in my locker-room office.

It's Art Modell, the boss in Cleveland. Says he's ready to make a trade that we had talked about for several weeks.

Guess what trade?

Joe DeLamielleure for draft choices.

I say, "Art, you couldn't have called at a better time."

We make the deal and send someone down to get Joe. Just
as he's putting on his helmet, the ball boy grabs him and
sends him back up to me, where I tell him to get dressed. Joe
went to the Browns and never made it back to the Pro Bowl.

The story of Joe DeLamielleure is a pointed reminder of
the three things every NFL player believes about himself: He's
underpaid. He's overworked. And he's better than he is.

DeLamielleure's problem was, he believed those three things
more than most people, more than he should have. So I made
his problem somebody else's problem.

And that's how we started the 1980 season.

> *Reggie McKenzie: At first that year, we all just felt sorry
> for thin old Chuck because we were sure he was hiding
> cancer. But after a few days of practices, a few busted
> heads . . . after we saw DeLamielleure turning around and
> walking out of there, we knew Knox was not screwing
> around.*
>
> *He was always big on one-on-one pass-protection drills—
> maybe he told you that—but this fall he was even worse.
> We would do one-on-ones until our breath smelled of grass.
> And then Chuck would yell, "You pissed off? Let me see
> how pissed off you are. Maybe, just maybe, you're pissed
> off enough to do it right."*
>
> *One-on-ones are Chuck's way of finding out what he
> can get from a guy when the game is on the line in the
> fourth quarter. Most every game on the line in the fourth
> quarter that year, we won.*

From that first game that year, I had a feeling we had
something special. By now I was certain. In our first game
we upset Miami, the defending Eastern Division champions,
17–7, breaking a twenty-game losing streak against the Dolphins. Perhaps more impressively, we sold out Rich Stadium—eighty thousand seats. The first sellout there in five
seasons.

At the same time, the city was being bombarded with this Chamber of Commerce slogan: *Talking Proud*. It was designed to make the city, usually the butt of ugly jokes, feel good about itself. I got to thinking pro football should not be so isolated as to forget that its highest duty is just that—to make a city feel good about itself. I began using that theme with our team. I got the stadium people to start playing this silly "Talking Proud" theme song after we scored touchdowns.

In the off-season I started making more and more appearances on behalf of the team that felt like appearances on behalf of the city. I helped raise more than a million dollars in a Children's Hospital telethon, the first time that had been done. For the first time, too, the money collected exceeded the money pledged. I know I'm bragging, but I'm as proud of that stuff as I am of anything that has to do with helmets. That stuff has to do with the rebirth of a city, with good, hard-working people.

"Buffalo and the Bills are talking proud." That's what I would say. I still get a little charge out of saying it, hammering it out in that frying-pan-over-the head voice of mine. I used to give out Talking Proud buttons, peddle Talking Proud belts. Pretty soon I felt like a city councilman or something. Big businesses that were thinking about relocating in Buffalo were told to call me. I would try to convince them what a great place it was.

I used my spiel like it was a forearm. Sometimes it worked, sometimes they thought I was just weird. I guess sometimes I *was* weird. I would say things like, "When it's fourth and goal, you got to be bold. It sounds like fourth and goal for your growing company, and it's time to take that chance. Take it on Buffalo—we're a city that's talking proud." At the time, this was a town that was economically whipped. The Bethlehem Steel Company had shut its works down from twenty-three thousand employees to five hundred. This town's welfare lines were longer than its grocery lines. The town needed a jolt, and I was lucky enough to be the head of a group that could give it that jolt. In talking proud, I felt I was just fulfilling a responsibility.

> *Budd Thalman: Whatever Chuck was doing, it worked. He did more for the Chamber of Commerce than even the Chamber of Commerce. He took that theme and made it his theme, and pretty soon people around Buffalo weren't taking those bad jokes sitting down.*

I guess pretty soon the city was believing. I know the team was believing. We won our first five games and nine of our first thirteen games. Three were in front of sellout home crowds; three more were in front of home crowds of more than sixty-five thousand. We had huge guys like Sherman White dancing on a tiny locker-room chair after wins. Sometimes I would dance with him. "Shoes" they called him. Whatever they called me, I got the hell out of there before I could hear it.

In our fifth game, a battle of the unbeatens with San Diego (I love to play in games marked by that phrase, "Battle of the unbeatens"), we won 26–24 after forcing a Chuck Muncie fumble late in the game. But we lost both of our safeties, Rod Kush and Jeff Nixon—both with knee injuries. Now what? We'd won number five; how were we going to win anything more without our good safeties?

How did that line go, about playing the hand you're dealt? I went out and called Bill Simpson, a former Ram who hadn't played in a year and a half and at that moment, in fact, wasn't playing for anybody. I threw a uniform on him in time to make practice on Wednesday. Four days later he started at safety and stayed there the rest of the year.

I know this book seems full of Doblers and Whites and Simpsons. You're saying, Where are our heroes, the guys from Hollywood, the guys from the headlines? I'm sorry, but I guess my favorite players have never been anyone else's favorite players. I think that's why the 1980 Buffalo Bills were one of my favorite teams. You never heard of them. You never thought they were much of anything. But get down in there and take a lick from a Reggie McKenzie or a Freddie Smerlas, and you'd know they were there. My favorite players—you never much saw or heard them, but you certainly felt them.

What you do speaks so well, no need to hear what you say. That's a cliché I picked up way back, when it became apparent nobody was going to listen to the words of a Dixon Flats flattop. I use it just about every day now: Do it, don't talk about it. Eighth-grade Sewickley.

There were a couple of other guys in Buffalo during those years whom you've never heard of, but whose actions spoke volumes. They were the Bills equipment managers, first Tony Marchetti and then Chuck Ziobert. Tony was there for twenty years, greatest man in the world, but he retired with no visible sign of appreciation. So I figured, Let's make this franchise like the old neighborhood, let's throw this guy a party and get him something to retire on.

I got it going with a little buffet and a little raffle, and before you know it, we're giving this guy a huge shebang with five thousand dollars in cash. A couple of years later he died of cancer, but I like to think he was happy. I know that watching him leave the team well-fed made my players happy.

After Marchetti, I hired Chuck Ziober, another unique equipment guy, a retired Marine Corps sergeant-major from California. Strange world. He got cancer, too.

I always like my players to appreciate the feeling of doing something for somebody else, because—just like the rest of us—a lot of them sometimes don't think of anybody but themselves. So we throw this stag for Ziober, too, just like Marchetti. I got all of them to chip in for a color television set with a remote control so Chuck wouldn't have to get out of bed if he was sick. We put the television set on top of a locker and called him in to the locker room. All the players started chanting his name.

Chuck got tears in his eyes, and he stood up in front of us and promised that he was going to fight the cancer to the end. I know this probably sounds a little sappy, but it was all part of the kind of team we had in Buffalo. The year 1980 stands out in particular. We had a certain inside thing going, which came in handy when we got to the fourteenth game of that incredible season.

Reggie McKenzie: We went into game fourteen needing wins in two of our last three games to take the Eastern Division championship. It was our last home appearance of the season, an opportunity for a big win.

Oh, fate. We were scheduled to play the Los Angeles Rams, Chuck's old team. The first time he had faced them since leaving. He was quiet the whole week, didn't say anything. But on Friday, at his daily team meeting, he stood up. He spoke real soft. He said, "Those guys lining up across from you on Sunday, those used to be my guys. Now you're my guys." Then he sat down. And we went crazy. Guys came out of the meeting throwing chairs, beating on each other. We all knew the name of this game. It would be the biggest in his career.

Yeah, I guess it was kind of a big game. Here was a Rams team that had hurt me. Here was a team that had gone to the Super Bowl two years after I left, gone with a coach, Ray Malavasi, whom I had hired. I got only a few salutes for putting them together, and a million laughs for walking away. I had left this great team to come to a place in shambles, a place where nobody said I could win. I had come to Carroll Rosenbloom's Siberia. But I had survived long enough to put my team in a position to win a division championship. And now we met, my past and my present. Yeah, I guess I was kind of excited.

The actual game, well, no big thing. In front of a screaming sellout crowd, we won by a field goal. In overtime.

Shirley Knox: It was the most unbelievable game I've ever seen. I was up in the press box nearly crying the whole time. Chuck wanted it so bad. It was so close. Afterward I had to be with him. I rushed down the elevator and waited for him outside the locker room, then when I saw him I nearly jumped into his arms. Something felt wet. He was crying, too.

I couldn't help myself. I cry. That wasn't the first time, and there will be many more times. I don't cry out of extreme happiness or grief. I cry when something hits me so hard in my gut, there's no other place to release the emotion.

And this win hit me. We had done it. We had been beaten down by the Rams, all of us who had worked there, from my long-time secretary, Mary Phillips, to Norm Pollom. And we had all come back to bite them in the heart.

We got to the locker room and the players surrounded me and started chanting, "Chuck, Chuck, Chuck." One of the greatest compliments in life is respect from the people who work for you. So maybe that was one of my greatest.

Reggie McKenzie: Knox probably didn't tell you about my postgame speech. After our chant I stood up in the locker room and grabbed the game ball and handed it to Knox and said, "We're just giving one game ball today. They may not have wanted you over in Los Angeles, Chuck, but we want you here."
Sure enough, Knox cried some more.

So what would you have done? And while I may have looked a little ridiculous crying, you should have seen the fans.

Budd Thalman: Call it one of the first demanded encores in professional football history. The players had left the field and were in the locker room dancing circles around Chuck. One of them, Baby Johnson, was singing a little

> *Super Bowl song he wrote. By this time the tears had*
> *stopped, and Chuck was singing and dancing along with*
> *him, actually moving his feet and everything. Then the*
> *equipment guy runs in. He screams "The fans won't go*
> *home!"*
>
> *Now, we're talking about 80,000 fans. If they won't go*
> *home, we've got a problem. So I suggest we send out Nick*
> *Micke-Meyer, who kicked the winning field goal, and we*
> *do, but the noise only gets louder. So Reggie stands up*
> *and says, "C'mon, guys, I think they want all of us." And*
> *out they go, all of them, into the freezing cold.*

The player's shirts were off, their pants were unbuttoned, and none of it mattered. They were running around the littered field in their socks and slippers, waving towels. The fans were waving back.

They had not had much to cheer about since their team's last trip to the play-offs, in 1974. And this was only the second time the Bills had made the play-offs in fifteen years.

The Rich Stadium sound was the sound of relief, but most of all it was the sound of—don't laugh now—love. It's true. I could hear it, I could *feel* it.

At that moment there, I didn't want to leave Buffalo for as long I could breathe that love.

Of course, the next week there was another game. Both the best and worst thing about my life is, there's always another game. We were cleaned out in New England, 24–2, which meant we had to win the last game of the season, in San Francisco, just to make the play-offs.

By this time, we were numb to all pressure or excitement. We beat San Francisco 18–13 in one of the better games I've seen an outside linebacker play. That's because he was playing inside linebacker. It was old man Phil Villapiano, a rushed replacement for Shane Nelson, who had broken his arm. Phil had not played inside linebacker since college, but you'd never have known, because he made ten tackles.

We ended the season as division champions at 11–5, a four-game improvement over the previous season and almost four times as many wins as the season before I took over.

On the cross-country trip home, our flight was delayed. For the sake of a good party, thank goodness it was delayed.

> *Budd Thalman: Before that night I'd never waited with Chuck for a plane after a win. I'm not so sure I could survive it again. Instead of gathering the players together and warning them to act like gentlemen in the public domain of an airport, he simply herded them into an airport cocktail lounge and threw a five-hundred-dollar bill on the bar. "It's on Chuck!" he shouted; then he left to sit in the terminal lobby with his coaches.*
>
> *At half-hour intervals, a different player would walk in with another five-hundred-dollar bill. "It's on Chuck!" the player would shout, and the other players would cheer, and the drinks would be poured. For the next three hours it went on like this.*
>
> *I don't recall what happened first, whether the plane was fixed or the bar ran out of liquor and food. But I know Chuck did not run out of money.*

Probably the most amazing thing about that San Francisco game was arriving in Buffalo afterward at five o'clock in the morning. There were 7,500 people waiting for us at the airport. That's five o'clock mid-winter, as in, five degrees. I thought to myself how hard it must have been for these people to get out of bed and come here. Then I took a couple of whiffs of the crowd and it dawned on me: they had never gone to bed. Wacko people. Lovely people. And people who deserved better than what was about to happen.

We had two weeks off before our first play-off game, in San Diego. One of those weeks included Christmas. I wanted to practice in Buffalo, to keep my people near their people during the holidays. I would have been able to do it, too, if Ralph Wilson had kept a promise he made to me when I signed on in 1978.

"Please," I had asked Ralph, "get me an indoor practice facility. We live in the city with the worst winters in the National Football League. We can't properly practice when we can't feel our fingers."

At the time, Ralph said he would.

Later he said we didn't have the money. While we were losing during those first two years, I didn't dare ask again. But when we returned home after the 1980 regular season to find it zero degrees and snowing like hell, I wished I had. The facts hit me like a wet snowball in the eye: We couldn't practice here for the play-offs, nor could we stay home for Christmas.

We were about to play one of the most important games in this franchise's history, and we had to make like gypsies. We had to go to Vero Beach, Florida, to the Los Angeles Dodgers' spring training complex.

Say what you want about men adjusting to the elements. The element that takes the longest to accept is not rain or snow, but unfamiliarity. After one quarter of football, a man gets used to being wet, to slipping, to having his hands blown cold. But when that man has stayed a week in a hotel over the holidays, and then plays on a field three thousand miles from home, sometimes *four* quarters are not enough.

Against the Chargers, they weren't. Led by a fullback we picked up off the waiver wire, Roosevelt Leaks, we took a 14–13 lead into the late stages of the game, when suddenly San Diego's Dan Fouts hit this guy named Ron Smith for a fifty-yard pass with just 2:08 left. It was only Smith's fifth catch of the year, and it was on a wrong pattern.

I know that's souring it, but it was obvious to anyone who had studied the Chargers like I had, the guy was supposed to run an "out" pattern. We defended an out pattern. The guy got confused and ran a "post." The Chargers went to the AFC championship.

Sometimes in a big game, even when my opponent is wrong . . . he's right. Or maybe it's me that's all wrong. After games like that, I wonder.

We got home and found seven thousand fans waiting for us at the airport. We had lost, but there were seven thousand people there to welcome us home. It made me think, If these Bills ever get to the Super Bowl, the Buffalo airport authority better insure against death by trampling.

I flew with Shirley to our Palm Springs condo for the next few weeks, deciding, yes, I would eat fried foods and fatty foods and everything sweet. What's more, if I chose to, I would drink. No more dieting, no more Mr. Mean. For a while, at least, we were going to take it easy. The disappointment of the championship notwithstanding, we knew we were established now. We knew that back in Buffalo we had found a home.

Thinking back, one of the things I liked best about Buffalo was that it was close to western Pennsylvania and the cities and people who knew me when I was nothing. For five straight autumns there was a constant weekend caravan from Sewickley to Buffalo. The Munizzas, Big D, Bummy, Jumbo. Sewickley was close enough—about five hours—that you could climb into a motor home on Friday afternoon and be in my city in time for a nightcap.

Some of them would occasionally stay at my house on Saturday. Some would watch the game from the sidelines with me on Sunday, hang around the locker room with me afterward, then drive back south in time to get a good night's sleep before work next day.

Budd Thalman: His old friends were everywhere. More than once I had to answer a question from higher authorities, like, who were these people? I would always say, "These are Chuck's people, and you don't mess with Chuck's people." And that was the end of that.

My father told me, make new friends but never forget an old friend for a new one. I strongly believe that. It's always good to get back to where I came from, even though sometimes it scared the hell out of me.

One night, just as they got to the outskirts of Buffalo on a visit, Big D and Midget ran out of gas. It's freezing cold outside, but Big D tells Midget, "You walk two miles to the next exit and get the gas, and I'll stay in the car." Big D must have figured a smaller body had an easier time staying warm.

So Midget goes out looking for gas, and while he's gone, a tow truck comes by and Big D waves it down. Big D takes the truck to the gas station, gets his gas, and goes back to the car. Everything is dandy, except for one thing: where is Midget? It's been an hour, and he is still out looking for gas.

Well, Big D drives up and down the highway and can't find Midget, so he panics and drives to my house, looking like he's seen a ghost. We wait another hour at the house, and now Big D is sweating hard, so I call some of my buddies down at the state patrol. They go out in force, trying to find my Midget on a dark freezing night. They can't find him, and now I'm getting worried. Then all of a sudden I hear a knock on the door. It's Midget. He had gotten back to the car with the gas, found no car, then *he* had panicked. In hitchhiking to a pay phone, he decided to just hitchhike all the way to the house. It had taken him three hours. Said he couldn't get anybody to believe that he was going to Chuck Knox's house. Everyone wanted to take him to the loony bin. Maybe there would have been a spare bed there for me.

Actually, about the biggest worry I had at this time was my son, Chuckie. He was well into high school, at the age of reasoning, and you could tell he was different. Not different from his friends or any other kid that age, but different from me. He had a nice house and money for nice clothes. Every night he knew where he would sleep, and how he would sleep, and was not afraid to sleep. From this knowledge had grown a comfort zone. My God, sixteen years old and already with a comfort zone. This was not how it was supposed to be. Oh, the house and clothes, sure, but not the comfort. My son was supposed to grow up tough. He was supposed to be the image of me. I was supposed to do for him what my father had done for me, only without the fear.

I had prayed and prayed for a boy, and by the time we had him, I had been through three girls and knew a little about raising kids. I was sure I could somehow keep him safe, yet make him tough as well. I even named him after my father, calling him Charles McMeekan Knox. That is why today, despite about two thousand newspaper references, he is *not* Chuck Knox, *Jr.* He is just Chuck Knox. Like me. That's how it was supposed to be.

But by the time he reached high school, I realized that was how he would never be. Safe and tough are mutually exclusive. If a boy doesn't go hungry, he can't become hungry. At the time, I thought, My boy is not a hungry boy, and I have failed.

Shirley Knox: I could understand Chuck's feelings about our son, but I couldn't understand how it was our son's fault, or how we could do anything about it. Did Chuck want us to send the boy to skid row? I kept asking him that. And I kept telling him his son was going to be tough, give the boy time, give him the right circumstances. He shouldn't have to run out and get a tattoo and try to join the Navy to prove it.

I had trouble accepting what Shirley or anybody else told me. Instead of letting my son's character shape itself, I had to stick my big fat hands in there and do it for him.

Chuckie Knox: So you want me to talk about my father? Is he going to read this? Oh, I don't care, I'm older now. It's over now.

Do you know that, when I was a sophomore in high school in Buffalo, he once bullied me into joining the wrestling team? I did it for a year and hated every minute of it. Worst experience of my life. I'm not a fighter. Only reason he made me join the wrestling team was because, much to his surprise, they didn't have a boxing team. I told him, "Dad, nobody has boxing teams anymore." I never said anything more about it because I was terrified of him. When I spoke to him, he would look at me with those eyes. Or he wouldn't look at me at all. It took me a long time to start telling him things.

I know he wanted me to be more like him, but I had advantages he didn't. Of course, he never let me forget them. Anytime I would borrow money from him, he would say, "Don't forget, you're not spending your money, you're spending my money." I remember once I needed to go somewhere and the car was out of gas, so I tried to get some money from my mother. She told me to ask Dad. I decided I didn't need to go somewhere that bad.

I'm the same with all the children when it comes to money. It wasn't just Chuckie. They have to appreciate a dollar the way I did. It's harder because they are exposed to more, but that doesn't mean I should just give it to them. Like I said, my daughter Chris once had a loan payment book for a new car. But I'm not all bad. After a couple of months, when she fell hopelessly behind on the payments, I tore up the book. And no, I didn't repossess the car. I would have, but I didn't have room for the damn thing in the garage.

Chuckie Knox: As I've gotten older and Dad has mellowed, I've realized that all he ever wanted was respect. He wanted us to understand what he had gone through, and be strong enough to endure when we went through our own hardships. All he was doing was loving us. And that's not so bad.

And for every bad time, there was a time like the time in college when he surprised me with a car. A used car— thirty thousand miles on it, you know my dad—but a car. Or the time I got into a fight in high school. I came home bruised, and my mom really bawled me out while my dad stood by and quietly agreed. But as soon as she left the room, he patted my back and whispered, "Way to go, Rocky."

So after the 1980 season I was sold on Buffalo the city, and pretty much sold on my life there. But no, I was not sold on the Bills' front office. I was always aware that to do what I did best, one day I might have to leave, no matter how much I loved it there.

The 1981 season started lousy. I don't know if it's a complacency that comes with being a team that has gotten farther than anyone dreamed, or what. This time out, we lost three of our first seven games. Then we recovered and went into a big Monday night game in Dallas with a 6–3 record. As it turned out, in the scheme of our season and the scheme of our lives, the game wasn't important. It is probably not even remembered by anyone who didn't butt heads in it. But something happened that night that has stuck with me like a war wound. It was the night one of my guys—and you know that "my guys" are often practically an extension of myself—was involved in a disturbing incident.

It was during the middle of the game, and we're holding on to a 14–13 lead. One of my guys suddenly gets off, and it costs us the game. I don't care if you get off, but don't let it cost me the game.

The guy was guard Conrad Dobler.

When I acquired him in 1980, I had ignored the fact that he used to bite players, that he used to kick and gouge and cheat like a dog. Yes, I know I teach football so that you do *anything* it takes to win within the rules. But you do not break the rules, if for no other reason than, it could cost you a game. I took Conrad, though, because I thought that under my system, where every advantage we extract is the result of hard work, he would change. And for a while he did.

But then Monday night, on national television, he was called for three straight unnecessary-roughness penalties. Three straight times he had leg-whipped John Dutton. The last one broke a blood vessel in Dutton's leg and this woke the Cowboys right up.

I never take a player out of the game during the middle of a series. No matter how bad he just got beat, no matter what crime he has committed, he is at least good enough to stay in there until a change of possession, or he wouldn't be out there in the first place. But with Dobler, for the first time, it was different. He was fighting his own little war with Dutton and it was killing us. I had to get him out of there before a fourth straight penalty moved them right next to our goal line.

So I did. I yanked him.

> *Ron Jessie: As Conrad came off the field, Knox told him to sit down until he had cooled off. No big deal, Knox does that a lot, talks to a lot of his players during the game. But Conrad doesn't sit. He throws his helmet. He turns to Chuck and says, "Damn you, you've just embarrassed me in front of sixty thousand people and on national TV! Damn you!"*
>
> *He crossed the line. He's turned on his daddy. You should have seen Chuck. He threw down his play card and took a step toward Conrad. We thought he was going to slug him. We'd heard of his getting into fights as an assistant coach, but we'd never seen him slug a player. We thought, This is it. But then Chuck stopped all of a sudden and went back to the game.*

How dare a man talk to me like that on the playing field. The bottom line is, I would never have talked to him like that. I yell at my players, sure, but it's always constructive yelling. And I never curse them just for cursing's sake. They're men, remember? I treat them as such, and I expect them to treat me the same. I wasn't mad because Dobler was disrespectful of a coach, I was mad because he was disrespectful of a man.

We lost the game 27–14, largely because of the momentum Dallas picked up when Dobler hurt Dutton. This only made the insult worse. I had to give the little postgame speech I always give when we lose on the road, the same ten words: "Let's get dressed and get the hell out of town."

Only this time, Dobler didn't listen. After everyone had gone, he was still in the locker room yakking to reporters, complaining about the officials, complaining about me. I stuck my head back in the door and said, "Conrad, I've had enough of this bullshit for one day. Get out of here."

The next day, in my prepractice meeting, I was still mad, and still at just one person.

> *Ron Jessie: In most of Chuck's accusatory speeches, he is really talking to just one or two players. Sometimes everybody wonders who it is, wonders whether or not he himself is guilty, which is Chuck's intention in doing it that way.*
>
> *But other times you can always tell who it is, because he is looking right at those players. That's what happened the day after the Dobler incident. He looked right at Dobler and said, "Some people have crap in their blood, I'm going to get the crap out." We had never quite heard it put that way before. It sounded bad. Conrad was dead meat.*

After that meeting I called Conrad aside and told him to meet me in my office. I told him I was benching him that week. I told him I realized it was a bad time for him, considering we were going back to the city where he once starred, St. Louis. I told him I knew I was depriving him of his time to show them. But this was *my* time to show *him.* A breakdown of respect leads to a breakdown of everything else.

Then I gave him these options: He could take it like a man, and be supportive of the new starter. He could be mad enough about this to quit and retire. Or he could be a complete ass, refusing to accept it but refusing to quit, which would mean going around making life miserable for everyone else. If that was the case, I would do something about it real fast. I would fire him or suspend him.

After the speech, I concluded with a thing I tell everybody after a chewing. It's even something I tell myself. I looked outside my office window and said, "Look, you know what's down there? That's the street. You are one floor from there. One false step and that is where you land—the street."

Dobler walked out of my office, jumped on the elevator, went to the locker room, and was greeted by a bunch of other players. According to my assistant coaches, all the players wanted to know what happened. Dobler said something like, "Today I learned pride is tough to swallow. But it will go down."

Conrad didn't play that next week, and St. Louis beat us 24–0. Maybe there's a connection there, I don't know. He formally apologized on the plane trip home. He said I didn't deserve what had happened that day. I told him, if he really felt that way, he should get himself ready for the next game. Not talk about it, but do it. He did, and he started that next week, and played well the rest of the season. At the end of the season he finally retired.

I've survived as a coach by giving everybody the benefit of the doubt. But once there is doubt, there are no more benefits.

The Dobler incident taught me a lesson that really didn't sink in until the 1987 strike, when I was in Seattle. Just because you give these guys everything—the benefit of every doubt and then more besides—don't expect the same in return. Just because you treat them like humans, don't expect them to treat you like anything other than a football coach. Most of the time, they will pay back your effort and your caring ten times over. It will be wonderful. It will be worth it. But it's those other times that you don't forget, that never leave you alone.

After those two losses, we were 6–5 and needed to win four of our last five games to get into the play-offs. The suddenly struggling New England Patriots were coming to town. We were ripe to get upset. But then fate interceded. Or was it faith? Or was it something even higher and stronger?

Whatever, on November 22, 1981, I had the most mystifying experience of my career. I say this without exaggeration.

It's like this. I'm on the Board of Trustees of Juniata College. Remember, the tiny liberal arts school I arrived at with boxing gloves and left with honors?

Well, I'm like the unofficial, nonresident alumni liaison, and this particular year I was helping the school raise $5 million to build an athletic complex.

But we have only about eight thousand living alumni, so raising that many bills is pretty tough. I figure, What the hell, I'm doing OK, so I pledge fifty thousand dollars.

About that time, Juniata College president Fred Binder and some other board members plan to come up to Buffalo for a game. It sounds like a good time to give them a first installment on the fifty grand. (You don't think I have ever had that much just lying around, do you?) I'd give them fifteen thousand dollars while they were there and save on a postage stamp. Unfortunately, they decide to come up for the New England game. It's the last game I want to see them. Our team is down and hurting and ready for embarrassment, and these are people I want to impress.

But Sunday morning they arrive. So I ask Shirley to give me a blank check before I leave the house for the stadium, and I figure, after the game I'll fill it in.

Then I get to my office and start thinking: If we lost, would I be in the mood to give somebody fifteen thousand dollars? I doubted it. The way our team was going, I had better fill that thing out right then or they might never see the money. So I pull out the check, write in the fifteen G's before the game, and put it in my money clip. It is burning a hole in my pocket during all four quarters.

Then the game's finish burns a hole through me.

We are down by four points with thirty-five seconds left and the ball on our own thirty-yard line. There are no time-outs left. We send four receivers downfield, and somehow our quarterback, Joe Ferguson, gets the ball to Roland Hooks, who makes it to the Patriots' thirty-yard line. Then Ferguson throws it out of bounds to stop the clock.

We've got one play left. We send three receivers to one side of the end zone for the Hail Mary, the Big Ben, whatever you want to call it. Ferguson tosses it up there, a mass of bodies knock it around . . . and Hooks comes down with it. Touchdown. We win. I don't believe in miracles, but since everybody else does, I'll say it: a miracle.

After the game, in the locker room, I surprise President Binder with the check. He is so stunned he sheds a tear. And I'm convinced: if I had not written that check before the game, we would not have won the game. If I had not given, I would not have received. When you give, you receive. That's a philosophy that transcends religion. It transcends anything the preacher can tell you on Sunday. What can I say? It's eighth-grade Sewickley.

We go on to win four of our last five games and make the play-offs. We then beat the Jets 31–27 in a wild-card game, but lose to Cincinnati 28–21 in our divisional play-off game. It was the same Bengals that one game later made it to the Super Bowl. And we lost on the same kind of mistake that Knute Rockne couldn't control. While driving for the tying touchdown, on a third-down play, our offense misread the thirty-second clock and cost us a big third-down pass because of a delay-of-game penalty. Haunted by more tiny mistakes.

Right after the season, with the franchise freshened up such that you'd think it had just been run over by a vacuum cleaner, with the team riding back-to-back play-off appearances, with attendance at an *average* of seventy-five thousand, Ralph Wilson called me into his Detroit office.

I've got two years left on my contract; he offers me two more.

"Sounds good," I say. "What's the raise?"

"Oh no," says Ralph. "There is no raise."

Looking back on it, maybe I should have stayed cool. Maybe I should have thought, The cost of living is pretty reasonable in Buffalo, the wife and Chuckie are very happy here, and I can probably handle a bad job as long as I have a good home. Maybe that's how I should have reacted. Maybe when the punch hit me and knocked me down, I should have stayed down. It would have been easier. It would have been safer.

But I got up. I thought about Tom Cousineau; I thought about the indoor practice facility; I thought about an impending salary battle with Joe Cribbs. I thought, To hell with it. And here's what I said:

"Ralph, you've just embarrassed yourself and me."

I turned around, walked out, got on a plane home, and decided before we hit the ground that after the 1982 season I would be gone. I knew I would have a year left on my contract and I would be breaking that promise. But Ralph had broken many promises to me, too. I was gone.

It wasn't too hard for me to keep quiet about it. The media are lucky if I tell them who my starting quarterback is going to be. Not overloading my ass with my mouth—I'm pretty good at that.

Maybe I should have tried to understand Ralph more, to be more tolerant of someone who didn't think exactly like I did. I'll be honest, there were some other things I should have thought about. Sometimes when I get a phone call from some friend in some bar in Buffalo, telling about how cold it is but how warm his liquor and his buddies make him feel, I'm almost certain I should have stayed.

But it's an old problem—my daggone vision. I see only one direction for my family, my team, and myself. I see only a single path to follow, the path that is the one best way to getting the job done. Those who don't want to get the job done, well, I don't see them. And if they insist on blocking my vision, then I am the one who must leave. I decided that unless something drastic happened in 1982, I was gone.

Well, something drastic did happen. And it made me wish I had left sooner.

We had gone a long, long way in just two years with running back Joe Cribbs. He was AFC Rookie of the Year his first season and All-Pro the second. So in the winter of 1981 he went to Ralph and asked for a raise. Ralph agreed, but the raise he wrote down was so small, Cribbs didn't know if the man was talking merit or cost of living. So Joe held out, wouldn't come to training camp, and said he wasn't going to show up at all during the season.

Now, I normally won't get involved in contract negotiations. Owners don't want guys like me in there who believe a man should get all he can because a man is only worth what he can get. If I do go in, I end up acting like the player's agent, and the owner ends up looking at me horrified, as if to ask, Are you crazy? So normally I stay the hell out of it.

But the Cribbs case was ridiculous. If I was to continue coaching like I had coached this team to two straight playoffs, I had to be given Cribbs. Without him I wouldn't have a stinger. So I got Ralph on the phone in Detroit—most of our arguments were conducted by phone—and I told him a few things: He was being penny wise and pound foolish. This was going to be just like Cousineau. He'd save money now, but it would cost us down the road. That raise might seem like a lot for the moment, but in a couple of years—the way the salaries were escalating—it wouldn't be anything. And you'd have the services of the guy for all those years. Why make such an important part of this team unhappy? We were winning, weren't we? And putting people in the seats?

Ralph wouldn't budge. I realized then he was the kind of

person who will put money into a franchise to build it up, but then once it is built up, he'll back off. It happened before I got there, and it has happened since.

With Ralph ignoring me, I went to see Joe Cribbs toward the end of training camp. I didn't plead with him to come back. I would never ask a player to accept less money just for me. He's got to think only of himself and his family, not me or his team. What if I got fired? Or what if he broke his leg and was finished before getting what he was worth? Who would feed his children then?

Together, Joe and I worked out an alternative contract that he liked, and that would have saved the Bills money on his original demands.

I showed it to Ralph. But again management could not come to terms.

At the same time, wide receiver Jerry Butler was holding out, and he didn't get his money until right at the end of training camp. So for our opening game, we didn't have our great running back, and our best wide receiver showed up only at the last minute.

And that, man, was *really* that. I was fed up and finished.

We won our first two games anyway, but I don't know how, because I was having an incredibly hard time just coaching. But as if sensing my distress, the team responded, even beating Minnesota 23–22 on "Monday Night Football" after being down 17–0. Then came the 1982 strike. So much for the season. The strike lasted what seemed like a couple of dozen weeks, although it was really only seven. But it was enough to split our team apart, cloud our vision, and end our season.

By design, my teams survive and win because of an underlying feeling of closeness among the players and me. Everybody uses the word "family," but it's not so much like a family as like a bunch of guys thrown together in a bunker. The vision is survival, the method is trust, and the victories and defeats are shared. You'll notice I'll never publicly trash one of my players. And my players will never trash each other. We're in it together. I'm like them and they are like me.

It is with this fine thread that we stitch together our victories. It's a tricky thread to twine, and once it's there it is extremely strong, but some things can snap it apart. Like a players' strike. I remember seeing my team come out of pre-strike union meetings arguing with each other, talking about fist fights and such. I knew that if we went on a long strike, we wouldn't have a chance when we came back.

Sure enough, we didn't. Joe Cribbs rejoined the team after the strike without a contract, but it didn't do any good. We won only two out of seven games after the strike. The players were all still fighting among themselves. I can't convey my message to people who don't hear things the same.

> *Reggie McKenzie: The strike tore our team right in two. Some teams can win like that. But not a Knox team. Peace at home, war on the outside. That's what he preaches. That's the only way he and his brother, Billy, ever made it. That's the only way his teams can make it.*

I think my Buffalo career ended in Tampa Bay, in the fifth game after the strike. We had won two of the first four games and were ready to win this one, down by one point at the Buc twenty-yard line with just a few seconds left. We were going to run one more play before the winning field-goal attempt. We gave the ball to Roosevelt Leaks and told him to run a few steps and fall down. He did. But he fell without the ball. Tampa's Lee Roy Selmon had broken through and ripped it from him, causing a fumble. They recovered and we lost 24–23. Remember, this was the same Bucs team that would win only two games the following year.

We lost our final two games after that, and I was history. Well, not exactly history. Not until I told Brent Musburger. I was asked to be on one of his CBS pregame shows before a play-off game. I knew the subject of my job would come up. I thought carefully about how to word my response. I wanted to make sure I didn't embarrass Ralph. But I also wanted to make sure the rest of the football world knew that, hey, I was available. I wanted to get my name out there as quickly as possible. I wanted to get my name out there because I felt, with my record, I was employable.

So I went on with Musburger, and right away he asked me if I was going back to Buffalo. He lobbed it right in my wheelhouse. I was ready for it.

I told him, "I'm going to consider my options." I figured that should do it. That should tell the NFL world, in its own little secret code, that I was gone from Buffalo.

It did. And I got lucky. One place on the West Coast immediately called me, and I immediately made plane reservations to go visit.

You may not believe this, but remember where the chapter started? That's where it will end. With me preparing to board a plane from Buffalo to discuss a head coaching position with the Los Angeles Rams.

8

Seattle

"The Los Angeles Rams would like to welcome back as our new head coach, our old head coach, Chuck ..."

It sounded crazy, but when you feel you have no options, crazy *is* an option. I know, I tossed around at night with this after the 1982 season. Finally, I made arrangements to fly cross-country to interview with Georgia Frontiere, C. R.'s widow, about taking over the Rams head coaching job. Why interview there again? Simple. They called me. I really didn't want to go, but I had already decided I couldn't stay in Buffalo; and seeing as I was no longer fifteen, I could not try to sneak in the Navy. I had mentally cornered myself and knew of no other angles out. At least on this Rams interview I could bring more than one suit with me.

It was the second week of January, a Monday, and I had made arrangements to fly out for the interview on the upcoming weekend. The reservations were notable in that they included a seat for Shirley. If I got the job, it would be the first time Shirley had ever seen a place we were going to live *before* we moved there. Imagine that. Six moves, six complete changes of life, and not once had she known where she was going. Her only road map had been that of trust. The only problem this time was, it was the one time she *didn't* want to go on a job interview.

Shirley Knox: I have to admit it, I loved Buffalo. It was so much like us. I wasn't sure I was ready to move back to Southern California. Although I would have followed Chuck anywhere, I was privately hoping for another way out.

Instantly, out of the Perry Como blue, that way appeared. A couple of days before our flight, we get a call from Seattle, from a guy named Mike McCormack. He had just given up an interim head coaching job with the Seahawks to become the general manager. Earlier in 1982 the club had fired long-time coach Jack Patera, and now McCormack's first duty was to replace him. Why did they think to call me? Because somebody out there had done the one thing I constantly preach against: somebody had spoken out of place, somebody had whispered to the Seahawks that Ralph Wilson was allowing Chuck Knox to be interviewed by other teams. Although anybody who saw me with Brent Musburger that fall could have guessed my intentions, the Seahawks had somehow heard it from an inside source.

Seahawks manager Mike McCormack: Chuck wasn't on our original list of coaches because he was still under contract with Buffalo. We had already interviewed four or five different people, and had not even thought of him. Then we heard through the grapevine that Ralph Wilson was allowing Chuck to be interviewed by LA. So we called Chuck. He told us it was true. We called Ralph Wilson, obtained permission, and then called Chuck back. We asked him if, on the way to LA, he could stop by and see us. It was a hassle, sure, and we were worried about imposing on him and his wife. But Knox said not to worry. In fact, he almost shouted to us not to worry. He and Shirley jumped on the next plane out of Buffalo and pulled into Seattle on the Wednesday night.

I wondered if Mike heard my sigh of relief. Not only was he talking about a head coaching job, he was talking about one that wasn't in Southern California. I had heard about Seattle's rain, its gray, its dreariness. I had read about it being so far from the rest of civilization that back in the 1800s businessmen on the East Coast would ship women out there by boat so the lumberjacks would have someone to talk to. It sounded like the perfect place to get my kind of job done.

We flew to Seattle, and when we got off the plane it was so foggy, we could hardly see our hands in front of us. They put us up at the Sorrento Hotel, a wonderful old place, solid and well-made, yet small and elegant—a near-perfect description of the city. By the time we got to the front door, it was raining all kinds of animals. And we were loving it. One night for dinner we met the team owners, the Nordstrom family. The next night we had dinner with the McCormacks at a trendy place called the Juanita Cafe. In between I learned some things about the Seattle Seahawks—like, this was a program upon which it was raining all kinds of animals.

This was a program that in the previous three years had gone 14–27. In the seven years of the franchise there had been only two winning seasons, and no play-off appearances. The way things were run, it seemed they hated the idea of succeeding.

Most certainly, my kind of team.

> *Mike McCormack: We knew right away it was Chuck's kind of team. We had worked up a profile of what we needed. We needed a teacher, a player's coach. We needed somebody who would walk through the locker room. Not to knock Jack Patera, but he would never walk through the locker room. After just a couple of conversations, it was obvious we needed Knox.*
>
> *I drove him to the airport Saturday morning and popped the question right there, like I was asking him for a stick of gum. Right there in the terminal, I asked him to be the second full-time head coach of the Seattle Seahawks. His answer, I later learned, was typical of him. He told me he first had to keep a promise. He had told Georgia Frontiere*

that he would go down and have dinner with her, and he had to fulfill that promise. I would have to wait.

Imagine me telling McCormack he had to wait. I'm surprised I said that. After just three days I respected him as much as any general manager I had ever worked for. The reason was simple: He had walked the sidelines. He had been a Hall-of-Famer for the Cleveland Browns from 1954 to 1962, and as an offensive lineman at that. Chuck Knox working for an offensive lineman—what more could I ask? I told Mike I would call him Sunday night with a decision after my weekend with Georgia. But I had already decided; that weekend in LA would be nothing more than the keeping of a promise. No way was I going to southern California when I could take over a bare-bones program and work for an ex-offensive lineman—and all in a rain that felt like Sewickley. I was definately going to Seattle, I was definitely going to call him. Only at dinner over at Georgia's house, we got talking and I never got to a phone. I figured I would just call Mike on Monday, no big thing.

Mike McCormack: Knox said he would call on Sunday, and we waited and waited, but he didn't. We thought, Oh no, maybe we've lost him. But then Monday morning the phone rang and it was Chuck. He said if everything was still the same as when we parted Saturday, he would like the job. He said he only had to stop by Detroit and see Ralph and get out of his contract.

The next day he called from Detroit, saying he had met with Ralph, and that he would come to work for the Seattle Seahawks. It was January 26, 1983.

It was a Tuesday, and I told Chuck we had to announce it that day. I asked him how soon he could be out there for the press conference. He said, "Well, I've got to fly to Buffalo tonight to take care of some things . . . how does Wednesday morning sound?" Talk about anxious.

In a heartbeat I went from anxiousness to anxiety. From a hotel in Detroit, where I had accepted the Seahawks' job offer, it was on to Buffalo for the official announcement—and some very unofficial emotion.

> *Shirley Knox: It was terrible. I loved Buffalo. Sitting there in the Detroit airport brought the realization home to me. In a sense we weren't going back to Buffalo ever, except for a change of clothes.*
>
> *By the time we got on the plane out of Detroit, the Buffalo media had been alerted. We landed at the Buffalo airport and reporters were waiting, ready to surround us. I saw a few of our old friends standing in the back and I couldn't help myself. I started to cry. I have never cried like that in public before, but I have never loved a place like I loved Buffalo. So here I am crying. And the cameras are rolling. They are getting it on television, all of it, every tear. I wanted to hide. I wanted to run back to our house and sit on our little lake and hide.*

In a way, I was lucky: I spent a few minutes with reporters, then packed a new bag and hopped another jet to Seattle. Compared to Shirley, who had to stay in Buffalo another couple of months until Chuckie's school was out in the summer, I've always been lucky. It's easier to leave when you leave right away. When it comes to my work, I've never had much use for a rear-view mirror, it only distracts from your forward vision.

When I landed in Seattle on a January Wednesday afternoon, it was obvious that most of the horde of newspaper reporters had never seen me in person. They suddenly started comparing my appearance to that of General Alexander Haig. I wouldn't have minded, if I had had his clout. Later I wondered if they were comparing us because I had walked into an out-and-out war.

I spent the first couple of months living in a suite in the Bellevue Red Lion hotel and working with the Seahawks front office. Things were fine on that end. The staff were receptive to my ideas and vision. Still, it helped that of my ten coaches, I had brought six with me from Buffalo. They knew how I did things, and they quietly spread the word—it works better that way. We even felt comfortable enough to work out a nice draft-day trade, giving up a second- and third-round pick to Houston for their top pick, which became Curt Warner.

When my first group of Seahawks arrived that summer, the comfort vanished. This was an organization that, while aiming toward the big, Super Bowl-type goals, had forgotten the little things. Despite working on a lush practice field on the shores of a lake, despite working in a facility isolated from the rest of the world by thick brush and an almost-hidden driveway, the players were not placed in an atmosphere where it was easy for them to succeed.

We made changes. We added water breaks during practice. We promised them sweats and gloves when they were cold. We gave them advance notice on days off, even informing their wives so there would be no confusion. I instituted an open-door/closed-door office policy: the players could come talk to me and the door would close behind them. No one else, not even an assistant coach, would know what we had discussed. Building the little bridges between me and my players was important that first spring because I wanted us, as a team, to cross that big span to the play-offs as soon as possible. In Buffalo, I had waited two years before making a push. I was getting too old for that now.

> *Former Rams and Seahawks tight end Charle Young: Chuck came in and said, "I'm throwing out the two-year program. I'm not coaching losers again. The losers here are gone."*

Sometimes that first year I still felt like a loser, only it had nothing to do with my teams. We're talking about something a bit more important here, my son. You might remember that I wanted a six-year contract in Buffalo so I could allow my son, Chuck, to start and finish high school in the same place. If you were counting, you might have noticed that I only stayed five years.

During that time Chuck became very comfortable in the very fine Orchard Park High. He made good friends, he played football, he did a pretty good job of growing up. He was so happy there that when I told the family we were going to Seattle, he asked me if he could stay behind. He said he would stay with the parents of a good friend, just for his senior year. I knew the particular parents and I knew my son, and I had great faith and trust in them both. And I certainly felt bad for leaving Chuck in the lurch in the first place.

But I told him no.

I didn't think a boy his age should be without his proper guardians. I told him that there was too much out there to cause him trouble. I made Chuck join me the way I made Colleen forgo San Diego State and join us in Buffalo. Looking back, did I really mean this about a boy who had hardly caused an ounce of trouble in his whole life? Maybe, and maybe not. Maybe it was that same old feeling that if I didn't take strong steps to protect what was valuable to me, I would lose it. Maybe I made a mistake. But if I did, it was almost as if I had no control over the matter.

Suffice to say, often those days I felt better on the field than at home. The players were attentive, receptive, wide-eyed. I'm not sure why, other than that one of the first things I told them was, they weren't that bad. Whether I had a right to believe that or not—and let me tell you, these weren't the 1986 Giants we're talking about—I still told them. And maybe they hadn't heard that before. I was simply trying to give them a vision, my vision, one which you can figure out yourself, standing in front of a mirror at home. It works like this:

Hold your left hand above your head, parallel to the ground. Hold your right hand down around your waist, also parallel to the ground. Your left hand is your vision; your right hand is current reality. Winners bring reality up to their vision. Losers lower their vision down to reality. I consider myself the kind that brings the right hand up. The only players I ever have problems with are the ones who insist on bringing the left hand down.

If I come in and look at you and see a Pro Bowl-type player (right hand up), and all you see is just an average player (right hand down), then we're going to have problems. You're going to take the path of least resistance; you're going to allow my left hand (vision) to drop down to your right hand (reality), while I'm going to fight to make that reality match my vision.

There will be disagreements, and we may have a fight or two, but as a coach it is my job to fight until that vision and reality are on the same plane, or you are on a different team. In the playbook that first year, I wrote these words, which serve as the beginnings of my vision: "Winners form the habit of concentrating on what they want to have happen. Losers concentrate on what they don't want to have happen. In pressure situations, winners call up past wins, losers call up past losses, and both are self-fulfilling."

The Seahawks were an average team that first season, yet they went all the way to the American Football Conference championship game. Some say it was Curt Warner, others say it was Steve Largent; I say it was all of us fighting together to make reality match vision.

Not that the vision didn't need a little enforcing now and then, as even big football players occasionally need to be reminded what is good for them. That is why, before we ever played an official down, I instituted our fine system.

When I arrived in Seattle there were fines, but not many, and at the end of the year, the players would use the money to buy a stereo system for the locker room, or some other toy. I changed that. Our fine money is now distributed to charity. If someone is fined, I don't see much use in rewarding him six months later with that same money. We'll give it to those who can truly benefit from his mistakes. In my five years in Seattle, through fines, we've given more than twenty-five thousand dollars to charity.

In my perfect football world, everybody is on the same page, and you don't need fines. But by the time I arrived at the Seahawks, I had been around long enough to realize there is no perfect football world as long as humans are wearing the helmets. You can talk about pride and unity until you are Seahawk blue in the face, but goals will be ignored, rules will be broken, and people doing the right thing will want to see punishment. I don't fine for those doing the wrong thing, but for all the other ones. Think about yourself. If you are doing the speed limit in a 25 MPH zone, isn't it comforting to see the guy going 40 MPH get a ticket?

I developed a set of punishments and told my players, *I'm not fining you, you are fining you.* For example, *Overweight: twenty-five dollars a pound.* Others think, This guy has no self-discipline, why should I? *Late for meeting: fifty dollars.* Others think, We can't count on this player Sunday, he's not taking this game seriously, or he'd be here on time. *Weapons in training camp: five hundred dollars.* I take these items from them, no questions asked, and give them back after camp.

Once the 1983 games started, as I had hoped, the players realized that our new vision would work. We won three out of our first five games, including victories against Cleveland and the New York Jets. The players were saying it had started feeling good to be a Seahawk again. A couple of weeks into that season, they got a somewhat more vivid glimpse of what I meant by vision. It was late in the game, we were winning by a couple of points, and there were just a few seconds left on the clock. All at once, my Seahawks started to storm onto the field. I thought, Hey, wait a minute, if we get a penalty for this, it will give them a chance to run for another play. I've seen careers finished on one play.

I screamed, "Get back! Get back!" I saw a huge body run past me, and out of instinct I turned and slugged him. It was

Mike Tice, a tight end who's about a foot taller than me and fifty pounds heavier. I landed my punch directly in his gut. He doubled over. I looked up to see a couple of pairs of eyes get like fried eggs. Everybody shut up and ran back. Once Tice caught his breath, he stumbled back, too.

"Coach," he said, gasping. "You almost knocked me out!"

"No, I didn't," I told him. "If I had wanted to knock you out, I would have used my right."

Give the players credit for a little vision, too. The next day at our weekly special-teams awards, I was given the Hit of the Week award.

It was that kind of spontaneous first year. Curt Warner was incredible, winning the AFC rushing title with 1,449 yards. Receiver Steve Largent, who should one day be my second player voted into the Hall of Fame (Merlin Olsen was the first), caught for more than a thousand yards again. The young defense was strong. Yet still, in other areas we were struggling. We go into the season's thirteenth week just 6–6. Then we defeat Kansas City 51–48 in overtime in one of the wildest games I've seen since the existence of the AFL. But then we lose to Dallas, which means we need to go into the Meadowlands and beat the Giants if we are to reach the play-offs for the first time ever. We do it, 17–12, and before you know it, we have beaten Denver in the wild-card game in Seattle.

Thus was set up one of the biggest upset wins of my career. We traveled to Miami in the conference semifinals to play the mighty Dolphins. We were young and impressionable; they were Dan Marino and great. Nobody said we could win. Nobody gave us a chance. And the football-watching nation that had sort of adopted us that season now turned on us. Everybody said we were out of our league.

After sixty minutes the Dolphins were out of the play-offs. We had won 27–20 in a game that forever sold Seattle on its Seahawks. We had been leading when Dave Krieg threw a big interception late that allowed Miami to tie us. But then we drove sixty-six yards in five plays to win. Largent had been held without a catch for fifty-eight minutes, but he caught back-to-back passes for fifty-six yards in that last drive.

The season before this, the Dolphins had played in the Super Bowl. The following season they would play in the Super Bowl. But not this time.

The Orange Bowl was filled with seventy-one-thousand fans. They cursed us. They threw things at us. They even harassed the Seahawk fans that had flown down for the game. But we did it. We won. One of the Northwest's favorite jokes was suddenly a single game from the Super Bowl. Their first. My first.

> *Reggie McKenzie: Right before the final gun I turned around so Chuck would be on my right side, away from my bad left shoulder. Then I picked him up. I don't know why, he didn't ask for it—I just followed my heart. I guess that picture of Chuck on my shoulder has become symbolic of the Seahawks' success. They should have taken more photographs in the locker room, after the game. Our safety Dave Brown stood up and gave a little speech, and then all the players started chanting, "Chuck, Chuck, Chuck." He starts crying, just like he did in Buffalo when we beat the Rams. Only then did I realize what this win represented: he had taken a terrible losing team and placed them on the threshold of greatness in one season. Imagine that. One season.*

When I really wanted to cry was later after that game, when Don Shula came out with this comment: "I knew Chuck Knox would get the job done up there. But I didn't know he would do it this soon."

After my initial celebration period, the first thing I thought of was, How can I make my players understand this win? Of course it meant we were going to the AFC championship game, but that's not what I meant. Nearly as important as experiencing a big win is understanding *how* you won, *why*

you won, so you can go on to win again. While I was thinking up different speeches on the plane ride home, a pilot passed
the word back: I wouldn't be needing a speech. There were
ten thousand fans waiting for us at the Seattle airport. Anything I might say, those people's presence could say for me.

> *Reggie McKenzie: It had been a long flight and we were
> all very tired. Normally when fans met Chuck Knox teams
> at the airport, he would order a couple of team captains
> to go out and meet them, and then put the rest of the
> team on a bus to avoid the hassle.*
>
> *But not this time. Chuck stood up and said, "Let's do
> the right thing and walk through this. All of us." So we
> did. It was kind of scary. I thought people were going to
> tear our clothes off. But by the time we got to our cars, I
> guarantee you, we knew we had just placed ourselves one
> game from a Super Bowl.*

Seeing all of those people pushing and pulling and making
us out to be daggone rock stars made me understand: This
team does not play alone, we play with an extra man, a twelfth
man—our fans. I said something about this to reporters and
soon people were running around wearing Seahawks jerseys
with the number 12 on the back. By the end of the next season, our franchise had actually retired the number, becoming
the first pro franchise to retire a number in honor of fans. So
the only number 12s I'll ever have will be that guy about ten
rows up, that woman in the loge boxes, and—hey, I'll take
those people on my team anytime.

It wasn't as if the fans in Seattle needed a jersey to make
them nuts. Everything there has always been all Seahawks.
The nightly fifteen-minute training camp report that ran after
the news on local TV attracted more viewers in that time
slot than Ted Koppel's "Nightline." When we opened our new
headquarters a couple of years back, people waited two and
a half hours in line for a tour. A quick tour, during the summer. That's nuts.

This means whenever we come home from a good game, there are fans waiting for us at the airport. Unfortunately, the entire team can't walk through that crowd every time, like we did after returning from Miami. So the next day there are always complaints.

Let me explain: We walked through the crowd after that Miami game because it was the first big franchise win, and I wanted the fans to know that they were part of it. But normally we will not walk through, not all of us, because we are just too emotionally drained. We are whipped. It has been a long, long day and here we are, usually late at night, just wanting to get home. Our bodies and minds can't withstand being beat on and touched and grabbed for five thousand autographs. It's suffocating. And often it's not secure. We often avoid the fans simply on orders from the airport people.

We love the fans, don't get me wrong. We just wish somebody would invent a better way to get to know them.

A week after the Miami game, we got to know ourselves a little better when the predictable happened. We were beaten 30–14 by the future Super Bowl champions, the LA Raiders, down in the Coliseum. No excuses offered, none needed. According to all the wise prognosticators, we shouldn't have been involved in the game in the first place. If they had their choice of teams, ten out of ten coaches in this league would take the Raiders squad over our squad without even thinking. At the time, the talent differential was huge. And two weeks later the Raiders defeated Washington in the Super Bowl.

We had made it to that Raider game largely on heart, but often in a big game like that, you need more. You need that extra bit of ability, that extra bit of talent that will get you the big play at the big time. The guy who can throw the eighty-yard bomb. The guy who can break through with the sack. Maybe we just didn't have more. Maybe I didn't have more. You would think that the longer you coach, the less you wonder about those things, but it's just the other way around.

On the subject of hearts, by the end of the 1983 season, one special one had finally warmed up.

> *Chuckie Knox: I guess my first year in Seattle, like my dad's, ended up OK after all. My high-school football team won the state championship for the first time in the school's history, and I was the starting running back. I used this to help get a full scholarship to the University of Arizona.*
>
> *When I left Buffalo I left my friends and girlfriend, and everything, but I ended up gaining a whole lot more. I learned how to adjust to change. I learned how to adapt to my environment. I don't know, maybe my dad really did have a good idea by forcing me out there. Maybe it brought us closer.*

The settling of the team and my family all served to set up 1984. My second season in Seattle, it was going to be a great season, everybody was back and healthy from our surprise year and . . . Foolish me. In the first game of 1984, against Cleveland, Curt Warner tripped and tore up his knee. He was out. For the season. The first game.

As we left the field following a 33–0 win, I was not thinking about the win, because I could only think, What is going to happen to the career of Curt Warner? That thought was followed by, What is going to happen to us?

> *Steve Moore: Losing Warner killed Chuck, just devastated him. You could see it in his face. He didn't say anything, never does, but you could tell. The first two days of the next week, he walked around looking white.*

I thought long into the next three nights about how to console this team. I couldn't think of anything, perhaps because I was a bit inconsolable myself. I walked into the Wednesday meeting, looked at all the players sitting in their little desks, and thought, *OK, just be me.* It's worked before. It's the only thing that works. I rolled my hand into a fist and threw out the following:

"The absence of Curt Warner will never be an excuse for anyone on this football team not to play up to his best. It will be no excuse for the coaches, myself included, not to win. Surely our defensive football team can improve and get better, because Curt Warner does not play defense. Surely our special teams can improve, because Curt Warner does not play on them. And surely the offense can pick up the slack, because two or three people can be used to get Curt Warner's yards, and two or three are always better than one. Gentlemen, it's simple. We are going to play the hand we are dealt. Period."

> *Seahawks assistant coach Joe Vitt: I've never seen a team more embarrassed. Guys who were already planning excuses for next week hung their heads. Guys who had been openly moaning about Warner suddenly shut up. The message had been received.*

To make sure that message would sustain itself in the locker room, I went out and hired a guy who understood what I was talking about—Franco Harris. The former Pittsburgh star was only with the team eight games, but he did what he was hired to do. He settled things down. He was like one of those big old comforters that can get you through a night of cold. Our young guys clung to him until they understood that their world did not begin and end with Curt Warner.

> *Charle Young: Signing Franco was a brilliant move. It picked morale way up. He didn't stay long, but he set the season in motion in the right direction.*

The first game after losing Curt, we beat San Diego 31 – 17. Then we traveled to New England and took a 23 – 0 first-half lead. The players were following my plan, believing in

my vision. Things were going amazingly well, considering
we had lost the heart of our offense. Then, as if the difficulty
of our task had finally hit us, we blew that halftime lead.
New England scored 38 unanswered points to whip us 38–
23. Give the Patriots credit for one of the best comebacks
I've witnessed. Don't give us credit for anything. I consider
the act of playing harder when you are ahead as important as
not giving up when you are behind.

The next week in practice I decided, That's it, enough talk.
The one thing I had not yet done was *show* them how Curt
Warner's loss wasn't going to affect us.

> *Joe Vitt: Chuck calls us coaches together and says, "Men,
> I damn well guarantee you, that's the last time we blow
> a lead like that." Then, in Thursday's practice, he turns
> his hat backward, walks to where the huddle had been
> forming, and yells at the offense as they are breaking up
> after a play, "Get back here! I'm calling the plays now!"*
>
> *He calls one play, then another—fifteen straight plays,
> bam-bam-bam. He is grunting and sweating, and the of-
> fense is so upset it's doing the same. I think Knox finally
> just scared the Curt Warner memories right out of them.*

Not to say I ever could have been a quarterback—I'd probably have killed some wide receiver—but something happened that afternoon in the huddle. We lost only one of our
next eleven games and made the play-offs, earning a wild-
card date with the Los Angeles Raiders. We were 12–4 and
playing on reams of emotion, yet these were the Raiders, the
defending world champions, and it was 1983 in Miami all
over again. The experts gave us as much chance of winning
as Curt Warner had of being the hero. They claimed we
couldn't run, because Warner was gone and our starting running back was Dan Doornink, who in his spare time was
studying to be a doctor. They claimed we couldn't pass, and
then were seemingly proved right just before kickoff, when
standout tackle Ron Essink got the flu. We were forced to

use a kid named Sid Abramowitz, who was making only the second start of his three-year career. Lining up across from him would be Lyle Alzado, looking even meaner than he looks on television commercials. The quarterback was dead.

So we ran. And ran. We ran fifty-nine times for a season-high 205 yards on the ground. Doornink gained a club play-off record of 126 yards. Alzado beat on Abramowitz for only two sacks, mostly because we dropped back to pass only twelve times. We won 13–7 in one of the most fun games I've ever coached. We didn't out-talent them or out-flash them. We just outworked them. Did I hear somebody say Ground Chuck, that cute newspaper phrase used to describe my offense? Call it what you want, it landed us in the second round of the play-offs for the second straight year.

A week later we traveled back to Miami for the divisional play-off game. It wasn't even close, which I'm sure made those people who lost money on us in 1983 laugh, but let them. Our wonder season collapsed in a 31–10 loss to the Dolphins, but a bottom piece of the NFL power structure had been pushed aside and the Seahawks had squeezed in. Two ways you could tell: They made two straight play-off appearances, including one without their best player. And rumors about their head coach were being spread on national television.

One night after the season, shortly after I won my fourth NFL Coach of the Year award, I received a phone call from a business friend asking if I had watched O. J. Simpson on television.

"He's saying you're going to be the next head coach of the Detroit Lions," said my friend.

"Is that so?" I said.

I thought it was a joke, and maybe it was. But it advanced so quickly from joke to rumor to unconfirmed report, people started believing it. I never heard from Detroit. In fact, the first person with whom I discussed it in an official capacity was the woman whose title is Coach's Wife. About a week after the rumor began—and by this time more newspapers were running it than ran crossword puzzles—Shirley approached me. "I've heard the rumors, and whatever you do, I'm with you," she said, repeating those same words she first spoke twenty-five years ago when I was leaving Kentucky for the New York Jets. "But I love Seattle. I love our life. I am tired of moving."

"I haven't heard any more than you've heard," I assured her. "But I guess from now on I won't listen."

The only good thing about this was, the Seahawks had been hearing those rumors, too. The next day Mike McCormack, who had talked about giving me a new deal long before any rumors, called and said, "Let's do something about your contract *now*." I suggested he call around the league and find out what the other coaches who ranked in coaching's all-time top ten were making these days—you know, fair market value.

Mike did call around, and then a couple of days later we held a press conference. I signed a new contract with a nice raise and that was that. As quickly as they left O. J. Simpson's mouth that night, the rumors stopped. It's funny how that works.

Like O. J. I've been holding forth regularly on television, once a week, one hour a week. It's not national television, but I bet I get more phone calls than he does. It's called "The Chuck Knox Show," which isn't too original, but then people don't want originality; they want my comments on the previous week's games, and they want a chance to scream in my ear. My show comes on a Seattle channel immediately after the Monday night football game, so I have to wait in the studio and watch the end of the game. Then I am on the air for anywhere from twenty minutes to forty-five minutes, always ending at 11:00 P.M.

Recently, as the NFL games have gotten longer, my air time has grown shorter and shorter. Once, a couple of years ago, I was asked to stay past 11:00 P.M. because otherwise my show would have been reduced to just a few minutes. I politely declined because Shirley was in the car waiting to take me to dinner. My show may just be once a week, but during the season I find time to have dinner with Shirley just once a week, too.

I am also on the radio about once a week, when I take call-in questions about every move I've made that week. Or almost every move. At least I answer from my heart. The way it works in other radio talk shows, somebody calls in with a question, a bunch of producers run around and find an answer, and then they put it up on a big screen in front of the guy doing the talking. He reads the screen and says, "Uh, well, if my memory serves me correct, your answer is Johnny Unitas, and the year was 1964."

If only every question could be about an old quarterback. During the 1985 season, less than a year after we were unquestionably heroes, the phones on my TV and radio shows were ringing off the hook, and for a different reason. No longer did a caller begin his question, "Chuck, you're the greatest thing . . ." Suddenly it was "Why was this . . ." And "What were you thinking about on that . . ."

The myth about 1985 was, Curt Warner was healthy, and with the addition of a player like that, a 12−4 team should go undefeated. Wrong, Curt Warner was not completely healthy yet; it would take him another full year to gain back all of his mobility from such an extensive knee operation. Thus it was the season of 8−8, featuring the birth of the "terrible twos": we'd win two, lose two, win two—all season long until we had knocked ourselves right out of the playoffs. People wondered why it was such a consistent inconsistency.

I can explain that about as well as I can explain our 20−13 loss to New England that season, when quarterback Dave Kreig's late pass at the Patriots' two-yard line was tipped and then intercepted and run back to our two-yard line. I can explain it about as well as I can explain the three-point overtime loss in Denver, or the three-point loss to the Jets. It was an unreal season, that's how I explain it.

A season like that, when every game is an unknown and

every outcome is unexpected, when jumping out from behind every wall is another question, even after you've exhausted the answers . . . it all makes for long weekends.
Contrary to the headlines, we don't have game *days*, we have
game *weekends*. They are a collection of moments that travel
at the approximate speed of a John Elway pass, but inside,
they burn slow. Every move is calculated, every hour ac-
counted for, yet as hard as you try to control everything,
sometimes you can only watch and hang on. Here, let me
show you one.

Saturday night: We check into our hotel, even if it's a home
game, which surprises some people, but actually it's eighth-
grade Sewickley. You want your players to think only about
the game, so all the guys need to be on the same turf, under
a common denominator. You don't want a guy coming to a
game Sunday morning tired from staying up all night with
the baby, or worrying about the milk his other child spilled
on him that morning, or upset because he and his wife are in
the middle of a fight.

On home games, my players show up at the hotel at 8:00
P.M. This is when, home or away, we begin our final meetings. My quarterback sits on an elevated chair in one of the
hotel conference rooms and goes over the game plan, fielding
questions and problems and whatever else comes up. Some
players say our quarterback looks like a king, sitting up there.
I say, "Fine, keep that in mind tomorrow."

From 9:00 to 9:30 it's the special-teams meetings. With
the Seahawks, many show up for those, even those not on
special teams, because the speaker is special-teams coach
Rusty Tillman. Those fans who have watched him on the
sidelines—and the TV cameras invariably do—know how
charged-up he can get. The players see the same thing at his
meetings. I think some of the guys come along hoping to see
him burst a vein.

From 9:30 to 10:00 P.M. the offense and defense break up
into their final meetings. This is when I encourage the coaches
to identify key little tendencies in the opponents. I want them

to bring up things that would have gotten lost in the information overload earlier, but now have dramatic impact. My defensive coordinator, Tom Catlin, might say something like, "Every time they make a receiver substitution, the ball is going long." Or, "Every time they get near the goal line, they start running on the right side." We want to tie a mental string around each player's finger, giving him something important that, with the game just fifteen hours away, he won't have time to forget.

After that last meeting, it's time for our hamburger buffet, a ritual I began in Los Angeles. It's a nice informal time for guys to relax together with the coaches and clear the air and their heads. I know it sounds like a little late to be eating dinner, but this isn't dinner. Call it a midnight snack. Big kids, remember?

The next thing on the schedule is bed. The only time I extend the meetings is before the first game of the season, when I bring together the rookies. I give them a little speech about what it's like to play Seahawks football, and talk about the responsibility of the uniform. I warn them about trying to fool the referees or me or, worse, themselves.

By 11:00 P.M. on game eves, the players must be in their rooms. I run a standard curfew. The players' rooms are checked by an assistant coach or trainer, along with a security man. It doesn't take long because we put all the players on the same hotel floor. Watching the floor always is a Seattle police officer, standing guard the entire night. The last thing we need is unwanted visitors. We'll be seeing enough of those the next day. But generally there is no problem, especially not with the players. Most players are no longer stupid enough to ignore their homes and families and futures for a few more minutes of drinking. The reason we want them in at 11:00 is so we can make one last trip around their rooms to make sure nobody is kept awake with pain from an injury, and anybody who is sick has the right medication. We make sure everybody can sleep because the hardest thing in the NFL sometimes is not the hitting, but the sleeping.

We still get young players who don't understand the rule and would like a nightcap. I tell them, even though we try to treat the players like businessmen—even referring to road trips as "business trips"—this is the one area where a football player is different. A businessman can come home drunk and get up hung over and fake his way through the day. If a football player tries to fake his way through one of our days, he's going home on a stretcher.

> *Reggie McKenzie: What Chuck always says is, "Don't throw it so far over the fence tonight that you can't get it back in the morning. Remember, you got to hit with that head."*

Sunday pregame: The players are required to be at the park by 11:00 for a 1:00 P.M. game. I get there about the same time, though at home I usually arrive a few minutes earlier to allow time for autographs while walking into the Kingdome. That's why I use Midget to carry in my briefcase. While I don't see much of him during the week—even though he stays at my house—Midget is my constant companion during the games. He brings me water, a towel, and, if you believe some observers, good luck. Because of his size, some writers call him my leprechaun. I prefer to call him a good friend, which, when you get right down to it, is the same thing.

Just before the National Anthem, timing it so we can be on the field for the song, I give my pregame speech. Because I talk to the team so much during the week—every workday except Saturday—this final speech is almost anticlimactic. It never lasts more than a couple of minutes and always ends with "I don't care if you're ready—are you prepared?" That's how I feel about it. If they aren't prepared, nothing I can say will get them ready.

Halftime: This goes by so fast, I can hardly remember what we are doing when we are doing it. I know we set up chalkboards around the room, and after offensive and defensive coaches meet, they gather individual groups of players around each chalkboard and discuss adjustments. I usually have an assistant coach run in and tell me how much time is left in the halftime activities. He'll come in and with hand signs signal, "Eight minutes," then "Six minutes," and so on, almost like he's a game-show host. Then with two minutes left, I give my halftime speech.

With all due respect to Knute Rockne, the speech does not come from the top of my head, nor from the sweat of my brow. It is as impromptu as our first offensive play in the second half. I'll admit it, it is one of two different speeches I have written *before* the game: I think up one speech for if we are leading and one for if we are losing, and carry them in separate pockets, ultimately pulling out whichever is appropriate. What with all the strategy that must be worked out, all the new situations and plays that have come up after thirty minutes of football, there is no time to think of anything meaningful. The only impromptu or emotional thing that enters into my halftime speech is—which one do I use if we are tied? Sorry kids, life ain't Notre Dame.

Postgame: For me, this is the most emotionally difficult time of the day. Win or lose, I must hold the same composure, keep the same cool, show the same face. When we lose, it's hard. When we win, it's damn hard. I can get away with an occasional ecstatic slip after a great or surprising victory—witness the emotional wins with both Buffalo (over the Rams) and Seattle (over the Dolphins)—but normally I can't. And never with a loss.

After the final gun I walk into the locker room, and when everybody has gotten inside and the doors are closed, I instruct my players to "Grab a hand, take a knee," and we kneel and say the Lord's Prayer. Then I tell them not to overload their butts with their mouths, hoping that this is fair warning of the impending media rush, in which reporters and cameras and microphones will crowd our space until all of us have dressed and gone home and left the locker room to them.

If we are on the road, I encourage the players to hurry up and get dressed so we can get the hell out of town: win or lose, I want them to look at our opponent's place as an unfriendly place, so that at our next destination they will not forget why we are there. After home games, I encourage players to get home to their families so they can come back Monday at least a little refreshed. Already, I am thinking about next Sunday's opponent. I make sure my players are, too. Before I open the locker-room doors I might add, "Don't let me hear you saying what you did or what you should have done today. Today is over. Too much looking back, and you're going back."

I meet with the media and then go home for dinner with Shirley. I used to go out after every game—all the coaches and their wives would take over some back room in a restaurant and stay up late breathing sighs of relief over having survived another week. Not anymore, I'm just too tired. Seattle has great restaurants on every block, but during the season I might go out to one, and just once.

> *Ken Meyer: He used to party so hard. We'd have such great times. Now though, we hardly see him outside of work anymore. He might go upstairs to one of the press box lounges for a drink with us while traffic clears out, but that's it."*

After dinner I settle down on the den couch and watch the game on videotape: I know I shouldn't, but I do, again and again. By the time I get off that couch, often it is Monday morning, 6:00 A.M. Let's see, that gives me thirty minutes to get in to work . . .

It's always essentially the same routine, and the weekend never seems any easier, just harder. Like in 1986, a season that began by making me think 1985 was easy, and ended by making me long for 1987, which was another mistake. Whatever it was, 1986 was a season that carried its own myths. We won just five of our first eleven games, and everybody thought we were going down the tubes. The Jets defeated us 38 – 7. Kansas City beat us 27 – 7. New England beat us 34 – 7. People thought the Chuck Knox system should be placed in the back of the garage with the other old rusted appliances, complete with a warning to the kids not to play near it. People were throwing all kinds of garbage on us. They were saying Tom Landry has fallen, Don Shula has fallen, Chuck Noll has fallen, now it's Chuck Knox's turn to fall. People were honest-to-gosh uncertain if I could win another game. I wondered if I had any more of those crisis speeches left in me; I was certain only that I had to find out.

> *Reggie McKenzie: Chuck stands in front of the team one Wednesday and gets real red and says, "Well, the boat is in so much trouble this time, there are no oars, and somebody is drilling a hole through the bottom. Nobody believes in this team but this team. And you have to keep believing. We don't have to change what we're doing, we just have to do it better. Every little thing, we just have to do better. Somebody has got to tackle, somebody has got to hit the quarterback, somebody has got to catch the passes. If somebody does each of those things, everybody is going to win."*

I essentially told them what I told the Rams many years before: Just play the football you've been taught to play, and good things will happen. We did, and they did. We won our last five games, including beating the eventual AFC champions, Denver, 41 – 16 to end the season with what many believed was the best team in the conference. After all, just a few weeks earlier we had beaten the eventual world champions, the New York Giants.

I didn't realize how good we were until the final game in the Kingdome, when I received a death threat from a Denver fan. During the first half somebody called our people and said, "If the Seahawks win, Chuck Knox is dead." Rumor has it, earlier that year opposing fans were threatening to kill me if

I didn't get an extended contract. My security guys told me this Denver threat was not a joke. They asked me to leave the field in the first half and slip inside a bulletproof vest— they even had three different sizes. I refused. "Once you give in, once they see you walking inside," I said, "they've won. Some crazy will be calling every week."

So I stuck it out for the rest of the first half, and then, on that same principle, I refused to wear protection in the second half. Once they see you with that extra bulge in your sweater, they've won also. The police never had any clue as to the identity of the crazy caller, but I never felt any bullets, so maybe he was just that, a crazy caller. When I thought about it later—and thought about my wife and family—I wondered if maybe I was a crazy coach.

One of the craziest things of all was that we missed the play-offs that year by one game, which meant we missed them by one play in one of our losses, depending on how you looked at it. I was too frustrated to figure it out. I took it hard, probably harder than most close calls in my career. On the season's final Sunday—after we had finished by beating Denver on Saturday and needed a certain combination of other teams' losses to make the play-offs—I sat in my den, determined not to watch the games. I had spent an autumn's worth of emotion watching my own team; I didn't think I could stand watching anyone else's. But occasionally I would sneak out in front of the TV, nudge through members of my family, and peek. And peek some more. And finally I stood there with them as they alternately cheered and booed and finally, when the wrong team won the wrong game, sat down and looked like they were going to cry.

We had been eliminated without any final say in the matter, and I wondered why I had even bothered to look. I retreated to my den, where I had promised to stay in the first place, and closed the doors behind me. At that year's Super Bowl—we were the only team to have beaten both competitors that year—I took it even worse. I looked down at the Rose Bowl field and watched the Giants' Bill Parcells and

Denver's Dan Reeves and thought, What wouldn't I give to be there. I'd been so close to being there. I had coached several teams good enough to be there. And yet I was up in the stands for the fourteenth straight season. That day I discovered tears in my eyes and resolved that if such a moment were ever mine, I would never let it go.

First thing I would do if I won a Super Bowl? Anybody who knows me knows: I would grab my assistant coaches. Since most of my guys in Seattle have been with me at least ten years, my eyes could be doused in champagne and I still would know who I was grabbing. A head coach should know and respect his assistant coaches like he does his heartbeat. In my case, they *are* my heartbeat.

> *Joe Vitt: Chuck treats his assistant coaches differently from anyone else in the league. Ask anybody. He was an assistant for what, a thousand years? It's like he knows what it's like. He sometimes makes what seems to be unreasonable demands on us, places loads of responsibility on us, but it's only because he does the same thing to himself.*

A description of my management style regarding assistant coaches, beginning with the hire, which they think is the hardest part, but is always the easiest:

I hire a guy only after I have interviewed a number of coaches. Some coaches immediately hire old friends, or friends of friends, but while recommendations are important, I never discount a man because nobody big has spoken out for him. You'll remember, few big people ever spoke out for me.

I bring in the candidates one by one, and after a bit of small talk, I bring them to one of our coaches' meetings and send them directly to the chalkboard. I throw them the chalk and tell them to begin diagramming. My assistants will shout the defense or offense, and the candidate will draw it, or draw a way to stop it. My assistants will respond with, "What if so-

and-so does this?" or "What if this happens?" Now the guy has to draw an entire set of new plays.

One note here: our diagrams are not **X**'s and **O**'s. We use **X**'s and *squares*. There are a number of complicated reasons for this, the main one being, squares are easier to draw. With the increased average weight of the defensive linemen, it's also increasingly difficult to convince our offensive line-men—**X**'s—that they will be lining up against mere circles. Would you call William "The Refrigerator" Perry a circle? No way. He's a square.

This comes into surprisingly serious play during the job interview because I'm particular about the way my coaches draw their squares. I like them with sharp corners. I like them to be tight. Sharp, tight squares indicate a sharp, tight mind. The diagramming procedures can take as long as six hours, but they tell me what two days of interviews cannot. They enable me to see how coaches handle themselves on their feet: I called it "chalkboard demeanor." I understand that some guys are better field coaches, but on my teams, you need to show that you can think and organize and relate like a teacher. For this, my coaches can blame Blanton Collier.

Former Knox assistant coach Elijah Pitts: I'll never for-get going through the chalkboard session. After he and his coaches got through with me, I thought I had no chance. They were shooting me down from all sides. But I got the job, and it was then I realized it wasn't always the right chalkboard answer they were looking for. It was the cour-age to come up with an answer, any answer. It was the courage to offer an opinion with the chance that nobody would agree.

When interviewing a coach, I also want to find out how he feels about working with other members of the staff. Some-times a guy will want to know what his title will be. Bad question. I tell him, you want a title, join the service, get a job at the bank. Here, we are only looking for guys called *workers*. If we consistently win, and somebody offers you a head coaching job because of it, then you've got your title.

Once I hire a coach, I work with the general manager to handle his salary negotiations. Because I felt so underpaid for so long, I want to make certain my coaches will get what the market will bear. Also, each year I work to get my coaches raises equal to the raises of their top peers on other teams, no less, no more. This can be both good and bad.

> *Joe Vitt: I've heard of coaches going in with a bunch of reasons why they should be the highest-paid assistant in the league, and Chuck has thrown them out before they got through the list. But then I remember how, after my first year with him, I asked for what I thought was a good first-year raise, five thousand dollars. He got real mad. But for a different reason. "Five thousand bucks? Bull!" he says. "Your wife needs a new car and you need a new house, and every other coach in the league is making more than you. Don't you dare ask for a five-thousand-dollar raise!" He was so mad, he gave me a twelve-thousand-dollar raise.*

Because I have left two teams in the middle of my contract I won't give my coaches more than a one-year deal—that way they will never be as unhappy in the second or third year of a contract as I have been. My coaches like those one-year deals for two reasons: They know they will always get a fair raise, and they know of another bit of my management history: I have never fired a coach. Barring some unusual off-field incident, once they are hired, they are with me as long as they want to be. It's easier to develop continuity and vision that way. It's harder to hire, because I can't afford to make a mistake, but once they are here, it's easier to be their boss.

Once in Los Angeles, C. R. thought we should replace a particular coach with somebody more flamboyant, with more imagination. I told him flat-out I would not fire a coach for that reason. So C. R. went out and tried to find this guy another job to make it easy for him to leave. He found what he thought was an appropriate opening, but my guy did not want to leave and I was not going to make him. If a coach is not doing his job, the bottom line is, I brought him in, he's my responsibility, I've got to make him better. But in the end, they usually get the job done, even if I have to bribe them.

> *Joe Vitt: Once during the 1984 training camp, we were arguing about the defense. Chuck finally told Tom Catlin he would buy his coaches a suit for every shutout. It was Chuck's way of challenging Catlin to prove that his method was the right one. Catlin said, "Fine, you got it." And everybody forgot about it.*
>
> *That year we had three shutouts. One afternoon during the off-season, Chuck sticks his head in our office doors and says, "C'mon, everybody down to Nordstrom's."*
>
> *Somebody says, "What the hell for?"*
>
> *Chuck says, "Don't be dumb. We're going for those suits."*

I'd like to keep most of my coaches for as long as I coach—I've never failed to ask an assistant to join me in a new job—but if a coach wants to go on to something better, I am obviously the last person qualified to stand in his way. In fact, five assistant coaches from my various staffs became head coaches in the NFL—Ken Meyer, Dick Vermeil, Kay Stephenson, Ray Malavasi, and Leeman Bennett. All acquired the jobs on their own, but I was glad to be of help when I could, any way I could.

When I was coaching in Los Angeles, Atlanta was interviewing my assistant Bennett for their head coaching job. About ten days after the interview, Atlanta general manager Eddie LeBaron called me and asked for a recommendation. At that same time, I was trying to get permission to talk to Bill Ford about coaching the Detroit Lions, and even the newspapers already had me heading there. In the course of recommending Leeman, I told Eddie that I might take that Detroit job any day now, and that if I did, did he know who the Rams would hire to take my place?

"No," said Eddie, "who?"

"Leeman Bennett," I said.

That night, Leeman Bennett was offered the job, which he later accepted, making it his first head coaching job in the NFL. In looking back, I like to think Eddie would have hired Leeman anyway. This just got him off his dime. Part of my motivation for treating my coaches as if I were fully responsible for their welfare is that that's how I expect them to treat the players.

> *Former LA assistant coach Dick Vermeil: I remember the time I was bitching about my backs being good runners but bad blockers. Chuck just glared at me. "If they already blocked, I wouldn't need you," he said.*

Like I've talked about: you're smart enough if I'm good enough to teach you. And my coaches must be good enough. I encourage disagreement among them, and with me, just as Blanton Collier taught. I encourage them to think for themselves and not to be yes men. Of course, this has its drawbacks: I can't tell them what I'm going to tell the team in a meeting, because sure enough, one of them will argue about it and force me to pull off a motivational speech while second-guessing myself.

> *Norm Pollom: I remember one night in a hotel suite Knox jumped all over our scouting department, so I and some of his assistants jumped right back and drew him into a huge argument. It ended about four o'clock in the morning with all the coaches gone except Chuck and me. We were screaming and cussing each other out before finally leaving too, slamming the doors and yelling all the way down the hall. Three hours later Chuck pounded on*

*my door. He wanted to go down and have breakfast. Acted
like he'd forgotten all about it.*

Because I want other coaches' ideas so much, and am so
eager to encourage them, I'm careful never to say an idea is
a bad one. If a coach wants to put in a new play and it doesn't
look too good, I'll say, "Let's put it in a holding pattern."
That means just what it sounds like. We won't use it now,
but that doesn't mean we won't use it later. You never know
when a crazy play might suddenly seem pertinent, and I never
want to discourage an idea. Because of this, my coaches spend
a lot of time thinking and planning. Often they are in the
office as long as I am.

*Joe Vitt: I sometimes wonder if we aren't the only
coaching staff to eat our lunches on the toilet. We may
also be the only coaching staff to be on twenty-four-hour
call. I bet Chuck never talked about the times during
training camp when he calls us at midnight or one in the
morning just to talk football.*

I demand a lot from my coaches—but I like to think it
occasionally works both ways.

*Norm Pollom: I remember one year I had just arrived
at the Senior Bowl when I received a phone call from a
doctor telling me my wife had suffered an aneurism. For
the next couple of weeks I was a basket case. I'm not really
sure what happened. I know I flew back to Buffalo. A couple of weeks later she died, and we flew the body back to
her hometown. Suddenly, Chuck was there to speak at
the funeral. I still remember his words as he looked at
me: "She loved life, and she loved this fella right here."
The funny thing was, in the end I never got a bill from
the funeral home, or the airline, or anybody.*

In a job where the doling out of responsibility is often your
biggest responsibility, good assistant coaches will often make

your day, and can make your season. But then sometimes, like in 1987 with the Seahawks, nothing will help. The year began with the Seahawks favored to go to the Super Bowl; it ended up with the team as messed-up and off-color as a certain rookie linebacker's hair. It ended with an overtime loss in a wild-card play-off game that people considered such an underachievement, it was as if we'd never made the play-offs in the first place. I'm just glad it ended, period. One newspaper said I called it the toughest year of my coaching career. I was not misquoted.

I began the season by interrupting my usual preseason team speech to mention our goal of the Super Bowl. It was the first time in my career that I had spoken those two words—*Super Bowl*—to my team before the first game. Considering we were perhaps the best team in football at the end of 1986 and had not gotten any weaker, I found it as good a time as any to break tradition.

Normally I never think you should shoot any higher than your next immediate step, which for us is an AFC West championship. After sixteen games you win the division; only after eighteen or nineteen games do you win the Super Bowl. But I just wanted to put the Super Bowl in the back of their minds. If only it had moved forward from there.

But not only was it not a Super Bowl year, it was a year where some games didn't even seem to matter. It was a year of total distraction and, eventually, team breakdown. For me 1987 was the year of "The Boz" and The Strike and not much more.

I'll start with Brian Bosworth. Note that I am one of about three people in this country who do not refer to him as "The Boz." He's a player, just another one of my businessmen, and I call him by his given names, Brian or Bosworth. Understand, I am not going to rip him. He is a good person who is going to be an even better football player. But I will talk about his phenomenon, which swept through the northwest like a Chinook wind, only at times more forceful and uncomfortable.

It is June 12, 1987. It's 9:15 A.M. I'm sitting in my office with a visitor when Mike McCormack comes to the door. It appears he's attempting to jump out of his pants. "Chuck, can I talk to you a minute?" he asks. I excuse myself and walk into the hall.

"Chuck, we got him! We got him!" cries McCormack, pounding his fist into his open hand.

"Got *who?*" I ask.

"We got Bosworth! In the lottery!"

"Holy Hell!" I say. Those were my exact two words. I remember the words, the time, and the ensuing high fives with McCormack and the other coaches. The entire staff spilled into the hall, some beating on walls, others slapping each other on the back, everyone celebrating our good fortune. And good fortune it was. Through the complicated lottery system that gave every team a shot at the star Oklahoma linebacker in the NFL's supplementary draft, we had a one-in-thirty-seven shot at getting him. It was such a long shot that when the June 12 supplementary draft day rolled around—a day to pick players who are coming out of college despite their remaining eligibility—I had completely forgotten about it. But somewhere in New York that morning, out of a big barrel, they had picked a ball tagged "Seahawks." And now we had Brian Bosworth. All we had to do was sign him.

Sure. His agent Gary Wichard had already stated that Bosworth would not play in Seattle, and Bosworth had later confirmed the statement. Even if Bosworth could be convinced to play here, the job ahead of us was still difficult. He would likely cost the ownership as much as several of our present linebackers combined.

I figure that before we say anything, or Bosworth has a chance to say anything, we need to talk. So the first thing I do after the announcement is call Wichard. I knew him back when he was a senior quarterback at C.W. Post University; in fact, through a mutual friend, I actually helped get him into the Senior Bowl that year. We arranged for a meeting in Dallas as soon as possible. Four days after the draft, Mike and I climb on a plane, fly to Dallas, and meet Bosworth and Wichard at this private club called La Cime.

I had not seen Bosworth—did that make me the only one in the country at the time?—and I was impressed. It wasn't because he didn't have paint in his mohawk haircut—which he didn't at the time—but because he had no phoniness in his voice. He was all business and talked about being a team player and playing hard, as if he had sat in on some of my speeches. He graduated from Oklahoma in four years with a better than 3.0 grade-point average. After one meeting I could tell.

I think he felt comfortable with me, too, as if he knew that I had coached the Joe Namaths and the Isiah Robertsons—personalities that made Bosworth appear bland. He smiled when I told him, I don't care how you dress or how you cut your hair, as long as you get the job done. Two weeks after the first trip, we made another one: same club and conversations. Only this time, whenever McCormack and Wichard began talking about money, they would leave the room while Brian and I stayed and talked football. I liked it that way, partly because with the kind of money Bosworth would be making, I didn't want to know anything about it until it was done. I was so excited about Bosworth, I might have jumped in there and pleaded with McCormack to give him his own department-store chain.

The second trip to Dallas was also different because by then the media had learned of our whereabouts and had gathered outside the club's front door. This forced us to exit through the kitchen and out the service entrance, around the garbage cans. It was real cloak-and-dagger stuff.

He still wasn't signed after that second visit, but by then, after raising so many eyebrows and whispering so many sweet nothings into each other's ear, I knew we'd eventually get it done. And we did sign, to what I learned was a ten-year, $11-million deal. We didn't have time to celebrate, because the deal was so complicated and there were so many little things to haggle over, that the signing didn't occur until August 14.

That was three weeks after the start of camp. For a rookie linebacker, losing three weeks is like losing three months. The delay hurt Bosworth all the way into December. He was coming from a conference—the Big Eight—where they mostly run the football, and where he is bigger than most people he faces. The adjustments were too great, and his time to make them before facing regular season competition was too short. At our first meeting I told him, "Here in the NFL, it's like playing Nebraska every week. You have two-hundred-eighty-five-pound guards jumping down your throat *every week*. Welcome to a new world."

By that time I had already had another meeting with the team about Bosworth, *before* Bosworth arrived. With the size of his contract and his fan following, I felt some things needed to be spelled out: "Whatever Bosworth is making, all it can do is raise the standard of living for everybody." I told them. "And if the guy can help us win, which he can, it will mean even more money for everybody. All you got to do, therefore, is perform the job for which you contracted and worry only about that."

After that I didn't hear any sniping at Bosworth, but I'm sure it existed. We call ourselves a family, yet even in a family you like some people more than you like others, and I understand that. As long as when the game starts, my guys beat the guys across from them, and keep their mind only on those guys, I don't care who they hate in the locker room.

Bosworth caused only two uproars during the season, which was about twenty less than I'd figured. And his problems were simply due to overloading his butt with his mouth, which, as you know, has happened to all of us. The first problem actually happened before our season started, just before the season opening game in Denver. Bosworth came out in the newspaper and said he would hit John Elway as hard as he could hit him, and if Elway got hurt, so be it. Four writers heard this, and while three writers wrote it one way, the other wrote that Bosworth claimed he wanted to hurt Elway.

Even though I believed the three writers instead of the one, and even though I don't think Elway paid any attention, I called Bosworth to my office anyway. I just told him, "Don't overload it. Lie in the weeds. When what you do speaks well, there's no need to hear what you say." Who says there's not a Knoxism for every occasion? I told him I just didn't want to have to worry about what he was going to say next, and I didn't want his teammates mad at him, because he might give an opponent extra incentive. But I also assured Bosworth that I was not going to gag or even muzzle him. He could scream and shout and raise hell, as long as those words and actions wouldn't damage the team. I told him he needed to be himself so he could play like himself. He was very apologetic and humble, and that was that.

The other incident happened at the end of the season, when Bosworth told the *Washington Post* that he wasn't happy living in Seattle, that he wasn't having any fun playing here. It made great reading, and it got everybody wondering things like, *What is Knox going to do to him now?* Knox did nothing. Because Knox didn't care. I never care if a player likes the town—he can leave in the off-season. I don't care if he's having fun playing football for me either—he can have fun on his own time. All I care is that when the proper time comes, he gets his lunch bucket and goes to work and does his job. Bosworth had that lunch-bucket mentality; he did his job. And by the time that story came out, he was second on the team in tackles. That's all I cared.

Besides the Denver incident, the only time I invited Bosworth up to my office was when he and agent Wichard put up the big stink about keeping his college number, 44. The NFL said he couldn't be a linebacker and wear that number, but he and Wichard fought it. I guess Wichard had already developed this Bosworth company, 44 Blues which might not go over too big if Bosworth was forced to wear number 55. That was one distraction I could not stomach, and I finally called Bosworth in and told him. I reminded him that a rose by any other name smells as sweet, and that unless he did his job, he wouldn't make any money no matter what his number was. He was humble again and apologetic again, and once again that was that.

For reasons I still can't figure, Bosworth became a cause célèbre in Seattle. Newspapers ran polls on what to give him for Christmas. One TV station received 30,000 calls—the most ever—when it posed the question "Should Bosworth stay, leave, or just shut up?" Whatever happened to stories on feeding the hungry children, or questions about the Gaza strip, or talk shows about the fighting in Ireland? The only thing about this I understood was that what Seattle said about Bosworth said a lot about our society.

Bosworth was such a big deal up here, only one thing could have happened in 1987 that would even faintly overshadow him. And it happened: a five-week football strike.

I still don't believe the players walked out. Even as the players were packing their gear and leaving, our management team didn't believe they were walking out. Our unwillingness to believe in this strike ultimately gave us a new, hardened vision of the typical NFL football player.

Here's how we played it: during training camp, while many teams were signing their released players to thousand-dollar bonuses that would ensure their return as replacement players, we did not. I would not even mention a strike. I wanted the regular players to know it was their team, their season. I didn't want them to think we were trying to find replacement players while coaching them at the same time. No matter what happened, they needed to know that they were our top priority. At least, I thought that's what they needed to know.

Then the strike hit, and we scrambled. While our regular players walked the picket lines, we were thrown into a last-minute search for new ones. We had no idea who to get, or where to get them. Loyalty had cost us, and left us with a huddle full of strange ones. Our strikeball team featured, among other things, designated pass rushers. They were two guys—a medical student and a factory worker—who flew from their homes in different cities on Friday, played on the

defensive line Sunday, flew back home that night. Because
of their other commitments, they couldn't stay with us during the week. Designated hitters.

We also featured a barroom bouncer from Las Vegas named
Scoggins. In our first strikeball game, against the Dolphins,
he dislocated the index finger on his right hand. He was in
great pain, yet we didn't have anybody to replace him. As he
was running off the field, moaning, I jumped in his way.
"What? Do you want *me* to play?" I shouted. "Get back in
there!"

He went back to the field, this changing his stance from
the left to the right hand. On the next play we scored, and
he ran off the field in pain again. I jumped in his way again.
"Where are you going? You're on the extra point team," I
reminded him. "Do you want *me* to play?"

He ran back on, we kicked the extra point, and he came
off one more time. This time he didn't run anywhere near
me. We splinted the finger and he finished the game. Somehow Scoggins and the rest of the strikeballers survived it.
One of the reasons might have been an unusual tactic I em-
ployed: I kept the media away from them. My reasoning,
which went against NFL custom, was that we had replacements who didn't know any plays or formations. Some of
them didn't even know the fundamentals. Others weren't even
sure how to line up. I did not want the media taking pictures
of them and laughing at them like it was some kind of joke.
Our replacement players also had too many hassles with police escorts and such to put up with questions like, "What
does it feel like to replace Kenny Easley?" That player might
have said something dumb, then Easley would have read it,
and tensions really would have been high.

As pro-union as I am—and I have sat with my father in
the back of labor halls filled with the shouts of mill workers—I did not publicly complain about the replacements. I
could not complain. I had signed a contract to coach a Seattle Seahawks team. The contract did not say *what* team. I
could only do what I had been contracted to do. But when

the strike finally ended, there was no one happier than me, even though I now had to deal with the hard part—facing the angry, defeated, returning players.

On that first day of their return, I walked into the hot, restless meeting room and decided to throw the first punch. I told them, "The coaches had nothing to do with the strike. If you are mad at the coaches, you are mad at the wrong people. You've got to be mad at the opponent. We have to stick together and make the opponent pay for your anger, for your lost money, for your strike."

Sound good? It didn't work. Some of my players, emotionally drained from the strike, didn't have the ability to direct their anger. Some of them just didn't have the will. Some Seahawks were mad at everybody and played like they were mad at everybody, and that included the coaches, who we thought had previously treated them like family. After watching us go 9–6 and out of the play-offs in the first round, I have since changed my mind about team unity. Now, with the big contracts and egos, I'm not sure how much unity is a factor in winning or losing. In 1987 the teams with no strike unity were actually among the best in the NFL—San Francisco and New Orleans. The Seahawks stayed on strike as a unit; our strikeball team was terrible because we treated our players as a unit and ignored prospective replacements; and *still* we did not succeed. Still, personal feelings interfered with our vision.

What happened after our team came back from the strike was a shocking experience for me. I guess maybe football players really are just individual contractors, and should be treated as such. Maybe I've been doing it wrong all these years. Maybe as coaches we've worked too hard at eliminating our players' distractions and discomforts, and tried too hard to create the best possible environment in which they could succeed. Maybe we've worried too much about being a family. Maybe we should just make them play.

Even though the rules are basically the same as when I first played on the eighth-grade Sewickley team, I have to

understand that the game has changed. I know I've changed;
I've mellowed. I went to a bachelor party one night last summer and was home by nine. I don't let my players fight during practice anymore, and I allow married guys to spend more
training camp nights at home with their wives.

Some have said the most obvious sign of my mellowing
with age can be found in our very young, our rookies. I don't
let veterans pick on them anymore. I don't allow training
camp hazing. It's as time-honored a tradition as the coin flip,
and I may be one of the only NFL coaches to outlaw it, but
like a lot of things, it has just stopped making sense.

I made this rule after one particular Seahawk training camp
at Eastern Washington University. It was the morning we
packed up and broke camp. One of the maids called me over
to where she was standing outside a dormitory. Her face was
red and her words were tight, and then she showed me: The
entire rookies' dorm area was a disaster. Beds were over-
turned, talcum powder was on the walls, busted water balloons were lying in puddles, empty fire extinguishers were
scattered around like bowling pins—I had rarely been more
embarrassed for myself or my football team. It was obvious
the veterans had tried to haze the rookies right out of their
sleep. I decided, fine, now it was my turn.

> *Joe Vitt: Chuck stood up at that morning's regular
> meeting and began talking slowly about embarrassment
> and pride, and then his face got all puffy and he started
> shaking. Then he was shouting: "You veteran fools did
> not give these rookies a fair shake. If I was a rookie, right
> now I would want to kill you. As of now, no more hazing
> on any of my teams! None! It's over with." Everyone lis-
> tened to Chuck in complete silence. They knew it was
> over.*

For one thing, they were hazing rookies who might not
even make the team. How fair was that? Also, a rookie has
too much to worry about without needing to think of a song

to sing at a rookie show. He can't afford to drink some terrible stuff forced down him by a veteran that will make him sick for two days. It's not that I'm all that fond of rookies. But I am fond of common sense. Late that afternoon, Joe Vitt came by to see me, saying he and the coaches were worried about my health. He didn't know if I could take many more outbursts like that.

I said, "Joe, did I get my point across?" Joe answered, "Chuck, the frigging building could be burning down and those players would not touch a fire extinguisher."

I suppose it's OK if I am changing, because everything else I trust in is changing. Look at Sewickley. Down by Walnut Street some designer is putting bricks on the sidewalks, and the idle rich are opening boutiques with stuffed animals, maternity dresses, and charm bracelets. Across the street from my old flat is a hair salon with, for chrissakes, *ferns* in the window. My old grade school is a post office. My old candy store is a real-estate office.

I used to have an uncanny memory. I used to be able to go back there and tell half the old men in town what kind of shoes they used to wear, because I was the one who shined them. Now I go back, and nobody shines shoes anymore— and I'm one of the old men.

> *Bobby "Mook" Marucca: We went into the old Sewickley Hotel a couple of years ago, and Chuck just stopped dead in his tracks in the lobby. I asked him, "What's the matter?" He looks around and says, "You know, this is the first time I've been in here when I didn't know anybody."*

Twenty-three steps, right? I suppose I've gotten a lot of mileage out of those twenty-three steps that once separated my three-room apartment from Walnut Street. Yet I don't think a man's life should be measured in distance.

The older you get, the more you look back at your footprints. It's not how far you've come, but what kind of trail you've left. Sometimes I look back and see big, well-formed tracks that lead off to a happy family, successful children, and football players who somehow turned out as men. Other times I look back and see nothing. A storm has swept through during the night—a lost chance at the Super Bowl, a busted romance in Buffalo—and covered everything up.

The thing I've discovered is that life's results won't always fit neatly into a line score. Success and failure cannot always be judged by the films. All a man can do is walk straight and upright and believe that if behind him things don't look so good, around the corner they must be eye-popping wonderful. Now, that's eighth-grade Sewickley.

Index